Stop Forgetting

REVISED AND EXPANDED EDITION

Stop Forgetting

DR. BRUNO FURST

REVISED AND EXPANDED
BY LOTTE FURST
AND GERRIT STORM

DOUBLEDAY & COMPANY, INC.
GARDEN CITY, NEW YORK

ISBN: 0-385-15401-1
9 8 7 6 5

Foreword

Memory is the basis of all knowledge. We know only what we remember. It is an established fact that the average person forgets eighty per cent of all the information he receives through all of his senses during a lifetime.

Dr. Furst devoted his prime years to painstaking research in order to find out how our memory works and how it can be improved by using various techniques. He gave us scientific and educational guidelines for memory training and worked untiringly to apply all the knowledge of the past to his own genius in memory work.

In this book Dr. Furst's original concepts are vividly brought up to date by the people who were closest to him throughout his most productive years, his wife Lotte, and Gerrit Storm.

With this revised and expanded edition the authors have been able to present the most comprehensive volume on memory training in existence today.

It is especially gratifying to note how much care has been taken in preserving all the values of the basic principles and techniques laid down by the "Master," while at the same time adapting them to every phase of modern life.

Of inestimable value in writing this book have been the more than thirty years of experience in teaching and working with students who are counted in the hundreds of thousands. This brought about a constant updating of the material and teaching methods and presented countless opportunities to find new solutions to memory problems in various professions and occupations.

Rather than aiming at the performance of spectacular memory feats, Dr. Furst's primary interest was in teaching others the rules and principles through which they could improve their powers of memory and concentration.

For many years the Furst memory course was given and is still given in the Adult Education program at Brooklyn College, and through all these years it has been a thrill to me to hear how students were elated about this course and specifically about the results they were able to achieve when they put the techniques to work in their daily activities.

By incorporating the newest approaches in teaching and by covering a host of new applications, this volume has become, truly, a new book.

Its publication is both timely and fortunate.

ARTHUR SECORD
former Professor of Speech
and
Director of Community Service,
Brooklyn College

Contents

THE CHAIN METHOD

How to Remember Reading Material, Lectures and Speeches, Prose and Poetry

THE PRACTICAL APPLICATION OF THE CHAIN METHOD

THE HOOK METHOD

How to Remember Anything Connected with Numbers

THE PRACTICAL APPLICATION OF THE NUMBER CODE AND HOOK METHOD

APPLICATIONS OF MEMORY TECHNIQUES
IN VARIOUS PROFESSIONS AND OCCUPATIONS

Stop Forgetting

CHAPTER 1

Improve Your Memory

YOU CAN REMEMBER!

If you think you have a bad memory you are certainly not alone. Millions of people believe likewise. Still, believe it or not, there is actually no such thing as a "bad" memory or for that matter a "good" memory.

Let us take a closer look at what is really meant by the words "good" and "bad" in this respect.

Some well-known personalities, past as well as present, are credited with a so-called "good" memory. Napoleon, for instance, had a reputation for knowing every officer in his army by name. General George C. Marshall was able to quote from memory almost every event in World War II. Toscanini directed entire symphonies without using scores. James A. Farley, the former Postmaster General, knows thousands of people by their first and last names.

Such memory feats may make you feel inadequate, especially if you are one of the countless persons who cannot remember the name of someone they have met a few days before; who cannot speak for ten minutes at a meeting without a manuscript; who forget where they left their keys in the morning or who cannot retain the contents of a book they have read only recently.

It is true that there are many persons who are famous for their prodigious memory in a particular field. But the emphasis should be on the words "in a particular field." The very fact that their fame is connected with the recall of specific data is an indication that their prowess is limited to that particular area.

You are likely to find the same thing among the members of your family, among your friends or your associates in business. A schoolboy may be able to give you the scores of several baseball games which were played quite some time ago, he may even cite the position of the players on each team, but he may at the same time be one of the worst students of his class in school. All this shows that the memory of anyone is at best one-sided. It may be good, perhaps even outstanding, in one particular field, but only average or even below average in other fields. The musician who can play a piece he heard only once before may not be able to remember you or your name; the man who startles you by remembering your name ten years after your first and only meeting may not be able to recall a melody which he has heard a dozen or more times.

To say that someone has a bad or a good memory is a generalization which is hard to prove. In order to find out how good one's memory is, we should ask the following questions:

How good is your memory for names and faces?

How good is your memory for numbers?

How good is your memory for errands or appointments, especially for those which are not connected with your business or profession?

How well and how long can you remember the contents of a book you read or a movie you see?

Can you remember how the cards were played in a bridge, canasta, or other card game?

Is there a difference in your ability to remember things that happened

  (a) last month?

  (b) ten years ago? (You will know that older people often remember events from their childhood much better than those of the recent past. We shall discuss the reason for this later on.)

Upon the completion of this survey, you will come to the conclusion that nobody can answer *all* these questions in the affirmative, unless you happen to come across someone who has already learned to master the various techniques such as are contained in this book.

Our ultimate goal is not so much to create outstanding abilities in only one particular field, as to bring your memory in general, in all fields, to a higher level. The difference between a trained and an untrained memory lies not necessarily in remembering only words, numbers, appointments, or business data, but in the ability to remember *all* those things we wish to remember in our business as well as social affairs.

All our knowledge rests in the final analysis on memory! You would not even be able to read this book if you could not remember the meaning of letters, words, punctuation, and sentences.

There would be no progress in civilization without memory, since every new invention rests on the amount of knowledge previously gained and remembered.

Would the Wright brothers, for instance, ever have been able to invent the airplane if they had not remembered the law of gravity, the manner in which birds fly, the functions of the engine, and a thousand other things? Of course, aside from all the memorized knowledge, this invention, like every other invention, took also a great deal of imagination and will power. We shall see in the following chapters that imagination and will power (concentration) are so closely related in our memory work that it is almost impossible to train our memory without training our imagination and will power at the same time.

TAKE A MEMORY TEST

Before going on, we recommend that you give yourself a memory test. Without such a test it is rather difficult to notice progress and to see for yourself how much your memory can be improved by proper training.

You see, one of the reasons why memory training has been neglected for such a long time, and is still neglected in our schools, is the fact that it is so difficult to compare the working of your own memory with the working of somebody else's memory, or to compare your memory at the age of twenty with your memory at the age of forty or fifty. Generalities such as "my memory grew better" or "my memory is growing worse" are not very helpful.

If your friend's eyesight is better than yours, you will notice it immediately because he can see a bird or a tree or a person, or read a sign, that you cannot recognize without your glasses. The same holds true with regard to hearing. But it is almost impossible to compare your memory with his.

No doubt at some time or other you attended a movie with a friend. Did you ever try to find out who remembered more details after one month, after two months, after one year? In the first place, you will admit that such tests are not often made and, secondly, even if you compared how much both of you remembered, it still does not mean much, because you tested only one particular field. And we have seen in the opening chapter that the outcome means very little for any other field, where the result may be entirely different.

Therefore you owe it to yourself to test your memory in several fields before you start training, and then to test it again—using similar devices—at the end of your training, say after two or three months. Naturally, in all these tests the time element plays an important role, and therefore it is necessary to look at your watch before you start.

Test No. 1. Look at the twenty words below for five minutes. Then close the book and see how many you can remember, in their proper order. It is not enough to remember fire engine; in order to be correct you must also know that fire engine is Number 5, etc. Give yourself one point for each word that you remember with its correct number.

1. theater	11. ticket
2. bookstore	12. circus
3. window cleaner	13. typewriter
4. vegetables	14. eyeglasses
5. fire engine	15. cake
6. ashtray	16. radiator
7. curtain	17. pillow
8. television set	18. stamp
9. sewing machine	19. photograph
10. notebook	20. chimney

My score is_____points

Test No. 2. Look at the twenty numbers below for five minutes. Then close the book and see how many you can remember, again in their proper order. It is not enough to recall 78; you must remember also that 78 is the fourteenth number, etc. Give yourself one point for each number that you remember in its correct place.

1. 22	11. 53
2. 48	12. 21
3. 87	13. 94
4. 96	14. 78
5. 14	15. 69
6. 75	16. 36
7. 33	17. 83
8. 56	18. 52
9. 62	19. 45
10. 29	20. 17

My score is_____points

Test No. 3. Look at the twenty items below and their prices for ten minutes. Then cover the prices with a piece of paper and write down the prices as you remember them. Give yourself one point for each price that you remember correctly.

electric blanket	$ 29	diamond ring	$742
room air conditioner	$205	used car	$875
power mower	$121	golf clubs	$120
refrigerator	$270	surf board	$ 80
color TV set	$625	binoculars	$ 80
electric knife	$ 19	cosmetic case	$ 70
washing machine	$251	skis	$ 76
outboard motor	$783	violin	$470
indoor jogger	$ 60	typewriter	$173
sheepskin coat	$140	living room set	$945

My score is_____points

Test No. 4. On the next two pages you see pictures of ten persons with their names underneath. Look at them for five minutes and try to remember each person's name. Then turn to the following two pages where you will find these same persons pictured without their names. Give yourself a point for each person whose name you remember correctly.

MR. LIPTON

MISS ALMOND

MRS. FULTON

MR. WAVERLY

MISS DIMPSON

MR. VILLANOVA

MR. ASHFORD

MRS. BALDINI

MR. SCHNEIDER

MISS TEIXEIRA

My score is_____points

Test No. 5. Look at the twenty historical dates below for ten minutes. Then cover the years and write down as many of these years as you can remember. Give yourself one point for each year you remember correctly.

First Congress met in Philadelphia	1774
Discovery of the Philippines	1521
Pilgrims' landing at Plymouth	1620
First telegraph in the United States	1843
Biggest earthquake in Japan	1703
First passenger railroad in the United States	1830
Death of Napoleon	1821
Invention of the cannon	1340
The great Chicago fire	1871
Founding of Washington, D.C.	1791
First English Parliament	1295
First printing machine introduced in England	1474
Death of Franklin D. Roosevelt	1945
First college degree for women	1841
Birth of Benedict Arnold	1741
Purchase of Florida	1819
Joan of Arc burned at the stake	1431
Lindbergh's flight across the Atlantic	1927
Inauguration of the Marshall plan	1947
Introduction of the Gregorian calendar in England and the Colonies (including the U.S.)	1752

My score is_____points

Test No. 6. Look at the twenty playing cards listed below for eight minutes and try to remember the correct order. Proceed in the same way as before and try to recall each card in connection with its assigned place. It is not enough to remember the 9 of hearts; it is necessary to know that the 9 of hearts was number 12, etc. Give yourself one point for each card you remember correctly.

1. 8 of diamonds	11. king of diamonds
2. 6 of clubs	12. 9 of hearts
3. queen of spades	13. 10 of clubs
4. 5 of spades	14. queen of diamonds
5. jack of clubs	15. king of hearts
6. ace of spades	16. jack of diamonds
7. 2 of diamonds	17. ace of hearts
8. 3 of hearts	18. 3 of spades
9. 9 of clubs	19. ace of clubs
10. 6 of spades	20. 4 of diamonds

My score is_____points

Test No. 7. Take fifteen minutes to read the following story, "Intrepid Airman, I," and then close the book and see how many details you can remember.

INTREPID AIRMAN, I*

1. I'll take three hours in the dentist's waiting room, with four cavities and an impacted wisdom tooth, in preference to fifteen minutes at any airport, waiting to get into an airplane.
2. You may class this as hysteria, you may regard it as ungenerous criticism of a system of transportation that has established itself as the fastest, safest, and most convenient in the world. But where airplanes are concerned I'm a case for quiet conditions in the padded room.
3. I'm all right at the terminus; indeed, when I see people queuing at counters labeled "New York," "Chungking," and "Bermuda," I feel a certain regret that I too am not bound for similar romantic destinations. But the urge for far-flung travel evaporates as soon as I get into the airport bus.
4. The first thing I do in the bus is to look around at the other passengers to see if they are the kind of people with whom I should be content to die. They always, for some reason, fail to measure up to my standards. By the time we arrive at the airport, I have lost about a pound in weight.

* Reprinted by permission of the London *Daily Mail* and the Reader's Digest Association, Inc.

5. At the airport I try to fall into conversation with the pilot or some member of the crew. I have a number of questions to ask—apparently offhand, casual questions, but they go to the root of the matter.

6. I wish to ask the pilot:
   a. Are the very best engineers even now checking every inch of our airplane?
   b. Have you, or any member of your family, ever been subject to giddiness, loss of memory, or nervous attacks?
   c. Are you going to drive it very fast?
   d. Will it be necessary for us to travel at much more than fifty feet above the ground?

7. To the radio operator:
   Can you, even if they send it out very quickly, be perfectly sure of understanding the Morse code?

8. And, finally, to the air hostess:
   If anything goes wrong, would you be so kind as to inform me personally, some time in advance of the other passengers?

9. Reassured about these matters—and I must admit that all air crews are immensely reassuring—I enter the plane. I cannot decide whether it is better to sit in the front and bear the full brunt of the impact, or in the back and run the risk of being carried away when the tail unit falls off. I choose a central position, where I can watch the wings and see that the propellers are going round.

10. Five minutes after we are airborne, I disentangle my fingernails from the upholstery of the seat and release the safety belt which I had drawn so tight that it stopped my breathing. I sit back to enjoy the cloud panorama.

11. The door of the pilot's cabin opens—and the pilot himself comes out! What recklessness is this? He has left some half-fledged boy at the wheel! I watch with horror as he strolls down the aisle, chatting easily with the other passengers. I know what he's doing. He's telling them it's all right. Both engines have fallen off but he's telling them it's all right.

12. When my turn comes, the pilot says, "Good morning—are you having a pleasant trip?" I merely nod, speechless. All I want him to do is get back to his work and remove that mad office boy from the controls. I relax as he shuts the door of his cabin behind him.

13. An hour goes by. I had a bad moment when the hostess leaned over and said something I was unable to hear. It sounded like,

"We are falling into the sea." I was halfway out of my seat when I realized she was asking me if I would like some tea.

14. Suddenly we are losing altitude. I look down and the earth is carpeted with railway lines, red brick houses, factory chimneys, and telegraph poles. This is it.

15. The percussion valve in the port cylinder has blown out. This is the emergency landing. I sink the old nails right back into the upholstery and close my eyes. There is a bump, a faint screech— we have gone through a cow?—and then all is silent and still. We are alive, but where?

16. I open my eyes, and we are sitting on the apron outside the terminal building. They are pushing up a ladder to the door.

17. I leave the plane with a slight swagger. A lot of openmouthed sightseers are standing behind the railings. Well may they stare. They are looking at one of the intrepid birdmen of the modern era—in Dublin a little more than an hour ago, now, as large as life, at Northolt airport.

18. What I say is that the airplane provides the safest, fastest, and most convenient means of travel in the world.

A good way to check how much you remember of the story you have just read is to retell it to someone else. This person should follow the story in the book, while you are retelling it, and see whether you cover all the essential points in it. You are not required to know the story verbatim, but no important thought in any paragraph should be left out.

Then test yourself again in the same manner three days later without having gone back to the story in the meantime, and see how much detail you still remember.

CAN WE IMPROVE OUR MEMORY?

Are you disappointed about your scoring average on the tests? You may have noticed that in some tests you did better—or not as bad—as in others. That is only natural.

Other students who took the same tests may have scored better in one particular test while doing much worse than you did in another test.

Don't be discouraged. If you go with us step by step through this book and do the exercises conscientiously, you will see an improvement very rapidly and you will enjoy your success.

Whether or not we can actually improve our memory is a rather academic question. You already know the answer: Yes, we can!

You do not have to take our word for it. In a little while you will be the best judge yourself.

After studying this book, doing the exercises, and comparing your scores, before and after, you will have undeniable proof that your memory has improved!

You do not have to wait until you have gone through the entire book in order to prove it to yourself. You will find your memory improving before you are halfway through, if not sooner.

There have been people, even highly intelligent people, who said that there is no such thing as memory improvement. Richard H. Rovere, author of a profile on my memory work in *The New Yorker,* made a statement to that effect when he wrote: "So far as is known, a man's memory, like his intelligence, remains just about constant most of his life. . . ." He continued: "Dr. Furst cannot increase the power of anyone's memory, but he can enable a person with a poor memory to make the best use of it. He cannot rebuild the motor, but by overhauling the ignition, adjusting the carburetor, and cleaning the sparkplugs, he can get more speed and mileage out of it."

If we take such statements at face value and apply them to the example of the motor, would not the final analysis be that you should not have your motor tuned up because it will never be the same as a new motor?

But let us now also see what some highly regarded men in the field of psychology thought about this subject. Professor William James, who is credited with raising psychology to the rank of a full-fledged science, said: "The one who thinks of his experiences most and weaves them into systematic relation with each other will be the one with the best memory." Dr. Roscoe Pound, professor of law at Harvard University, at one time was asked how it felt to possess such a wonderful natural memory as his. "Nonsense!" said Dr. Pound. "I remember because I must. I worked to develop my memory." Thomas De Quincey wrote: "It is notorious that the memory strengthens as you lay burden on it and becomes trustworthy as you trust it." Many similar statements could be added.

At one time I broke my left leg while ice skating. After several weeks I managed to walk on crutches. It took quite a while, however, before I could do away with the crutches. True, these crutches were an artificial help, but without their support I could not have walked at all; and finally, through the help of these crutches, I was again able to walk without them.

Well then, if someone calls the support that a memory system will give to our memory "crutches" or "artificial," it is not as bad as it may sound, for it ultimately does lead to memory improvement. Psychology has always distinguished three ways of memory improvement:

1. Mechanical methods—deepening, prolonging, and repeating the impression.
2. Intellectual methods—employing a logical, rational system and classification.
3. Ingenious methods—artificial systems of memory improvement.

On the face of it, then, there are three distinctly different methods. However, it is often difficult to determine where the one stops and the other enters.

For that matter the difference between a natural method and an artificial method often becomes academic. For instance, the telephone number of CBS in New York City is 765-4321. Is it a natural or an artificial method if we remember this number by thinking of the reversed sequence of the digits? If the house number of our friend is 1492, is it a natural or artificial help if we connect his house number with the discovery of America? If his house number is 43, is it natural or artificial if we remember it by the fact that he was forty-three years old when we first met him?

Such examples could be listed by the thousands. These few are sufficient, however, to prove that it is not so easy to draw a clear, straight line between natural and artificial methods.

Let us go one step further and assume for a moment that the method *is* artificial. What is so bad about that?

Every farmer knows that he must help nature by artificial

means if he wants a good crop. The soil of his farm may be too dry and therefore need irrigation. It may not be rich enough and therefore require fertilization. He may have a better harvest if he grows high-yielding strains. All these are artificial means, but for the world's steadily increasing population they may well spell the difference between survival and starvation.

If we use eyeglasses, don't we use artificial help for the sake of seeing better, a hearing aid for hearing better?

Is not the automobile actually an artificial substitute for walking? The airplane and the spacecraft an artificial means for flying?

In our daily lives we use thousands of artificial aids without even realizing that they are substitutes. Really, there is no valid reason why we should look down upon artificial means to achieve a worthwhile purpose.

The overriding factor is not so much which type of method we use, but rather whether it does accomplish what it was intended to bring about.

Whether our memory methods work is a question you will soon be able to answer, when you practice the first memory exercises and your memory grows steadily stronger as you go on working— not just reading.

Our approach to memory improvement consists of two elements:

1. A system that will provide you with the keys by which you can commit to memory anything and everything you wish to remember in your business or social life.
2. A system that will strengthen your powers of observation, concentration, and classification so that your memory will retain whatever you want to remember without much effort.

When you learn the rules given in this book and you become accustomed to applying them almost automatically in your daily life, you will be successful.

You see, the process is like learning a foreign language. In the beginning you still think in your mother tongue, translating every word into the new language. No doubt this requires conscious effort on your part. However, the more you read, hear, and speak the new language, the more you get used to thinking in that language. Gradually you find yourself thinking in it. That's when you start speaking it fluently without much effort.

The same thing happens in training your memory. In the beginning our rules and exercises enforce a new way of thinking— an effort similar to that in learning a foreign language. Soon you will realize the tremendous advantages of this system, and by continuous application you will get so used to it that it will become second nature to you. You will be using it automatically and as a result your memory will change from a sieve to a perfect filing cabinet.

Before we start applying the system we should know a few basic facts about memory and how it works. We mean how it works naturally, aside from using any system and without training. We should know the answers to such questions as:

What do we remember best?

How important is it whether or not we are interested in a particular subject?

How does our memory receive impressions?

What is the best time for learning?

What is the best interval of time between learning and repetition?

What influence has age on memory?

CHAPTER 2

How Does Our Memory Work?

WHAT DO WE REMEMBER?

Stop to think for a moment of all the things we learned in school. We devoted years and years to a variety of subjects. And how much of it do we still remember?

We devoted years and years to mathematics. But alas, if an eighth-grader comes to us with a rather simple equation, most of us are more at a loss to solve the problem than the student.

Take a foreign language as another example. No doubt you spent a few years in Spanish classes or French, or any other language for that matter, but let a foreigner ask you now for road directions in your own city, and you are at a complete loss in both understanding him and in trying to communicate with him. Yet you learned his language. Isn't it embarrassing how much you forgot, how little of it is left?

The same goes, in general, for what we learned in other subjects. In general that is. There may be exceptions. Some subjects we may remember very well. We remember not only the lessons but often the way in which they were presented, the voice of the teacher, the examples written on the blackboard, maybe even the questions asked by our classmates.

The same kind of experience can be found in everyday life. Of an entire summer that you may have spent at the seashore, one day stands out clearly in your mind, while you have no such vivid recollection of the others.

Have you ever watched a rerun of a TV show which you had seen before? And were you surprised that there were episodes, maybe whole segments, in the show of which you recalled hardly anything, while you remembered other parts in minute detail?

How come? There must be a reason for this. It is the same brain that is working; it is the same mind that received the impressions; nevertheless there is so much difference in remembering!

Of course, there is an answer, but the answer is not as simple as we would like it to be. Instead of one reason, there are scores of different reasons.

Let us find one of the most important ones first. When reminiscing about a picnic in the mountains a year or so ago, one person in a group may remember the scenery in every detail while another has forgotten all about it. The scenery itself, the object, is obviously the last thing that can be blamed for anyone's remembering or forgetting it.

So, if it is not the *object* itself that is to blame, it must be something that is *subjective*—which is in our mind—although, of course, in some way connected with the object in question. This something may be called "interest."

It is interest which compels us to give our undivided attention to a certain object; sometimes so much that we exclude all other thoughts that might interfere. Interest creates concentration.

Going back to your schooldays again, you find that there were subjects that interested you very much. You still remember quite a bit about them. However, there were others which did not interest you at all, and you have forgotten almost everything you ever learned about them.

It is the same in everyday life. If somebody approaches you with an attractive proposal that may be vital to your entire career, you listen very attentively, don't you? Your mind does not wander to other things; you concentrate on the issues at stake. Whether or not you accept the proposal is another matter, but you will remember it for years to come, if not for life.

From all this we conclude that one of the most important elements of memory and memory training is interest. It is fundamental. To concentrate on something without being interested is very difficult, sometimes impossible. The reverse is just as true. Interest somehow automatically results, to some degree, in concentration.

A common experience that we all have had is the following. We were reading a book that did not interest us too much and our mind started wandering while our eyes were still following the words and the lines. When the chapter came to an end, we had only a vague idea about its contents, perhaps even no idea at all.

On the other hand, you may recall that you went to see a ball game. It may have been quite some time ago. You had a particular interest in the game perhaps, because one of the players was a personal friend of yours, maybe a relative, or someone with whom you went to school. You can vividly remember the day and the place, the weather and the trip down to the stadium. You can still visualize the critical moments in the game, how the scoring went, the decisive plays and the players involved in them. You may never forget that game. The main reason, of course, is the concentration, the undivided attention with which you followed the game, which was a result of your interest in it.

Therefore, before we go further, make it your first rule to stop reading this book the moment your interest begins to flag. All the exercises described in the following chapters require your full concentration, and only undivided attention will result in success. There is no point in proceeding further if you fail in any one of the exercises. It may be necessary for you to repeat an exercise. It is not good to skip anything or to go ahead without mastering each chapter as you go along. It is useless to skip and jump. If you proceed slowly, but regularly, each new exercise will hold your interest. You will watch the improvement of your memory faculties with keen satisfaction and you will make the most out of every new chapter.

HOW DO WE REMEMBER?

How does our memory work? Assuming that we are interested in a certain subject, how does it register in our memory? Our senses are our media of perception. We perceive by our sense of sight, hearing, touch, taste, or smell. Most important are the first two, seeing and hearing.

We distinguish between eye-minded, ear-minded, and motor-minded persons, and it is of the utmost importance for anyone to know the type to which he belongs.

We call a person "eye-minded" if he remembers best the things he sees, the stimuli which are conveyed to his brain cells by means of his eyes.

We call a person "ear-minded" if he remembers best the things he hears, the stimuli which are conveyed to his brain cells by means of his ears.

We call a person "motor-minded" if he remembers best the things which are connected with a certain motion. This motion may be something he does himself, for instance writing, playing an instrument, or touching something. The motion may also be something that originates outside the person—anything that reaches him by physical contact, by taste, or by smell.

It goes without saying that the eye-minded person benefits most by learning from books or from anything presented visually. His memory retains the printed word, sentences, and paragraphs. He will remember that the paragraph on the first human heart transplant was printed on the left-hand page of his history book. When he sees a movie he will remember actions and incidents clearly while most of the spoken word tends to become vague and to fade away.

In contrast, the ear-minded person benefits more from lectures, the spoken word in general, and anything else produced by sound, since his memory retains better those things picked up through the ears. He may be able to repeat a conversation almost verbatim, while at the same time finding it difficult to describe the person with whom he conducted the conversation. If he sees a movie, the sound of the words and the music will stay with him, while the action may soon be forgotten.

Motor-mindedness refers to the remaining senses: touch, taste, or smell. With most of us they rank far behind sight and hearing, although there are exceptions. Blind persons often develop the other senses to a remarkable degree, far more in fact than people who have normal eyesight. This fact is important to notice, since it proves that every sense can be developed and improved.

It must be understood that no person is 100 per cent eye-minded, ear-minded, or motor-minded. We usually have all three qualities. The question is only which of these is preponderant in the individual. We know that approximately three quarters of all human beings are eye-minded, a fact which, as we said before, does not mean 100 per cent eye-minded, but anywhere between 60 and 80 per cent, while the balance is divided between hearing and the other senses.

Among people who are predominantly ear-minded we find many musicians. Some can play a composition they have heard but the score of which they have never seen. It is interesting to note that the same differences in type appear among the animals. The eagle, for instance, is predominantly eye-minded, being able to detect his prey from an altitude so high that man could not distinguish a hut from a church. The deer is mainly ear-minded, being able to hear the snapping of a twig from a great distance, whereas the dog is known to have a sense of smell that by far surpasses his sight and hearing.

How well we learn and memorize any given material depends to a large extent on the type to which we belong. It would therefore be quite meaningful to be aware of our own type. Astonishingly enough, very few persons know to what type they belong.

It is a foregone conclusion that a person who is preponderantly eye-minded should try to learn as much as possible from books, and that a student who is preponderantly ear-minded puts his time to better use by attending lectures as much as possible, or listening to tape recordings for that matter, in other words by listening to the voice of the teacher or professor.

However, as we said before, nobody is 100 per cent eye-minded or 100 per cent ear-minded. Therefore, it is of great help to the student who is ear-minded to read aloud. By doing so, his ear will come to the aid of his eye, and he opens two channels to his brain instead of one. An alternative would be to transcribe his notes by voice to a tape recorder or cassette and use the playback whenever he feels the need for it.

The motor-minded person will do best to put as much as possible in writing. The writing in itself will help him absorb the study material.

If he is eye- and motor-minded he might copy quite a bit from his books.

If he is ear- and motor-minded he should by all means rely on the notes he takes while listening to the lectures.

At any rate, you have an enormous advantage if you know your own type and arrange your learning and memorizing accordingly.

Again, there are not too many persons who are aware of their type as far as reception is concerned. Ask a pianist who plays a composition by heart how he does it. In most cases he will answer that he actually does not know.

You may ask several musicians this same question, and if they do give you an answer after giving the matter some serious thought, you will get a variety of reactions. One will tell you that he "sees" or imagines the score before his eyes while he is playing. A clear example of an eye-minded type. In contrast, the ear-minded musician follows his ear, and it is quite possible that he has never seen the score or that he would not be able to read it if he had, because he cannot read notes. Finally, the motor-minded musician would be able to play the composition even if the piano were mute. He relies neither on the score nor on the melody. What he remembers best is the *movement* of his hands.

The great Albert Schweitzer was the personification of all these types synchronized into one. He is the exception to the rule. When working among the natives in West Africa, he used to take time out from his rigid schedule as a physician to devote to playing the "organ." For lack of a real organ, he would take some wooden planks as imaginary keyboards. In this manner he "played" his favorite Bach pieces with visible gratification.

Only a very extraordinary man like Dr. Schweitzer combines all three types in one person. He was a genius. Most of us are not that versatile. In order to find out to which type we belong, we can follow two different procedures; one works best if you want to test yourself, the other works best when you test somebody else.

If you want to test yourself, select two paragraphs of about equal length from a book. Each of them may cover perhaps half a page. Read the first of these paragraphs silently to yourself. Check the exact time you need for reading it. Then write down on a piece of paper whatever you remember.

Having done this, ask somebody else to read the other paragraph to you while you listen. The time needed for the reading must be exactly the same as the time which you spent in reading the first paragraph. This is important. When your friend has finished his reading, write again on a piece of paper whatever you remember. Then compare your two papers and see whether you remembered more from the paragraph you yourself read or the paragraph you listened to.

This experiment should be repeated at least three times. With each new experiment the material used should be longer. If you used half a page the first time, choose a full page the second time and two pages the third time. Naturally the material used in one test—reading and listening—must always be of equal length.

The conclusion will be easy for you. If you find that you remember more of those paragraphs which you read for yourself, it means that you are preponderantly eye-minded; if you remember more of the paragraphs you listened to, it means that you are preponderantly ear-minded.

It is somewhat easier to test someone else, especially if he does not know in advance what the test means. Here's a list of ten words which you might read to your friend. Tell him only to write on a piece of paper the first word which comes to his mind when he hears a word that you call out to him. Here are the ten words:

1. wall	6. river
2. cake	7. letter
3. book	8. bird
4. noise	9. flag
5. file	10. hat

Then look at the words your friend wrote. Generally speaking, there are two possibilities: (1) he may have written words like these:

1. picture, paper, ceiling	6. water, boat, fishing
2. flour, sugar, icing	7. envelope, typewriter, stamp
3. page, illustration, text	8. feather, wings, egg
4. propeller, music, siren	9. cloth, stripes, stars
5. paper, drawer, box	10. ribbon, straw, felt

or (2) he may have written words like these:

1. hall, ball, vault	6. liver, ringer
2. make, bake, take	7. latter, ladder, ledger, lecture
3. look, hook, bug	8. flirt, hurt, birth
4. poise, choice, moist	9. bag, drag
5. pile, mile, fine, fire	10. bat, chat, flat

Of course, all these words are only examples, and the variety of words which your friend may have written in response to the words called out to him is almost unlimited. But whatever his response is, a survey of his answer will show whether more words are similar to Group 1 or whether more words are similar to Group 2.

As you see, the examples in Group 1 contain words which somebody with a vivid imagination may *see* if he thinks of wall, cake, book, and so on. The examples given in Group 2 indicate words which are similar in *sound* to the words which you called out to him. Therefore, if you check your friend's paper, you must compare the words that you gave him with the words that he wrote down. If you find more words which belong in Group 1, your friend is preponderantly eye-minded; if you find more words which belong in Group 2, he is preponderantly ear-minded. By checking the number of words belonging in each of these two groups, you can even find the approximate percentage of his eye- or ear-mindedness.

You can also see why it is an advantage for your friend not to know in advance the purpose of the test. If he knows it in advance, he will become too conscious of the associations which he forms. He will watch to see whether he tends more to visual or to auditory associations, and such watchfulness is detrimental to the purpose of the test.

THE BEST TIME FOR LEARNING

What is the best time for learning?

It depends to a large degree on sleeping patterns. We can roughly classify people according to their sleeping patterns into two broad categories: "evening sleepers" and "morning sleepers."

There are persons who fall asleep immediately upon going to bed, and after a very short time their sleep reaches its soundest depth. Toward morning it becomes lighter; they wake up instantly and there is no long-drawn-out transition between sleep and full awakening. The depth of their sleep is easily tested by the fact that noises which do not disturb them in the evening wake them up in the morning.

Just the opposite holds true with regard to the morning sleeper. At night he needs a good while to fall asleep, and during the first hours his sleep is so light that the slightest noise wakes him. During the morning hours, however, his sleep is deep, and the transition from sleep to waking takes quite some time.

Generally speaking, and admitting occasional exceptions, we may say that the evening sleeper learns and memorizes best in the morning. At that time his senses are at the height of their efficiency and his brain cells are wide open for new impressions. The contrary, of course, holds true for the morning sleeper. He feels more or less drowsy during the morning hours and reaches the height of his capacity toward noon or even during the afternoon. Naturally, for him the evening hours are the best time for learning difficult material.

Of course, there are other factors which enter into the picture. What is your mental capacity, and how much mental work must you accomplish during the day? If we compare two persons with equal mental capacities, the man who has to deal with difficult problems all day long will be less receptive to new impressions in the evening than his counterpart whose daytime work is accomplished in a more or less mechanical way. The conclusion which can be drawn from the above is that if we want to study and work at peak efficiency, we should take the various determining factors into account as far as practicable.

The Interval in Learning

The interval between learning and repetition is much more important than people usually assume. Ebbinghaus, a German professor, devoted much time to experiments in this particular line, and his tests have been checked and double-checked in almost every country.

It is wrong to assume that any subject matter which we once learned and mastered will remain our mental property forever. A person may have spoken a foreign language rather fluently but, by not using it for several years, may have lost the ability completely and be forced to admit that he can neither speak it nor understand it any longer.

That would not happen if he used the language constantly. Use is repetition, and repetition is necessary for everything which we wish to keep alive in our minds. But everyone knows this! What is not so well known is that the spacing of repetition plays a very important role in learning and remembering. Ebbinghaus found that a subject which requires 68 repetitions to be memorized if learned in one day requires only 38 repetitions if they are spread out over three days. A more complex subject which required 504 repetitions in one day could be mastered by repeating it 158 times the first day, 109 times the second day, and 75 times the third day. Thus repetitions for all three consecutive days add up to 342, effecting a saving of time amounting to approximately 30 per cent if compared with the 504 repetitions on a single day. Since time is, or should be, of great value to all of us, no one should fail to make use of such a timesaving device, especially if it is as easy to apply as the proper spacing of learning and repetition.

Whenever you study a new subject, do not force yourself to try to master it completely on the first day. Be satisfied if you acquire a fair knowledge of it, allow it to sink into your memory, and then repeat it on the two following days, and you will see that you can master it better with less effort.

It is one of the strange phenomena of the human mind that memory continues to work even when the actual task of learning has ceased and even when we are asleep. It is the same peculiar occurrence which helps us to solve a problem while we are dreaming, especially a problem on which we focused our attention before going to sleep and which proved too tough for solution.

The only possible explanation for both phenomena is the fact that our subconscious mind continues working and thinking while our conscious mind is asleep. The same mental power that produces dreams must be able to work on problems and to solve them. It is evidently wrong to think of our conscious and our subconscious functioning as two mental activities which are eternally divided. It is much better to think of them as two rooms whose separating wall is flexible and easily removable. It is figuratively accurate to speak of the "threshold" between the conscious and the subconscious mind, for every thought can easily flow from the conscious to the subconscious over this threshold.

Surely the following has happened to you as it has happened to almost everyone. You tried to think of the name of a person and found you could not remember it. You may have known this person for a long time, but at that moment the name would not come to you. It was not in the realm of your consciousness. However, if at that moment you had heard or read a name similar in sound or which had some other association to the name in question, then this similarity would have been enough to recall the name to your conscious mind.

What happened in between? We know that no impression which ever meets one of our five senses can be entirely lost. While we are not aware of it, it rests in our subconscious, where it may be buried for good or whence we may be able to draw it over the threshold into our conscious mind, usually with the help of some association.

Age

Must we accept a decrease in our mental efficiency as we grow older? This question is usually asked by people who have passed their fiftieth birthday. Younger people are not much concerned about the future of their brain cells, and they cannot or will not realize that their own memory may not always remain so reliable as it is at present.

Memorizing is partly a physiological and partly a psychological process; and this dualism is responsible for the innumerable varieties of ways in which our memory works. In the physiological sense memory rests on pathways connecting our brain cells, and both the quantity and the firmness of these pathways are decisive for its functioning. As we grow older, these brain paths become less firm, and there comes a time when the process of forgetting proceeds more quickly than the process of learning.

While such an unwelcome reversal invariably happens near the end of a lifetime, there is much we can do to delay its occurrence. It is certainly no coincidence that many people who used their brains more than the average person have kept their retentive and productive ability up to a ripe old age. Think of Bernard Shaw, of Goethe, of Thomas Edison. It would be a fallacy to think that in order to take proper care of our brain cells we should spare them every effort and preserve them unused. Just the contrary holds true. You can train your brain as you train your muscles, and you can prove this to your satisfaction by simple tests while you go through the exercises described in this book. You will see that experiments which call for effort when tried the first time become easy when you repeat them, and after a while you can hardly understand why they caused any effort at all.

If we realize that memory can be developed like a muscle, we must also accept the truth that its efficiency will diminish like a muscle if it is not properly used. It is a known fact that, after an illness which keeps one in bed for several months, walking is very difficult. The muscles of the legs forget how to move, and one has to relearn walking much as a little tot first masters the skill.

Why, then, should we be astonished when the same thing happens to our memory—when it loses its reliability if we don't use it? And yet the average adult is always afraid to trust his memory. There are notebooks and calendars, appointment books and telephone lists, memorandum slips and desk notes—all destined to unburden our memory and therefore all working in the wrong direction.

Thorndike, who devoted much time to tests concerning memory and age, found that there is no natural reason for a decline as we grow older except in the latest years of our lives. If our memory weakens before that time, we must blame ourselves. Most people, after they have finished their formal education, don't bother very much about further learning—that is, *learning* in the actual sense of the word, not just *reading,* which is merely passive and receptive.

Except in acting and similar occupations, there is little inducement or motive for learning anything word for word. That in itself involves the loss of good memory techniques, which are maintained only with steady practice. Still, this would not be decisive if we balanced it, at least, by remembering all the little things which occur in our daily business and social life. But we are too much afraid to "burden our memory" and many of us consider it a waste of time to remember names and addresses, telephone numbers and appointments, which are "so much easier" jotted down and looked up in notebooks.

Some people take daily walks when it would be "much easier" to use the car or take a bus, because they know that walking is healthier and they wish to increase or at least keep up their muscular strength. On the other hand, they write down every little reminder, thus steadily decreasing their powers of memory. If they try to remember something once in a long while, they are apt to forget it; as a consequence, they distrust their memory still more and they write down still more. In the end, they are astonished to find their memory failing them entirely, and they do not realize that they have only themselves to blame for this steady downward trend of memory and efficiency. All this, aside from physiological reasons, explains very well the fact that older people often forget important things which happened last month or even last week, while they remember perfectly every detail, even of unimportant events, which took place thirty or forty years ago.

CHAPTER 3

Association

INTELLECT AND IMAGINATION

We know what a line is. If we put four lines of equal length together, end to end, we can make a square. If we put six squares together in a three-dimensional shape, the result will be a cube. That is simple, isn't it? But nobody could understand the meaning of a cube without knowing what a line is and what a square is.

What is true in geometry is true in every phase of life. We learn and remember everything that is new to us only by connecting it with something that we already know. There is no other way of acquiring knowledge.

Just as the mason puts one stone upon another, connecting the two by mortar when he is building a wall, so must we connect every new idea with a familiar one if we want the new thought to stick in our mind. We are not always aware of this fact, but it is worthwhile to give it some thought.

You will immediately see the truth of this statement if you think of learning a foreign language. In order to learn that *light* is *lux* in Latin, we must form a connection between *light* and *lux,* and only if this connection or association is strong will it enable us to recall the foreign word whenever we need it. Once the pathway between *light* and *lux* is firmly established in our brains, we will recall the one or the other without conscious effort, and even without our will.

From languages let us turn to history. Suppose we know that America was discovered by Columbus, and we have to learn that he discovered it in 1492. In order to remember this, we must form an association between the discovery of America and the year or the number 1492. There are many different ways of forming such a connection, and we have the choice of which way to take. But we must choose one of these ways if we wish to answer the two questions: When did Columbus discover America? . . . What happened in 1492?

Throughout your life you have been making such connections, but seldom consciously. You may not have been aware of forming associations at all. You did it subconsciously, just as a little child connects the word *daddy* with the person of his father without knowing anything about connections and associations.

However, we will see in the following chapters that it is to our advantage to form our associations consciously, and to form our connections in a way which fits our type and the requirements of our own personal memory.

The old Greek, Roman, and medieval philosophers tried to find certain rules for these associations and to classify them. Aristotle and, later, Thomas Aquinas found three basic rules:

The *Law of Similarity* refers to things which are alike.

The *Law of Contrast* is applied if the relations of similarity are reversed.

The *Law of Propinquity* implies that nearness of place, time, or some other relationship of any object in memory recalls other objects that were connected with it in a previous experience.

Robert E. Brennan, professor of psychology and director of the Thomistic Institute of Providence College, combined the three laws in one sentence. He stated that any part of an experience which we had at a previous time has a tendency to recall other parts of the same experience whenever the first part comes into our consciousness.*

Granted that this one sentence covers every conceivable association which we have formed in the past, it is certainly not sufficient if we try to remember things by connecting them consciously and by establishing an association which is so strong that one item must recall the other to our mind whenever we need it.

For the purpose of learning and remembering, it is necessary to go into greater detail and to become aware of the various possi-

* *General Psychology* (New York: The Macmillan Company), p. 245.

bilities by which two objects or two thoughts can be connected. Of course, in theory these possibilities are almost infinite, but for practical purposes we may select ten laws of association which cover the ground and which are sufficient for everyday life.

If we think of the word *back,* it may recall a word like *lack,* or *pack,* or *rack,* or *sack* because they are all similar in sound. The same holds true for the words *prescription* and *subscription.* Words of the same sound very often rhyme, but not necessarily. *Memory* and *Memphis* have *Similarity of Sound* but they do not rhyme.

If we think of a member of our memory class, we may think of him as a student or a pupil or a scholar. These words are *Synonyms,* or words with similar meanings, and therefore one may easily recall the other.

The page you are now looking at is a part of the entire book; one paragraph is part of the page; each word is part of the paragraph; and each letter is part of the word. One recalls the other because they are related in the sense of *Whole and Part.*

This book may remind you of another book in your library, but it might also remind you of a magazine, a newspaper, or a pamphlet because they are all printed material, and therefore all *Things of the Same Species.*

However, your trend of thought when reading this book may be entirely different. You may think that this book is supposed to increase your knowledge about memory training and to improve your memory. Thus the book and its study is the cause of your action, and a better memory is the effect of it. Knowledge follows study as thunder follows lightning; crime and punishment; war and treaty—all obey the same eternal law of *Cause and Effect.*

Many readers of this book will be zealous students; but if you think of the most zealous, it is quite possible that his counterpart, the laziest, will come to your mind. The oldest member of a class often reminds us of the youngest; thinking of a giant often recalls a dwarf. The law of *Contrast* connects things just as strongly as the law of *Similarity.*

Many of our exercises require you to write something. To do this you need paper and pencil, or paper and ballpoint pen. During lunchtime you may order ham and eggs and you may use a straw to sip your soda. Since we are accustomed to think of paper and pencil or ham and eggs or straw and soda as belonging together, since they are matched in our brain cells, we call them *Matching Pairs,* and we realize that the thought of one of them may easily recall the other.

The ballpoint pen we mentioned may be new or old, it may be cheap or expensive, and the way it writes may be good or bad. All these are different attributes which could belong to the same object, the ballpoint pen. But we may change this trend of thought; we may start with one of the adjectives. Then we find that not only is the ballpoint pen expensive, but so also is our uncle's apartment, Fred's vacation trip, and Alice's fur coat. Very often a certain person (or a certain object) is closely connected in our mind with a certain characteristic, and the same happens with regard to objects. Thus we have found another association law, which we call *Subject and Quality,* or *Object and Quality.*

If you think of this book, its authors may come to your mind. If you think of the United States, you may recall the Stars and Stripes. Think of the Declaration of Independence, and it is almost certain that Thomas Jefferson comes to your mind. If we admire the Lincoln Memorial in Washington, our thoughts may wander to the Gettysburg Address. Why does all this happen? Somebody else could have drafted the Declaration, and Lincoln could have delivered his famous speech on another battlefield. But history, geography, literature have shaped all these events, and they are so inseparably impressed upon our minds that one will recall the other without any conscious effort. When it happened it was purely accidental, but since it happened this way, this *Accidental Association* is so firmly established that the same trend of thought exists in our brain.

However, there is another possibility. Suppose you were on an extended business trip and took a plane from Omaha to Cleveland. Your suitcase turned up in New Orleans and it was three days before you recovered it. This could have happened on any other leg of your trip. That it happened between Omaha and Cleveland was purely accidental, and so was the fact that your luggage went to New Orleans. But because it happened that way, the names Omaha, Cleveland, and New Orleans are so closely associated in your mind with the loss of your suitcase that you cannot think of this suitcase without being annoyed at hearing the names of these cities. Here again, we have an accidental association, but this time it works only in *your* mind; it is purely *subjective* and it does not apply to anyone else.

All of these association laws work whether or not you are aware of their existence. The thunder reminds you of lightning even if you have not heard of cause and effect or of the existence of association laws at all. It isn't the association law that creates the connection in the mind; this connection exists by itself, and the laws of association only serve the purpose of explaining why it exists. Which laws you prefer depends upon your way of thinking: the more rational your thoughts, the more important becomes cause and effect. And that may be the reason why some psychologists consider this association law of greater importance than all the others.

Professor Brennan, whose work was mentioned before, even goes so far as to state:

"Without the knowledge of general laws, memory must be burdened with ponderous items of information. The perfect mnemonic system is one in which phenomena are related as cause and effect. And because it is the function of philosophy to study such relationships, we can very largely supply the deficiencies of a poor memory by cultivating a philosophic turn of mind."*

The practical application of these laws of association and the method of using them for learning and remembering will be discussed later on. For the moment, it will be sufficient to mention that all these association laws are based on logic, on reasoning as contrasted to imagination and emotion.

C. G. Jung, the most famous of all the scholars who studied with Sigmund Freud, distinguishes three ways of forming associations:

1. The matter-of-fact associations, which are based on intellect and which are governed by the aforementioned laws.
2. The imaginative associations, which we shall discuss immediately.
3. The emotional associations, which are based on an affective state of mind.

* *Ibid.*, p. 257.

What is the distinction between intellectual and imaginative associations?

To explain this distinction, which is of immense importance for our work, let us go back to the words *mason . . . stone . . . wall.*

Intellectual thinking would reason like this: The mason needs the stones if he intends to erect a wall. We could add that we are accustomed to think of mason and stones as belonging together (matching pairs) and of the stone as being part of the wall (the whole and the part). We could also argue that the wall is the result of the mason handling the stones (cause and effect).

The contrast of this way of intellectual or constructive thinking is to *see* with the mental eye a mason or a group of masons piling one stone upon another and to imagine the wall growing higher and higher until it is finished. In reality we may be seated at a desk with nothing around us but the four walls of our room, our furniture, our books, and our pictures; but our mental eye does not care about the actual surroundings. It sees what we wish to see, and only the question of how clear and how distinct these images are remains in doubt. This faculty of our brain is called *imagination,* and we shall see that imagination plays a very significant part in our dealing with memory.

In contrast to intellect, imagination has the advantage of not being bound by logic. It happens too frequently in everyday life that we have to remember things which have no logical connection. Think, for instance, of names. We are introduced to Miss Chapman. There is no logical reason for her name to be Chapman. If the name of her parents had been Candlestick, her name would be Candlestick too. But still we must remember her name if we wish to address her correctly the next time we meet her. Often there is no logical reason for the name of any city, mountain, or river; and if there is one, we may not know it. But still we have to remember the name of the city, mountain, and river for one reason or another. So, to recall these things, we have to form an association which has nothing to do with logic.

Recognizing such a necessity means searching for something that can replace reason and logic as far as memory is concerned—and this is where imagination comes in. Chances are that you daydream once in a while. You see things which are not there and which may be based merely on wishful thinking. Therefore you know that imagination is not bound by logic. The mason, the stone, and the wall could be associated both by intellect and by imagination, but what about an eagle and a coal mine, or a Sioux Indian and your telephone? Of course, we can find a logical connection like this:

Eagle—raven—black—coal—coal mine.
Sioux Indian—old America—modern America—telephone.

However, this is a very roundabout way, and it certainly does not look like an efficient memory aid or a timesaving device.

Isn't it much easier to *see* mentally the eagle flying over a coal mine or to picture the Sioux Indian in his full regalia using your telephone? Don't say that you do not have a Sioux among your friends and that there is no chance for a member of that tribe to use your telephone. Imagination is not logical; and if you have a clear and distinct picture of the Indian with his headgear and his tomahawk speaking into the mouthpiece of your phone, you are pretty sure to remember it for a long time.

Imagination is an inborn gift, but it can be developed. Like memory itself, it is difficult to compare one's own power of imagination with that of others. If you were asked to close your eyes and imagine a ship, you could do it. But the clearness of this mental picture might vary to a considerable degree from someone else's. This degree is very difficult to measure, but you can test your imagination with almost every exercise given in this book. If you find that your power of imagination is inadequate, turn to Chapter 6, where you will find some exercises specifically designed for the training of mental vision.

But do not confuse imagination with knowledge. If somebody asks us to visualize a ship when we are far from any body of water, we are at liberty to think of an ocean liner, a Mississippi side-wheeler, a sailboat, or whatever comes to our minds. It goes without saying that a sailor who has spent years on ships of all sorts is in a better position to visualize details than the farmer in Mexico who never saw a ship in his life. But this difference is based only on personal experience concerning ships; it is knowledge and has nothing to do with imagination. Imagination is, as Prospero says in Shakespeare's *The Tempest,* "such stuff as dreams are made on." The farmer in Mexico who has never seen a real ship may visualize a dream ship. Every part of it may be wrong in a nautical sense, but still his mental eye may see "his" ship much more clearly and distinctly than does the sailor because the farmer's imagination may be stronger.

What holds true for the eye holds true for the ear. A musician may be away from his study and from his instrument, say walking in the woods, and still be able to "hear" any melody he imagines. His mind can produce a composition which is no more real than the farmer's ship. As far as memory is concerned, imagination is almost as important as reality.

The relationship between imagination and reality is a very close one. The following may serve to illustrate this point. Let us assume that you visited Washington, D.C., many years ago, and that in all those many years you never returned there and did not give it any thought. In all probability you do not even recall what the Capitol looks like. Had you gone back to Washington, say once every year during that time, the Capitol would have impressed itself more and more on your brain cells because of the effect of repetition.

However, if you had not had an opportunity to return to Washington, but had thought of the Capitol frequently, the repetition of your thought would have had the same effect as actually seeing it. The strength of each repetition depends on how close your mental picture comes to reality. The clearer, the more distinct your mental picture is, the easier and the better will it be as a substitute for the actual structure. But it still is your imagination that brings back the visual image; without it, repeating the image would be out of the question. Nothing is more important for memory training than a vivid imagination.

How is it possible that a boy who is a dunce in school and is always failing in class work can recall the baseball scores of his favorite team for the entire season and does not make a single mistake about runs, hits, and errors of the individual players?

William James gives the perfect solution to this question, which is not as easy to answer as it seems, since reference to interest alone certainly is not sufficient. James points to the fact that the boy's interest in "his" team makes him think of the games at frequent intervals. Each thought means a repetition of the first impression. Whenever he reads or hears about the most recent game, his thoughts go back to previous games, and every such thought means an additional association, which strengthens the recall of the statistics of each game. As a result, every score, every player, every game is anchored in his mind by many different associations and strengthened by so many mental repetitions that he is able to answer any question instantaneously, notwithstanding his lack of ability in other fields. The games were not repeated but his imagination made it possible to think of them repeatedly.

From all we have said, the following conclusions can be drawn:

1. Memory works through association. We can remember a new idea only by connecting it with something that we already know.
2. The question is not whether or not we form associations. The question is whether we form these associations consciously or subconsciously.
3. Association is formed either by intellect or by imagination. With most of us, imaginative association is stronger than intellectual association.
4. The forming of associations—both imaginative and intellectual—can be trained.

CHAPTER 4

Concentration

INTEREST AND MOTIVATION

Concentrating sounds like hard work, doesn't it? But it needn't be! It all depends, though, on many factors. We have already found that it is very easy to concentrate on something in which we are highly interested; something that captures our attention and holds it. When that is the case, we do not even realize that we *are* concentrating. It does not take any effort on our part. Millions of people were concentrating intensely during that historic event when man set foot on the moon for the first time. Millions in all parts of the world followed the activities of the astronauts from moment to moment. Many sacrificed their sleep in order not to miss out on any part of that awesome happening.

Was it hard for them to concentrate? You know the answer. Everyone was so interested in what was happening that it would have been ludicrous to ask whether anyone had trouble concentrating.

Since it is "interest" which induces effortless concentration and, conversely, since lack of interest is the basic cause of the inability to concentrate, it is of the utmost importance that we find out what it is that creates interest. In its broadest sense it is "reward." "Reward" can have many different meanings for different persons. There are many types of rewards, ranging from the material gain expressed in dollars and cents all the way to the other end of the spectrum, the purely intellectual satisfaction of learning and gaining knowledge. In practical life it means that if you take a self-improvement course—for example, one in memory training—you look forward to the reward of being able to remember all the things you used to forget so easily. The ability to remember will be rewarding in many ways, including better job performance and higher pay.

It is only natural that someone who enrolls in a computer-programming course will concentrate on his studies because he or she realizes that the direct result will be a job opportunity, a basis for livelihood, the prospect of proceeding to higher levels of computer study, to become a systems analyst and so on further up the ladder of success.

Sometimes however—or rather, most often—the relationship between effort (concentration) and result (reward) is not so immediately visible.

The student who has problems with his studies can be heard to say: "If only I could skip the subjects I hate, I would do all right. Why do I have to take biology when I want to become an airplane pilot?" Parents and guidance counselors devote quite some time and persuasiveness to try to convince young people that in order to get anywhere in life they need "an education," and that in order to get this education it is not enough to get just passing grades in the "easy" courses alone.

Some parents, I am told, offer their children all kinds of incentives for getting better grades in school, sometimes in hard cash. But I never heard of one boy who had to be induced by his parents to remember his school team's standing in the basketball, football, or baseball competition. Lively interest and reward go hand in hand in this case. The reward here is the pride in the team or the school, and the sense of belonging. No material reward, but a reward nevertheless. Sometimes the reward may even come from a negative angle, such as not wanting to belong to those who are not "in the know," in other words, a fear of losing one's status among one's peers.

As long as there is some relationship between the effort and the achievement, the connection between concentration and reward is very clear. Once the student can come to see that he has to put his mind to studying a wider range of subjects than only those he "likes," he has set the first step in the right direction. At this point the student is in a better frame of mind to tackle a heretofore difficult subject. The little extra concentration he then brings to his task nearly always results in the realization that the subject material is not as hard to digest as he had assumed.

Crucial for any student at this point is encouragement. Not so much the encouragement from parents and teachers, important as this is, but, more than anything, the encouragement that springs from tasting the gratifying sense of success. The success in having done something right, of having achieved something worthwhile, no matter how minuscule it may be in comparison to the large volume of knowledge that still is to be mastered.

The student draws strength from this gratifying sense of accomplishment. There is a great deal more determination in his attitude. He is now prepared to give his studies the needed concentration. More comprehension, better remembering, is only a natural result from this greater concentration.

However, there is still another plague to be dealt with. Interest may slacken after a while, and thus invite distraction, which is ever present in a multitude of forms. Distraction can come from the outside as well as from within. Environment has to do with it.

If you really plan to concentrate on your studies you will want to be in a room which is conducive to studying. Most of all, you will want to exclude any disturbing noise. Not only street noises, but also the sounds of radio, TV, voices of other people, the telephone, and so forth. It is best to be alone in a room, or if you have to share a room with someone else, it is best that you both agree not to disturb each other. The room, the chair you sit on, the posture you take, the lighting, the air, the temperature are all factors that can be either conducive or detrimental to concentration.

All these attributes play their role in a concerted effort to overcome restlessness, which is a known "killer" of concentration.

There is hardly any need to point out that personal habits play a role as well. Alcohol, even in small doses, and heavy smoking tend to diminish the capacity to concentrate. Improper diet, lack of exercise, lack of sleep can also cause a reduction in our mental capacities. In other words, there is no excuse for one's inability to concentrate when one grossly defies the elementary rules for normal healthy living, or allows all kinds of distracting disturbances to prevail in his or her environment.

Now for the distractions that come from within. One can make all the preparations carefully and still fail to be able to sustain the desired degree of concentration. This is a very real problem for many people. They start with the best intentions, but after a while their minds wander in any and all directions.

For one thing, the method of memorizing is to blame for this. All too often people try to "hammer" the material in their heads by parrotlike repetition, over and over again. The word *hammering* should in itself be indicative of their futile efforts. It is a pity that learning by rote is still the most universally practiced method of memorizing. The reasoning behind it is obvious. It goes like this: A little repetition is good, so a great deal of repetition must be better. The conclusion is, then, the more repetition the better. The results should have proved this reasoning to be entirely wrong.

Constant, humdrum repetition is the very cause of mind-wandering.

How much better is it to study, learn, and remember by way of association! Association stimulates the mind. If we only learn to think in pictures, our study material becomes colorful and so much more eagerly absorbed by our minds. Thus we need much less repetition for it to become our mental property.

The imagination should be given free rein, because it is boundless imagination that makes learning a pleasure instead of a drudge. Imaginative visualization can make the most difficult text material easy to digest, since it induces concentration and widens one's attention span to a heretofore unthinkable degree.

It is not only in the field of study that concentration should be diligently practiced. In the conduct of our everyday life we could well do with a healthy dose of concentration.

For example, let us look at how we handle ourselves in conversations with others. How much misunderstanding could be avoided if only we made an effort to concentrate a little more on what the other person was trying to say? We have come to talk about the faculty of listening as a gift or a talent. This fact in itself proves that a good listener is a rare thing. The hubbub of modern-day living may in part be blamed for that, but it is hardly an acceptable excuse for not listening with due attention to anything worth listening to.

Concentration is also a prerequisite for observation. It is through observing the whole as well as the details of any object, any scene or happening that we become aware of the nature of things, living or inanimate. There is no denying that it pays to train oneself in the art of observing. It has its own reward.

Anyone who needs to be convinced of the value of accurate observation has only to attend a court session and listen to the widely varying and often conflicting testimonies of witnesses under oath, giving in all earnest their versions of accidents or crimes which they saw with their own eyes.

It is not only possible to improve our faculties of listening and observing, it can be an enriching experience as well, as we shall show you in succeeding chapters. Interested listening and observing will make us concentrate almost automatically. The will power to concentrate is generated without our having to make any extra effort.

Again, bear in mind that as you progress in your memory study, our goal is not to make you a wizard in performing any particular memory feats, but rather to improve your ability to remember in general, in all aspects of human endeavor, so that you can apply your memory power to any area you may wish to explore, with confidence.

CHAPTER 5

How to Study

Anyone who is willing can learn. How much one learns is, aside from the degree of concentration, largely a matter of efficiency.

In spite of all the many books that have been written on the subject of effective studying, the waste of time and effort on the part of students remains staggering. Even the most serious and most determined students are often unaware that, in their well-meant zeal to gather any and all information on a subject, much, if not most, of their time is wasted in trying to assemble reams of data without sifting the essential from the non-essential.

They all know that taking notes is very valuable, especially for later review. And for fear of missing any essential points of a lecture, they take down almost verbatim what they hear. This kind of "note taking" completely defeats its purpose.

To begin with, it is a fallacy to believe that one can listen, think, and write, all at the same time! The purpose of the lecture is to impart new knowledge to the listener. Therefore the listener must think while following the speaker, and try to absorb ideas, principles, definitions, and explanations. Besides, even if it were possible to transcribe the lecture word for word, what would be so good about that? Either one has to reread the entire transcript and condense it to a series of meaningful notes, or one can file it with all other transcripts for later review. Either way, there is a considerable loss of time, and time is a most valuable commodity.

As a result many a student accumulates volumes of transcripts and much too elaborate "notes," and when the time comes that he needs them he can barely skim through the mass of material, which leaves him with a feeling of frustration.

The other extreme can also be found. A student may take down so few notes that the gist of the lecture does not come back to his mind when he reviews them, even right after the lecture! This is just as much a waste of energy.

The art of effective note taking has to be learned. It makes no difference whether it concerns a lesson in high school, a lecture in college, a classroom discussion, a speech at a social or civic meeting, or a dissertation over the radio or television, the rules are the same.

In order to take notes one has to listen! This is such a basic and self-evident factor that it seems rather strange to restate it here. However, it is really not superfluous to mention it once more, because nothing is of more crucial importance than the *listening* factor. There are many excuses given for poor listening. The subject may be uninteresting. The lecturer may be dull, his delivery may be unimaginative, monotonous, or hard to understand. In addition, we have to deal with the fact that our listening capacity is four or five times greater as far as *speed* is concerned than the average speed of speaking.

In other words, there is ample room for distractive thoughts while we are listening to a speech or a lecture. To cope with all these hindrances we had better come to the lecture hall with the proper armor, lest we be defeated before we start.

The entire arsenal of modern transcribing methods, from shorthand to tape recording, is useless in the pursuit of knowledge if we are not prepared to engage our mental powers actively. The ultimate purpose of studying is and will always remain to acquire knowledge by making it our personal property, by storing it in our memory. Our memory absorbs ideas and information only by activating our brain cells and our mental acuity.

The function of our written notes is to recall to mind the central points of the information we digested earlier, whether it was weeks, months, or years ago. This "information retrieval" is more miraculous than the working of the computer, in that one's "memory bank" not only produces the limited data "bits," as in our case the "note," but also the associative information, be it the reasoning behind the data or the explanation or any other matter that was connected with it at the time we recorded our "note." Notes, then, must be concise, comparatively short, and representative of the essence of a point made in a lecture.

This also means that much of what is said may not be worth recording. That which is worthwhile should be taken down in a condensed form. Not everybody will make the same notes, and the kind of notes taken also varies to a certain degree depending on the subject and on the manner of delivery by the lecturer.

But before everything else it is important to approach the lecture with a positive attitude, with the determination to distill whatever is worthwhile from it. Passive listening to what is said will get us nowhere. In this respect the adult often has a definite edge over the young student. The realization that the subject forms an integral part of the program of learning, no matter how uninteresting it may be in itself, or how poorly it may be presented, comes more naturally to the adult and makes for a more eager attitude.

It is the attitude that makes the difference. An interested and keen attitude puts us in the frame of mind that is needed for attentive listening. In order to cope with all kinds of distractive thoughts, the good listener will assume a posture that reflects his determination. He is, so to speak, aggressive in his listening.

There is such a thing as anticipatory listening. Since the subject is not completely foreign to him, there are likely to be moments when the listener's thoughts will wander about. To combat these distractions and to keep his mind on the subject, he keeps poised in anticipation that the speaker will inject a bit of knowledge that is new to him, or a viewpoint on an old theory that strikes him as different from the routinely familiar. It is at that point that he makes a note, short and to the point. Short, because otherwise it would take too much time and consequently he would miss the continuation of the lecture.

During the lecture one should try to sort and sift the important from the unimportant, and discern the thread of reasoning. Mentally, the listener can question the speaker. "What basis does he have for this statement?" "Is it fact or speculation?" Challenge him: "I wonder when he will come to the heart of the problem." "Why doesn't he stop here and explain the point?" Argue with him: "This point seems irrelevant to the subject." "I read a different viewpoint on this matter." "Now he goes off at a tangent which leads him nowhere." Even if the speaker later on deals with these very points and removes the listener's doubts and criticism, it is bound to make a deeper impression on his memory, exactly because of this mental interplay that keeps the listener alert.

The technique of taking notes is rather simple. Although there is ample room for personal preferences, it would seem a good practice to separate principles, main issues, and definitions from explanations and substantiating data and details. The former can be recorded on the left side of the note paper and the latter on the right side. This will facilitate later review considerably.

Normally it is not difficult to distinguish between the main points and the detail data. The attentive listener will notice the speaker's slowing down or an added emphasis in his voice when a matter of central importance is broached by the speaker. Often the speaker specifically announces that he is giving a definition or stating a principle.

Students in high school or college should without fail make specific notes when the teacher or professor uses such leading admonitions as: "One of the most important things to remember is . . ."; "Make sure that you know the following definition"; "If you do not know the application of this formula," etc., not only because the material is of such importance for understanding the subject, but because such emphatic phrases are subtle hints that they provide the answers to possible test and exam questions.

Upon the conclusion of a lecture our notes have an immediate function. If we only take a minute to look over our sheet, we may discover a hiatus here or there. In other words, we notice that, on going from one note to the other, there is a break in the continuity. This is a sure signal of a need for further information on a specific point. It is also the most appropriate moment, the entire lecture being still fresh in mind, to approach the teacher, professor, or lecturer and pose a specific question. And—to make an additional note to fill in the gap according to the answer we get.

Leave ample space between notes so that at any later time references from other sources can be added.

The complaint of so many students that by exam time their notes are of little or no help is due to the fact that they did not actively engage themselves with the subject when the lecture was given. Some occupied themselves with writing as much as they could, not allowing themselves to digest the material. Some satisfied themselves with jotting down an occasional point in a haphazard fashion only to discover that by review time their notes do not present a coherent record.

All these complaints must be attributed to their lack of attention and passive listening during the lecture. Those who listened with an aggressive and challenging attitude need only glance over their notes. Theirs is the gratifying experience of recalling all the essential material discussed during the lecture, thus gaining the confidence which is indispensable when facing exams.

Making notes from printed material is not much different from note taking during lectures. There is, of course, the facility of checking back immediately when something is not clear. Otherwise the procedure is similar. Instead of underlining words and sentences, it is much better to make annotations in the margin in one's own words. Also at the end of each section or subchapter one should take the opportunity to write down a few pointed remarks so chosen that they bring back the gist of the subject upon later rereading. It is a timesaving device that pays off in multiples at review time.

Anyone who desires to acquire the valuable skill of note taking should not fail to study carefully the chapters in this book under the titles "The Principles of the Chain Method" and "The Practical Application of the Chain Method."

CHAPTER 6

Exercises in Observation, Concentration, and Imagination

No doubt you realize by now that memory exercises can hardly be separated from exercises in observation, concentration, and imagination. Whenever we try to remember something new by connecting it with something that we already know, we must use our imagination in order to form an association and we must concentrate on both items in order to impress them upon our mind. But whereas memory exercises by necessity include all others, it is possible to devise some special exercises in observation, concentration, and imagination which should be helpful to those who are weak in any of these particular powers.

OBSERVATION

There can be no doubt that many people's powers of observation are poorly developed. Most people do not really observe what they see or hear, and there are thousands of examples and stories to prove this point. One of the best was written by Bernardine Kielty in the *Book-of-the-Month Club News* under the title "Public Hearing."*

George Gallup, the poll expert, tells about an experience in the Department of Agriculture, which proves how little people listen to what they're told, and how inaccurately they read what is written. At one time a Congressman was chiding the Department for its free and easy way with the taxpayers' money. "Look at the stuff it printed," said he, "hundreds of pamphlets in which no one had the slightest interest—*The Recreational Resources of the Denison Dam, The Wolves of Mount McKinley, The Ecology of the Coyote.* They

* Reprinted by permission of Bernardine Kielty.

print every last thing about nature but the love life of the frog."

Shortly after his harangue, the Department of Agriculture was surprised to find in the mail five or six letters from Congressmen asking for *The Love Life of the Frog.* Similar orders kept coming in so regularly that the Department was obliged to state in a circular, "We do *not* print *The Love Life of the Frog."* After the public announcement was made, requests for *The Love Life* were trebled. It got to be such a headache that the Department finally gave out a press release stating that it had never printed a pamphlet about the love life of the frog, and wanted to hear no more about the whole thing.

When this news item came out in the papers, requests began to number up into the hundreds. By now the matter had got out of hand and the Secretary of Agriculture himself was called in. Determined to stop the foolishness once and for all, he took time during an address on the air, on a nation-wide hookup, to deny vehemently that the Department had ever prepared any pamphlet concerning the love life of the frog, that to his knowledge there never was such a pamphlet, and that even if there had been the Department wouldn't have printed it. After the broadcast there were more than a thousand requests in the mail.

The story reveals how inattentively most people follow the news, and it proves at the same time how many people need training in observation, whether or not they are willing to admit it. We have five senses through which we gain impressions of what is going on in the world around us, and naturally we can train all five of them. But since taste and smell do not play as prominent a role in most people's lives, here are some exercises for eye, ear, and touch only.

Observation: (eye)

1. Choose an object like a telephone, a radio, a simple machine; look at it closely for a few minutes; wait about an hour and then make a drawing without looking at the object. Compare your drawing with the original, notice any mistakes, and correct them by again making a drawing without looking at the object.

2. Look for a few minutes at a picture in any book or magazine; observe as many details as possible; then redraw it from memory. If you have somebody to help you, you may skip the redrawing and, instead, answer questions put to you by your friend concerning details of the picture. These questions could

be: How many persons? What do they look like? How are they dressed? What is the color of these dresses or suits? How many houses? How many windows? Is there a clock in the picture? What time is it on this clock? And so on.

3. Extend this exercise to a room. Start with a room you are familiar with and proceed to other rooms you have seen only a few times. End with rooms that you have seen only once, but in each case go into details. Don't be satisfied in knowing that there was a bookshelf in the northwest corner, but recall how many shelves there were, approximately how many books on each shelf, what kind of books, and so forth.

4. Draw a map of the United States and put in the following:

> the boundaries of the state you live in
> the capital of the state you live in
> New York
> Washington, D.C.
> St. Louis
> Los Angeles
> Lake Erie
> Lake Superior
> the Mississippi River
> the Ohio River
> the Columbia River

Having done this, compare your drawing with the map. Notice where you made mistakes but don't make corrections while you have the actual map before your eyes. Rather, impress your errors and their corrections upon your mind. Then lay the map aside and make a new drawing. The more mistakes you made, the more necessary it is for you to repeat this exercise.

When you are sure of your drawing of the United States, proceed to the entire North American continent, then to South America, Europe, and the other continents. How many details you wish to include is up to you. That may depend upon your interest in geography and on the time you are willing to spend on this training.

5. Train your ability to estimate distances and quantities. While you are taking a walk, estimate how many steps it may take to reach a certain house, tree, monument, or the like, which you see in the distance. Count your steps and check yourself. If you

were wrong, do it better next time. Look at a big house and estimate the number of windows in it. Look at a store window and estimate the number of articles on display. Then count and check yourself.

Observation: (ear)

6. Identify various noises. While you are seated in your home or your office, you hear countless small noises of many kinds. Some of them have their origin in your own home, others in neighboring rooms, and still others on the street, a river, or wherever you are located. Most of these noises are familiar to you, and still it will not be easy to distinguish one from the other and to identify them if you have never tried this exercise before.

7. If you are a city dweller, listen to the sounds when you go to the country and try to identify them. If you live in the country, do the same with city noises.

8. Identify human voices. Certainly you will have no difficulty with members of your own family or with your friends, but you may have difficulty with voices that you have heard only a few times or perhaps only once. You may have noticed that voices change when heard over the phone and that they change in various degrees. Listen for the pitch, the inflection, the pattern, and the tempo of the voice. Try to identify it when you hear it again.

9. Another good means for training is the radio. Tune in at random to any station and listen to the voices you hear. If you recognize the voices, try to identify the speakers; then check whether you are right or wrong. You can do this also by listening to TV programs by turning off the picture, not the sound. In order to find out whether you are correct in identifying the voices you hear, all you have to do is turn the picture on again. If you do recognize the faces of the speakers but cannot recall the names, look them up in your program guide or wait till the end of the programs when the names are usually mentioned again.

This exercise should be repeated until you become more adept at recognizing voices.

Observation: (touch)

10. Touch various objects with your eyes closed. Decide what kind of material they are made of. Try to distinguish various qualities by touch without the help of the eye. Estimate the weight of objects like books, glasses, boxes, packages, and so forth.

CONCENTRATION

1. This exercise should be done at home. Stretch out in a comfortable position and try to relax as completely as you can. Choose a simple and familiar article like a pen, a pencil, or a book (without paying attention to the title or anything else printed on it). After having made your choice, close your eyes and try to visualize the form of the article in question. Exclude everything else from your mind and try to concentrate for a few minutes on this one article. In the beginning you will have difficulty because it is almost sure that associated thoughts will creep into your mind. If you try to think of a pencil, you may think of the hand which holds the pencil or words written with the pencil, and so on. But all this means that your thoughts are straying from the pencil itself and are not sticking to it as they should.

2. Trace your thoughts back while you are daydreaming. Suppose you are reading a book (not this book), a magazine, or a newspaper that does not interest you very much. Suddenly you catch yourself thinking of a bullfight you watched in Mexico about ten years ago. How did your thoughts get there? Looking at your book, you may discover that the last sentence you read dealt with an SOS of a ship in distress. By concentrating on your trend of thought, you may be able to retrace it in the following way:

The ship in distress made you think of ships that went down during World War II; some people were saved, others perished. You think of the famous four chaplains who died, leaving their life belts to the sailors; they were commemorated on a postage stamp; other reproductions on stamps and coins come to your mind, like the buffalo on the nickel, and this buffalo leads to the bull and the bullfight in Mexico.

This is one example in a thousand. But since almost everyone indulges in daydreaming from time to time, it is a concentration exercise which can be done practically any time and anywhere.

IMAGINATION

Training of the imagination is more difficult than training of observation and concentration abilities, but it can be done. Try this exercise when you are alone and undisturbed:

Read one or more paragraphs of a story or play or poem, preferably an imaginative one, like the following:

MERCUTIO: She is the fairies' midwife, and she comes
    In shape no bigger than an agate-stone
    On the forefinger of an alderman,
    Drawn with a team of little atomies
    Athwart men's noses as they lie asleep. . . .
    Sometimes she gallops o'er a courtier's nose,
    And then dreams he of smelling out a suit;
    And sometimes comes she with a tithe-pig's tail,
    Tickling a parson's nose as 'a lies asleep;
    Then dreams he of another benefice;
    Sometimes she driveth o'er a soldier's neck,
    And then dreams he of cutting foreign throats,
    Of breaches, ambuscadoes, Spanish blades,
    Of healths five fathom deep; and then anon
    Drums in his ear, at which he starts and wakes;
    And, being thus frightened, swears a prayer or two
    And sleeps again.*

Put the book aside and try to visualize what you have read. It is not a question of repeating or remembering it. If ten or twelve lines are too much, take three or four. The real task is to *visualize* what you read. With your eyes closed, you must *see* the fairies' midwife. You must visualize her "no bigger than an agate-stone." You must see the courtier sleeping and the fairy galloping over his nose. Visualize the soldier and see him "cutting foreign throats." Hear the drums and try to visualize him praying while

* From Shakespeare's *Romeo and Juliet*, Act I, Scene 4.

you "hear" at the same time the words of his prayer, which are left to your imagination.

Let us return to daydreaming. You have read these lines from *Romeo and Juliet* or other lines in some other play or story. Now put the book aside and think of a continuation of your own. Of course, for this exercise you must not know the end of the story, as you probably know the tale of Romeo and Juliet. Imagine that you are the author and create a continuation of your own. Visualize the characters and let them do things. Visualize what they are doing and don't be satisfied until your mental eye can see things just as clearly as your real eye.

These exercises have been designed to sharpen your powers of observation, concentration, and imagination. But in effect they will also carry over in your daily life as you will increasingly apply these powers to whatever activity you happen to be engaged in. They become second nature, thus providing greater fulfillment and a keener sense of awareness.

Classification

HOW TO ORGANIZE MATERIAL
FOR BETTER REMEMBERING

CHAPTER 7

The Principles of Classification

MEMORY AS A FILING SYSTEM

It was language that originally distinguished man from the ape. When man started to give names to animals and objects around him, he started to distinguish one from the other. Soon he must have found out that it was useful not only to speak of the ocean, the lake, the river, the brook, but to employ the word *water* as comprising all of them and hence to distinguish them from the earth and the air. Thus classification was created.

Very soon afterward he must have found that the nouns designating the animals around him were not sufficient to distinguish one horse from other horses; so he invented the adjective. Then the horses could be big or small, white or brown, fast or slow; but still all these were horses as clearly distinguished from cows and dogs and any other animals. Thus classification was continued.

When we classify things we put them in order, for classification means nothing else but the arrangement of complicated material in such a way that those things are put together which are alike in one respect or another.

The following example will show you how effectively classification facilitates memorizing things.

Look at the names of these sixteen objects for not more than twenty seconds. Then close the book and see how many of them you can remember.

1. magazine	5. pencil	9. plate	13. spoon
2. ink	6. knife	10. eraser	14. corkscrew
3. bottle	7. glass	11. book	15. newspaper
4. fork	8. pamphlet	12. ice	16. pen

Whatever your score was, look at them again and you will find that they can easily be classified in four groups: reading, writing, eating, and drinking. Now you have:

Reading	*Writing*	*Eating*	*Drinking*
1. book	5. ink	9. fork	13. bottle
2. magazine	6. pen	10. knife	14. corkscrew
3. newspaper	7. pencil	11. spoon	15. glass
4. pamphlet	8. eraser	12. plate	16. ice

You may not need more than five seconds to impress each group on your mind, and therefore you will easily score 100 per cent after twenty seconds spent on those four groups. In all probability your score on the first attempt was lower, and the conclusion which we can easily draw is that organized material is more easily memorized than disorganized material. This is by no means a new discovery. Trees, flowers, and insects have long been classified because the botanist as well as the zoologist found that it is much easier to write about them and to memorize them if they are grouped together in a way which seems logical and sensible.

One would think that a system, the value of which is so easily recognized and tested by everybody without much effort, would find widespread use in school, college, and business, but unfortunately this is not the case. For each example of material presented in an organized manner we find numerous other examples of material offered without any regard to order and classification.

To make sure that the idea of classification is understood, let us give you sixteen new items and leave it to you to classify them again into four groups. You will notice that the very effort to classify them is in itself enough to keep them in mind, and a special effort for memorizing them is hardly necessary.

1. window	5. car	9. airplane	13. receiver
2. steamer	6. wire	10. dial	14. train
3. number	7. hat	11. table	15. door
4. coat	8. chair	12. dress	16. suit

You will find the correct classification at the end of this chapter. These words were chosen in such a way as to make their classification simple.

However, it isn't always so easy. Just look for a moment at the following twelve words:

1. parrot	5. goldenrod	9. buttercup
2. dog	6. vulture	10. wolf
3. carnation	7. cat	11. rose
4. tiger	8. eagle	12. canary

At first thought we may classify these twelve items in the following way:

Animals	*Birds*	*Flowers*
1. cat	5. parrot	9. carnation
2. dog	6. eagle	10. goldenrod
3. tiger	7. vulture	11. rose
4. wolf	8. canary	12. buttercup

However, another classification of the same items is possible and correct from another point of view. You might think of wild life, and consequently classify these twelve items in two columns: one column indicating wild animals, birds, and flowers the other indicating domestic ones. In doing this, you arrive at the following classification:

Wild Life	*Domestic Life*
1. tiger	7. dog
2. wolf	8. cat
3. eagle	9. parrot
4. vulture	10. canary
5. goldenrod	11. carnation
6. buttercup	12. rose

Needless to say, we could use the distinction of wild life and domestic life as subdivisions of the first classification. Then it would look like this:

	Animals	*Birds*	*Flowers*
Wild Life	tiger	vulture	goldenrod
	wolf	eagle	buttercup
Domestic Life	dog	canary	carnation
	cat	parrot	rose

Such subdivision plays a very important role in classification. The wider the field covered, the more important the subdivision becomes. As you probably know, scores of volumes have been written about the classification and subdivision of books in libraries. It is no exaggeration to say that the value of any library depends to a large extent upon its catalog, and the catalog depends upon classification and subdivision.

A library could contain millions of books and yet be of no value if the reader were not able to find in a short time what he was looking for. Suppose a library were classified only according to the names of the authors arranged in alphabetical order. Let us further suppose that you want to read some books on memory training. In that case the catalog of authors wouldn't help you a bit. You could use it only if you already knew the names of those who have written on this subject. Therefore it is necessary to have another catalog which is classified according to subjects. In that case you are able to look up *Memory* and find the books you are looking for without previous knowledge of their authors' names.

However, even a classification by authors and subjects is not enough. Take the last classification example cited: it is obvious that we can find material about a tiger in books dealing with animals just as well as in books dealing with wild life. Furthermore, we will find material about the tiger in books dealing with cats in general.

As you probably are familiar with libraries and their cataloging system, it is hardly necessary to go into further detail. It may be sufficient to point out that classification and subdivision are by no means restricted to libraries. Every enterprise, large or small, has a filing system, and the more detailed the divisions and the subdivisions in this filing system are, the easier it is to work with it. Finally, the brain is like a library. Here and there knowledge is stored, and our ability to reach that knowledge at any time we want it depends very much upon whether or not it is organized and classified.

The following geographical classification may serve as a final exercise. Reclassify the twenty-five items in a way which is entirely different from the given classification.

Countries	*Mountains*	*Rivers*
China	Rocky Mts.	Rhine
Egypt	Himalayas	Nile
Switzerland	Alps	Mississippi
Canada	Atlas Mts.	Murray
New Zealand	Townsend Range	Ganges

Lakes	*Cities*
Erie	St. Louis
Eyre	Melbourne
Tanganyika	Cairo
Dead Sea	Hong Kong
Ladoga	Trieste

You will find the solution at the bottom of this page.

Solution to the problem on page 59:

Transportation	*Telephone*	*Room*	*Apparel*
1. car	5. number	9. door	13. coat
2. train	6. dial	10. window	14. hat
3. steamer	7. receiver	11. table	15. dress
4. airplane	8. wire	12. chair	16. suit

Solution to the problem above:

Europe	*Asia*	*Africa*
1. Switzerland	6. China	11. Egypt
2. Alps	7. Himalayas	12. Atlas Mts.
3. Rhine	8. Ganges	13. Nile
4. Lake Ladoga	9. Dead Sea	14. Lake Tanganyika
5. Trieste	10. Hong Kong	15. Cairo

America	*Oceania*
16. Canada	21. New Zealand
17. Rocky Mts.	22. Townsend Range
18. Mississippi	23. Murray River
19. Lake Erie	24. Lake Eyre
20. St. Louis	25. Melbourne

CHAPTER 8

The Practical Application of Classification

Suppose you are a resident of Manhattan and you want to call up a bookstore to find out whether they have in stock a new book that a friend of yours recommended to you.

You take out the Manhattan Classified Telephone Directory, also called the Red Book or the Yellow Pages. The Quick Reference Index of the Red Book tells you that bookstores can be found under the heading: Book Dealers-Retail. Under that heading you find, among others, Doubleday Book Shops listing several shops in various parts of Manhattan. You notice that one of their stores is located downtown at 14 Wall Street, which happens to be not far from the place where you work, making it easy for you to pick up the book in your lunch hour. So you dial 732-5040 and get Doubleday, Wall Street, on the phone.

All this is a simple and familiar procedure to you. But would you ever stop to realize that you had used the principle of classification three times?

The Quick Reference Index, as well as the Main Section, uses classification according to business, profession, and occupation, and subsequently also according to the alphabet.

But you also availed yourself of the help of classification when you made your phone call. How is it that your dial instrument finds the Wall Street shop of Doubleday among all the millions of telephone numbers in New York City? Well, it works by selecting one class of numbers given by the first digit, then proceeds to the subclass given by the second digit, and so on until it reaches the last subclass of numbers which leaves only one single choice. This is classification in its highest development, and it shows how great an achievement can be reached if classification is properly used.

You will encounter another application of classification when you enter the bookshop. The books can easily be located as they are grouped by category, such as fiction, arts, economics, sports, travel, languages, etc.

This is by no means common practice in bookstores. Quite a few of them are decidedly less than perfect with respect to classification. And that is putting it mildly. If the books are classified according to subjects and subdivided again according to authors, there can be only one shelf and only one place on that shelf for any particular book, if it is in stock at all. A clerk would not have to search through half the store, while the customer in the meantime finds the book more or less accidentally on his own.

What has been said about bookstores can also be said about many books themselves, as far as the organization of the text material is concerned. Certainly every book that is intended to convey knowledge or information to its readers would be remembered much longer and better if its chapters responded to the laws of classification. However, one glance at the table of contents often convinces us that these laws are entirely disregarded, and this is one of the reasons why so many books are forgotten in such a short time.

What holds true for books holds true for any kind of merchandise. The better the classification, the easier to survey the shelves, the catalog, or the price list; and the easier it is to remember and to find the various items.

At one time one of the largest wallpaper companies published a style book containing 182 different designs. It was bound and made up in rather expensive fashion and was certainly meant to impress the customer as favorably as possible. It would not have been difficult for the manufacturer to apply classification since wallpaper can be easily grouped according to color and subdivided according to design or in the reverse order. However, nothing of the kind was to be seen in this book. There were blue, red, and brown colors at the beginning, in the middle, and at the end; there were flower designs alternating with abstract and geometric designs of all sorts but without any visible order or arrangement. All the wallpapers carried the same price. Needless to say, how much time could be saved if such a book were arranged in proper order, classified in one way or another.

The need for classification in many areas of society is progressing at a rather fast pace as forced by the advances in technology in our time.

The robot—the artificial man or, better, the artificial brain—rests on the same principle. Quite some time ago Dr. Vannevar Bush, director of the Office of Scientific Research and Development, wrote in an article in *Life* magazine:

Consider a future device for individual use, which is a sort of mechanized private file and library. It needs a name, and to coin one at random, "memex" will do. A memex is a device in which an individual stores all his books, records and communications, and which is mechanized so that it may be consulted with exceeding speed and flexibility. It is an enlarged intimate supplement to his memory.

It consists of a desk, and while it can presumably be operated from a distance, it is primarily the piece of furniture at which he works. On the top are slanting translucent screens on which material can be projected for convenient reading. There is a keyboard and sets of buttons and levers. Otherwise it looks like an ordinary desk.

In one end is stored material. The matter of bulk is well taken care of by improved microfilm. Only a small part of the interior of the memex is devoted to storage, the rest to mechanism. Yet if the user inserted 5,000 pages of material a day it would take him hundreds of years to fill the repository, so he can be profligate and enter material freely.*

It is clear that Dr. Bush envisioned what we now know as the computer. Both business and science are utilizing its capacities extensively and it will be only a relatively short time before the computer enters our household.

There are numerous fields in which classification is used and where it would be unthinkable to do without it. In the previous chapter we mentioned the libraries and pointed out that their usefulness relies entirely upon good classification of the catalog. The first practical system of cataloging libraries by classification was developed by Melvil Dewey as far back as 1873. This system has been expanded and improved ever since.

Many libraries still follow his pattern, which in its basic elements looks approximately like this:

* Reprinted by permission of Dr. Vannevar Bush and *Life* magazine.

Dewey Decimal Classification   17th Edition—1965
Classes: 0   Generalities
1   Philosophy and related disciplines
2   Religion
3   The Social Sciences
4   Language
5   Pure Sciences
6   Technology (Applied Sciences)
7   The Arts
8   Literature and rhetoric
9   General geography, history, etc.

These ten classes are each divided into ten divisions by adding digits from 0 to 9 after the class notation, as for example under 6, "Technology":

Divisions: 60   General
61   Medical Science
62   Engineering and allied operations
63   Agriculture and agricultural industries
64   Domestic Arts and Sciences
65   Business and related enterprises
66   Chemical technology, etc.
67   Manufactures processible
68   Assembled and final products
69   Buildings

In turn each of these divisions consists of up to 10 sub-divisions. For example 62, "Engineering and allied operations," has the following:

Subdivisions: 620   General
621   Applied physics
622   Mining engineering and operations
623   Military and naval
624   Civil engineering
625   Railroads and highways
626   ———
627   Hydraulic engineering, etc.
628   Sanitary and municipal engineering
629   Other branches

Every one of these subdivisions can be further detailed by adding another decimal digit if the need arises. In fact, some subdivisions require four digits after the three-digit subdivision to identify a particular item. It is obvious that the Dewey Decimal System greatly facilitates the search for any book, magazine, or article.

We must bear in mind, however, that classification is not something which is done once and forever. It is an ongoing thing. As the world changes and whole fields of knowledge are further explored, there is a continuous need to classify and reclassify things and materials. It is worth noting, for instance, that the above extracts of the Dewey Decimal system were taken from the 17th edition. One glance at the successive editions is enough to convince us that librarians and scientists have been working and are still working on solutions to ever changing problems. And this work will never be finished because the ideal, the perfect classification will never be attained.

In previous editions of this book the *Standard Filing System* of the American Institute of Architects was used as an excellent example of classification. Since 1966, however, it is no longer available as a separate publication. Other related business and professional organizations came to realize that, since they were working with the same materials and documentation as the architects, important benefits could be obtained by all concerned if they all adopted a certain classification system. And thus the *Uniform System for Construction Specifications, Data Filing and Cost Accounting** came about, which now serves as a guide and cost-saving tool in the recording and filing of data, preparation of bids, cost accounting, etc., for the various contractors and others in the construction industry.

In comparing the new *Uniform System* with the predecessor documents, such as the *Standard Filing System,* a remarkable phenomenon comes to the fore. Instead of a more elaborate use of numerical features, as one would expect in such a greatly expanded system, there is actually a de-emphasis on numbers in the new version. While formerly there were 41 major divisions, the new system has only 16 divisions.

---

* Published by American Institute of Architects, Associated General Contractors of America, The Construction Specifications Institute, and the Council of Mechanical Specialty Contracting Industries.

Moreover, only the Cost Accounting Guide uses a four-digit numerical index; the Specification Outline and the Filing System use headings only, as the following excerpt from Division 16 shows:

ELECTRICAL   DIVISION 16

Specification Outline Page 1.41	*Filing System* Page 2.15	*Cost Accounting Guide* Page 3.7
General Provisions		1600 Alternates
Basic Materials & Methods		1610 Basic Materials & Methods
	Raceways & Fittings Busways Conductors Electr. Supporting Devices	
Electrical Service System		1620 Electrical Service System
	Electr. Substations Electr. Entrance Equipment Standby Electr. Equipment	
Electr. Distribution System		1630 Electr. Distribution System
	Panel Boards Wiring Devices	
Lighting Fixtures	Lighting Fixtures	1640 Lighting Fixtures
Communication Systems	Communication Systems	1650 Comunication Systems
Electr. Power Eqpmt.	Electr. Power Eqpmt.	1670 Electr. Power Eqpmt.
Electr. Comfort System	Electr. Comfort System	1680 Electr. Comfort System
	Heat Pumps	
Electr. System Controls & Instruments	Electr. System Controls & Instruments	1690 Electr. System Controls & Instruments
Lighting Protection System	Lighting Protection System	1695 Lighting Protection System

These headings are further detailed in alphabetical order under Part One and Part Two, while only the Cost Accounting Guide, mainly because of computer applications, has a numerical refinement into only four digits, as, for example, *1650 Communication Systems:*

> 1650 Communication Systems
> 1651 Telephone Equipment
> 1652 Intercommunication System
> 1653 Public Address System
> 1654 Paging System
> 1655 Nurses' Call System
> 1656 Alarm & Detection System
> 1657 Clock & Program System
> 1658 Audio-Video Reproducers
> 1659 Closed-Circuit Television
> 1660 Radiotelephone System
> 1661 Commercial Projection System
> 1662–1669 unassigned

Because of the excellent cross-reference table included in the *Uniform System,* it is easy for anyone, whether he is a manufacturer, architect, builder, or otherwise professionally involved in the construction industry, to find what he is looking for. Knowing how to work out and apply classification to actual and practical situations should be a rewarding ability for the executive as well as for the clerical staff and the plant workers.

The connection between memory and classification should be evident to everybody. In the preceding chapter we saw how much easier it is to remember and recall classified material. Therefore we should make every conceivable effort to arrange things which we have to remember in our line of work in such a way as to help our memory, not to hinder it.

We should also not overlook the opportunities for classification in our own immediate personal environment. Did you ever think of arranging your own books or gramophone records by classifying them in groups? If you make a little effort you will see that it is much easier to remember in what section a particular book or record *must* be found than without classifying them. How to do it is a highly individual matter. One person may want to arrange his records according to the type of music: classical, neo-classical, opera, jazz, etc. Another person may want to go by the instruments: organ music, piano, violin, vocal, orchestra, and subdivide the vocal section into soloists and choirs, the orchestras into ensembles and large orchestras. Each section can further be arranged in alphabetical order of the names of either the composers, the orchestras, or the musicians.

For the lady of the house there is ample opportunity to apply classification in her kitchen. When properly and sensibly arranged, she will have little difficulty remembering what is where when she needs it.

The Chain Method

HOW TO REMEMBER READING MATERIAL, LECTURES
AND SPEECHES, PROSE AND POETRY

CHAPTER 9

The Principles of the Chain Method

HOW TO LINK THINGS AND THOUGHTS

How much do we retain of everything we read?
How much do we retain of everything we hear?

It is a generally accepted fact that we lose, on the average, more than 80 per cent of all the information we receive through all our senses during a lifetime. Obviously, we do not want to remember everything we read or hear. But it is nothing short of tragic if we forget so much of the things which we do want to remember.

Think of the student, who diligently pores over his textbooks and faithfully does his homework, only to discover that by examination time a great deal of what he learned eludes him.

Think of the storyteller at a gathering of family or friends. Everyone is hanging, so to speak, on his lips. And then watch his visible embarrassment when he fumbles the punch line because he does not remember how to lead up to the climax.

How often have you listened to a lecture or a speech or an important conversation and a few weeks later were at a loss to recall most of what you had heard?

The same applies to the reading and retention of articles and books.

The solution to these problems is the use of our Chain Method.

A chain is constructed by selecting "cue words," applying the following two rules:

1. The cue words must be selected in such a way that each will recall the sentence or the thought or the paragraph for which it has been selected.
2. The cue words must be selected in such a way that it is easy to link them together to form a "chain."

The Chain Method resembles an outline, but only in part. The chain goes one step further than the outline, and this step is of the utmost importance as far as memory is concerned. Both chain and outline contain cue words which are most important for recalling the story or the article. The outline puts one of these cue words beside the other regardless of their relationship or continuity. The Chain Method, however, emphasizes the continuity of cue words and links them together in such a way that one of them must unfailingly recall the next one, thus forming a chain.

How do we find the best cue words?

In the first place, we must realize that a cue word does not necessarily mean one single word. It may be a little phrase or a short sentence.

Secondly, a cue word does not always have to be a word or words which are part of the printed text. Although this will often be the case, it is not a requirement that must be rigidly enforced.

When a thought or paragraph deals with abstract material, it is preferable to substitute a word of a concrete nature. Abstract thoughts are not as easy to link as are concrete objects. For instance, patriotism (an abstract thought) can be easily symbolized by the flag (the concrete object); relaxation by a rocking chair or a hammock; financial problems by a dollar bill; etc. There is quite a variety of word symbols available to us and they will not be the same for everyone, since different persons have different thought patterns.

Concrete objects are easy to visualize and need little imagination to connect them with other concrete objects. This is important since the "linking" of the cue words is the essential feature of the chain. We accomplish this linking by applying the laws of association, which were explained in Chapter 3. We look for relationships, such as cause and effect; whole and part; contrast; similarity; subject and quality; matching pairs; etc. In this connection you will find it often helpful to ask leading questions, such as: Where? What? Who? When? How? These little questions tend to guide you along in constructing your chain. Once you have selected your cue words, you should repeat them one after the other. A story or an article itself follows a certain thought pattern of its own, which will be very helpful to you. When repeating the cue words to yourself, you should by all means try to visualize the sequence of the cue words. In that way you will strengthen the logical chain of thoughts immeasurably.

How many cue words are needed? This depends on several factors. First of all, it depends on how familiar you are with the subject in question. The length of the article or chapter also has something to do with it, although a 20-page article does not necessarily require ten times as many cue words as a 2-page article. Another factor is the amount of detail in which we want to cover the topic. Also, it is only natural that highly technical material will require more cue words than a run-of-the-mill subject.

Most of all, however, the number of cue words varies according to one's experience in forming chains. The beginner uses too many. There is nothing wrong with that. As you gain more experience and become more proficient you need less and less cue words. Your chain will become shorter and often at the same time stronger.

In addition, do not forget that you also have a natural memory which helps you to recall many details which are brought to your mind by the cue word.

As you will see in the following chapters, the Chain Method is a most effective tool, not only for remembering short stories or articles, but also for remembering entire books. And not only for reading material but also for remembering speeches and lectures you hear and movies you see.

It is also a perfect system for constructing and remembering a speech which you have to deliver.

The Practical Application
of the Chain Method

CHAPTER 10

How to Remember Stories and Books

It is easy to see that the Chain Method should be useful to everyone. How useful it will be to you will soon be evident. The more you put it to work, the more you will derive its benefits. And you will enjoy doing it.

Let us see how a chain works in actual practice and construct a few together.

For our first chain we'll use the story entitled: "Intrepid Airman, I," which you will find on page 11 in Chapter 1 (Test no. 7). Turn back to the story and read it over so that you have a rough idea of its contents. When you have done this you will be able to sense the meaning which the author is trying to convey to us and it will not be difficult to recall the main points which form the framework or skeleton on which the entire story rests. The sequence of the plane trip, which is familiar to anyone who ever made a flight, gives us the guidance from one event or feeling to the other.

The framework then looks as follows:

The introductory theme is the comparison of the anxieties endured in the dentist's waiting room and at the *airport*.

The trip starts in the *terminal*
from there we go by *bus*
which brings us to the *airport*
where we have conversations with *3* persons *pilot*
radio operator
hostess
thereupon we *enter the plane*
choose a seat
take-off

while airborne we have the *second*
conversation with 2 persons: *pilot*
                                 hostess
            then follows the   *descent*
                                 landing
    and we are surrounded by   *sightseers*
and we boast about flying as the *safest means of travel*

Here you have the framework of the story which you can follow in your mind step by step. When you now read the story again, you will be able to fill in more details which add charm to the story.

It is not imperative that you select one cue word for each paragraph. Sometimes you may be able to cover several paragraphs with one cue word and, conversely, sometimes you may want to use more than one cue word for one particular paragraph.

Bear in mind that you are not required to know the story verbatim, but still in as much detail as possible. (We shall deal with verbatim remembering in Chapter 12.)

If we look again over the framework we constructed of the story we realize that we already have most of the cue words at our disposal. We now have to see whether these cue words are sufficient to recall the details, not only right now, but in months to come. Some people do not have too much difficulty in re-telling such a story in detail right after reading it. However, the purpose of the cue words is to bring back the gist and the flavor of the story if we want to retell it say three or six months from now.

Let us now complete our chain together by adding some cue words that cover the happenings on this plane trip. The cue words are numbered in the same way as the order of the paragraphs. Of course, the paragraphs were not numbered by the author; this was done to make it easier for you to check the cue words with the paragraphs to which they belong.

INTREPID AIRMAN, I

Par.	Cue Words	
1 & 2	Dentist chair	
3	Terminal	
4	Airport bus	
5	Airport	
		first conversation with 3 persons; who?
6	Pilot	
		4 questions:
		about: his plane
		his person
		how fast
		how high
7	Radio operator	
		Morse Code
8	Hostess	
		forewarning
9	Entering plane	
	Choice of seat:	
		front?
		back?
		middle!
10	Take-off	
11 & 12	Airborne	
		second encounter with 2 persons; who?
	Pilot	
		"office boy" at the wheel?
13	Hostess	
		tea—sea
14	Descent	
		crash landing?
15	Landing	
16	Terminal	
17	Sightseers	
18	Flying	
		moral of the story:
		Flying—safe, fast, convenient.

Do we have too many cue words for a two-page story? For a beginner a chain of this length would be quite normal. You may even have selected a few more cue words than we did. As you become accustomed to "chaining" fewer and fewer cues will be needed.

You won't have much difficulty in remembering this chain once you have made the various links clear in your mind, by visualizing the sequence of events, step by step, so that the one cue word promptly recalls the next.

Now that you know how a chain is constructed, why not make use of it right away and see how easy it is and how useful it can be? Go over your chain and run through it in your mind to check whether you touched upon each cue word.

The next thing to do is to retell the story to someone else, anyone who wants to listen. For a beginner it will be a gratifying experience. A few days later, and again a few weeks from now, you should repeat the same feat to prove to yourself that you still remember the story in all its detail. This accomplishment will prove to you the value of the Chain Method.

Since the Chain Method is of such great importance and since it can only be put to good use by practice, let's go over a few more stories, to guide you in developing your skill in constructing chains.

The next story was selected not only because it lends itself so well as an exercise for the beginner but also because it is so true to life. Again, skim through the story first, then read it more carefully and write down the cue words of your choice.

UNPACK YOUR SUITCASE—AND LIVE!*
Ibbie Bryan

Mrs. Dowell is an old woman now—old and a little tired. Her children are all married, and her husband died several years ago. She potters about, trying to fill empty hours.

The other day she said to me rather wistfully, "You know, I've never really made myself at home in the world. I've always been like the person who stops overnight in a hotel and decides it isn't worth while unpacking for so short a time. There were so many things I wanted to do—little things—and I kept telling myself I would, but I never seemed to get settled."

Listening to her, I thought of all the people in the world who are waiting to unpack their suitcases. They're going to do a lot of real

* Reprinted by permission of Ibbie Bryan, *This Week* magazine, and *Reader's Digest*.

honest-to-goodness living when . . . well, when the children grow up
. . . when they have more money . . . when they find a better apartment . . . when they get into the sort of work they really like. They're
going to read, take up that hobby, take that correspondence course,
keep in touch with their friends. They're going to unpack everything!

But right now there isn't time. So the days drift by, and then weeks.
Fifty-two weeks make a year.

Why put off doing all those little things that you're dreaming about?
Flowers on the table in that cubbyhole apartment will be just as pleasant as they would in the house you're going to build. You may not be
able to settle down for long hours of reading now, as you're going to
when the children start in school, but you *can* snatch fifteen minutes
now and then.

Certainly England is not living a normal life. One might expect the
English to live catch-as-catch-can until things get settled. But the other
day I read a letter from a woman in London, and she said, "One
can't neglect the small details that make for pleasant living even in
these times. So much must be held in abeyance that we have fallen
into the habit of not making plans at all, but just enjoying each little
portion of time to the fullest."

Perhaps that's best after all. There are a lot of things that can be
enjoyed right now. Not anticipated, but experienced.

In my home town there was an old doctor who was constantly at the
beck and call of his patients. Yet every night he would go home, put
on his slippers and smoking jacket, and settle down before the fire
with his pipe and book, exactly as though he had the whole evening
before him. Once I asked him, "How on earth can you settle down so
comfortably when you know someone's going to call you any moment?"

He chuckled. "Well, my dear, if I waited until I was sure there
would be no interruptions, I'd never have any free time at all. As it is,
I get in quite a few snatches of good solid comfort." So saying, he
went to answer the telephone.

I used to plan and plan what I was going to do when I furnished my
own apartment. I had a lot of little things stuck in my trunk that I
would use. But in the meantime I lived in a furnished apartment and
wished every day it didn't look so much like every other furnished
apartment. Then one morning I went to the trunk and got all those
pictures and vases and my big illustrated map of Texas—and set to
work. By noon my apartment didn't look "furnished" at all. It isn't
exactly what I plan to have someday, but it does have a charm of its
own.

Right then I decided to "unpack my suitcase." I went to the library and got three books I'd been intending to read for the last five years. I made a card index of my friends, and now each night I telephone a couple of them, just to say, "Hello—I've been thinking about you." I've even started taking a walk every day. Of course, I still have plans for the future. I'm working to realize them. But in the meantime, I'm going to live!

A lot of people go through life too wrapped up in the dream of what they're going to do to accomplish anything at all. Last night on the radio I heard a particularly lovely new tune. It was composed by an up-and-coming young songwriter we'll call Johnny. A few years ago Johnny worked in an architect's office. His friend Tom worked there too. They were both trying to get a stake, because Johnny was going to quit and write songs, and Tom was going to paint pictures.

Johnny did start writing songs. Tom's still talking. He hasn't unpacked. And when he's sixty, he'll say regretfully, "When I was a kid, I wanted to be an artist. Had a touch for it, you know. Never got around to it, somehow."

There's really no reason to go through life as a stranger in a strange land. Make yourself at home here. Unpack your bags and get settled—instead of waiting for a "better time" that may never come.

Now let's review the gist of the story.

We start with the thought that Mrs. Dowell potters about and has never made herself at home in the world. Following the introductory sentences, the writer uses a metaphor—a figure of speech—and compares this woman with other people whose entire lives are like overnight stops at hotels, where they never find the time or the opportunity to "unpack their suitcases." The reason for this behavior is the fact that they do too much daydreaming. They are always planning things for the future but never for the present. They are planning—in the words of the author—for the time

> when the *children* grow up
> when they have more *money*
> when they have a better *apartment*
> when they are doing the sort of *work* they like.

These four "when" sentences are important for the repetition of the story, but their sequence is unimportant. Connect them in the sentence: "In order to rent a better *apartment* and to raise *children,* we must *work* and earn *money!*"

Corresponding with these four "when" sentences are four things which these very people contemplate doing in the future:

They are going to *read.*
They are going to take up that *hobby.*
They are going to take that *correspondence course.*
They are going to keep in touch with their *friends.*

These four thoughts may be linked in the sentence: *"Read a correspondence course dealing with your hobby together with a friend!"*

The next thought in the story is a warning by the author that *time is fleeting.* She refers to days and weeks and continues with the sentence: *"Fifty-two weeks make a year."* No repetition of the story should omit this sentence because its very simplicity accurately conveys the idea which the writer is trying to impress upon our mind, namely, the days and weeks easily add up to years and years.

The contrast to daydreaming is actually *doing things,* small things which can be enjoyed right away and not only anticipated. Among such small things, the story mentions *flowers and reading.*

The second part of the story gives us examples of various persons. These persons are a *woman* who wrote *from London,* an old *physician* who lives in the author's home town, the *author* herself, and *Johnny and Tom.* We remember these five persons by thinking of

2 women—1 old man—2 boys

For somebody whose memory retains images of objects more easily than images of persons, there is another possibility in linking:

London (the woman from London)—fireplace (the
old physician)—apartment (the writer)—song
writing (Johnny)—painting (Tom).

The association of these objects should be easy. If we think of London burning during the blitz, we can easily connect it with fireplace. The fireplace is a part of the apartment. This apartment belongs to the writer of the story. This writer reminds us of the song writer, and song writing and painting are two arts which are easily linked.

There remain to remember only the four things (again four!) which the writer is doing and enjoying now. These are:

> decorating her apartment
> reading
> taking walks
> telephoning friends

By comparing these four items, we notice that two of them— *decorating and reading*—take place *inside the apartment,* while *walks* are *outside,* and so are the *friends* whom she calls up. The fact that we have two inside and two outside activities makes it easier to remember all four.

Thus we construct the following chain:

Cue Words	*Linking Thoughts*
Mrs. Dowell potters about; never has made herself at home in the world	
	Comparison (metaphor)
Overnight stop at hotel	
	Reason: daydreaming

Real living starts *when*
  children grow up
  more money
  better apartment
  sort of work they like
(In order to rent a better *apartment* and to raise *children,* we must *work* and earn *money*)	

	Then what?
Read Take up that hobby Take that correspondence course Keep in touch with friends (*Read* a *correspondence course* dealing with your *hobby* together with a *friend*)	

Cue Words	Linking Thoughts
	Time is fleeting
Days—weeks—years (Fifty-two weeks make a year!)	
	Contrast: *doing things* instead of *dreaming*
Little things can be enjoyed now (not only anticipated) flowers—books	
	Two women—one old man— two boys
The woman from London	
The old physician The writer	
apartment books inside	
walking friends outside	
Johnny and Tom	

As a third exercise, try constructing a chain for a somewhat longer story and at the same time try to reduce the number of cue words. Again, first scan the contents, then read the story and choose your cue words as you go along. In this case, ask yourself those leading questions which we discussed in the preceding chapter, such as: Who? Where? What? When? Which? It will help you greatly in finding the best cue words.

MY HUSBAND BOUGHT ME FOR $40 AND A CHICKEN*
by Suellen McAndrews

When the Peace Corps director in Liberia assigned me to teach in the jungle village of Kpaiyea (Pie-ay), some 200 miles inland from the West African coast, he said that I wouldn't have any trouble. "You'll be the only white woman living in the village," he said. "But there are two Peace Corps men there already, and the villagers are

* Reprinted by permission of Suellen McAndrews and *Reader's Digest.*

very friendly." He didn't tell me that they would also be untiring matchmakers.

When I arrived in Kpaiyea, seven children appeared from the underbrush, hoisted my bags onto their heads and pulled me toward the center of the village, laughing and calling out, "Come quick, yeah! The new teacha can be coming-o!" The women, too, bubbled with warmth and curiosity. As we got to know each other their interest left me little privacy. Each morning, on their way to the rice fields they'd stop to watch me do my curious chores. I had to boil all my water before I could drink it, and the women always teased me. "White teacha waste hot water so! She drink it when she should please Teacha Bob with hot bath. Then he would ask her for friend business."

Teacha Bob was Bob McAndrews, a volunteer from West Hollywood, Calif., who had been running the school with George Radcliffe, of Plymouth, N.H. "Friend business" actually means a trial marriage "to see each other's ways" and determine compatibility. "Americans don't have friend business," I tried to explain, but the women only laughed and patted me on the back.

In time, though, an American-style romance did blossom between Bob and me. And immediately everyone in the village began giving us advice. Kpaiyea women often conceive before they wed to prove their fertility. After I had assured the women that I had no such intention, their husbands took Bob aside and said, "We want you to be a happy man, so we have anotha fine, fine woman for your friend business."

Bob declined the offer and asked me to marry him. But when we told the villagers we planned to have a church wedding in Monrovia, they asked, "How can we know that something is a true thing if it cannot come into our own eyes?" So we decided to have a tribal wedding ceremony, and the villagers helped us prepare.

Before the ritual could take place, they explained, Bob had to convince my father and mother (who were flying over from Colorado) of his love for me by offering my father the best presents he could find or afford. A village man sometimes saves for years, only to have his prospective father-in-law refuse to give away his daughter because he does not consider the gifts substantial enough. To save Bob from such embarrassment, the chief advised him to give the best gift of all—a cow. But Bob couldn't possibly afford the $120 needed to buy the animal. So the elders compromised on less expensive gifts.

The day of the ceremony, I pulled over my head my bubba, a sleeveless blouse with a ruffle at the bottom, and wrapped the matching lappa, or skirt, around my waist so that it hung just below my knees. And we set off for the center of the village. Most of the inhabitants had gathered there in a circle. I was directed to sit next to my parents on a mat on one side of the circle, and Bob sat across from us.

Chief Gbigbi walked out from his hut looking regal in his new embroidered white gown. I noticed that his white goatee had been clipped. The villagers fell silent immediately when he raised his arms. He spoke in Kpelle (the tribal dialect), which a prominent villager translated into English: "This is an honorable thing for Kpaiyea and for Liberia," the chief began. "It is the first time a white man and woman can come to be married in our village. Now all eyes can see that it is done properly."

He motioned toward his hut, and two elders emerged carrying parcels wrapped in intricately patterned purple and yellow cloth that had been woven in the village. They stood with Bob, and the chief chanted, "Teacha Bob has seen Suellen walking about in the village and likes her ways. He is here in good faith to buy her for his wife."

Now it was time for Bob to present his gifts to my father. Taking one of the parcels from the elder on his left, he handed it to the chief, who unfolded it to reveal a blue, tan, black and white striped gown with intricate orange embroidery at the neck. The chief motioned for my father to raise his arms and carefully placed the gown over my father's head. The villagers clapped their hands and cheered. "Teacha Bob can do a good thing-o!" they shouted.

Next, a bundle of American dollar bills was given to Bob. He gave the money to the chief, who slowly counted it, then gave it to my father one bill at a time, saying, "We know that it has been a heartache for you to raise a daughter all these years and then have her leave home with another man. In our custom, the man who wants your daughter must give you $40 as compensation for the loss. This is the payment that binds a Liberian marriage. If Suellen leaves Bob, he can ask you for the $40 back for all the trouble she caused him."

My father smiled and thanked the chief and put the money deep into the pocket of his new robe.

Fresh meat is rare in Kpaiyea, and so it was with pleasure that the chief asked Bob to present the final gift, a very large white chicken that had been brought from a nearby village. The chief took the struggling bird from Bob, held it high for all to see, then thrust it into my father's hands while he intoned above its squawks, "This fine white chicken is the symbol of Bob's pure heart. Do you accept it and the other gifts as payment for your Suellen?"

My father nodded, and an elder triumphantly took the bird to the cooking hut to be added to the delicacies of the coming feast.

Then the chief asked me, "Teacha Suellen, can you know the good and bad parts of this man, Bob McAndrews, and are you happy to live in his same house with his bad and good altogether?"

"I am," I replied.

The chief raised one arm toward Bob, the other toward me and said, "You people of Kpaiyea and America have seen Teacha Bob's fine gifts, and you have heard Teacha Suellen say she can see the ways of this man and be happy to live with him. Also, Suellen's father is satisfied. Now it is my turn to say my part of this marriage business."

He led me by the hand to Bob and we sat close together.

"Love can be an easy thing now," said the chief in loud, clear words. "But we can all see with our eyes that every day I, as the chief and judge of Kpaiyea, have to sit for many hours and hear the palaver between husband and wife to see who is right and who is wrong when they vex each other. That is not a good thing. So I say to you that marriage should be the same as this story:

"Two friends lived far apart in separate villages. One night the rain was pouring hard, and no moon was there, but one friend woke up and thought to go to his friend. He walked and was always afraid of the lightning that might catch him or the night ghost that could eat him. However, he did not stop until he had reached his friend's hut. By that time he was as wet as if he himself had been a river. But he brought dry firewood, made a fire and fixed some new rice to offer a hot meal to his friend, who by now was awake. 'Why did you come in this bad rain and at night?' asked the friend. 'Because I wanted to be near you, my friend. Come, let us eat,' he replied.

"So, Teachas Bob and Suellen, I tell you this thing—you should remember this story and be happy to love the other person, even when he does not ask for it, and before taking care of yourself." He raised his arms, threw back his head and shouted, "Now all hear! Let us cheer and sing and dance, for our teacha, Bob McAndrews, has bought himself a fine, fine woman!"

The villagers whooped, clapped and yelled, "Fine-o! Fine-o!" They rushed to shake our hands and pound us on the back. The drums began to beat, and after a feast of rice, chicken sauce, fruit and palm wine, we all danced in a frenzy of happiness far into the night.

Next morning we drove my parents to Monrovia. There Bob and I were married again in a small and quiet church ceremony. Yet to both of us, the most significant symbols of our marriage were 40 one-dollar bills and one white chicken—and the age-old wisdom of Chief Gbigbi.

After you have completed your chain, check yours with the

one appearing below to see whether you can eliminate some of your cue words and still retain the essentials of the story.

Cue Words	Linking Thoughts
Peace Corps teacher Suellen	
	where?
West African jungle village	
	what about her?
only white woman	
	met whom?
teacher Bob McAndrews from California	
	what happened?
villagers matchmakers	
	how?
"friend-business"—trial marriage	
	contrast
Americans—no "friend business"	
	what instead?
Bob proposes	
	what followed?
tribal wedding	
	what happened?
wedding in tribal dialect (villager translated in English)	
	what else?
presents for father: gown 40 one-dollar bills for Liberian marriage chicken (no cow)	
	who performed ceremony?
chief	
	what was his message?
love "can be easy" now; story of two friends	
	how did it all end?
next day church ceremony in Monrovia	

At this point you may ask: "What about stories of ten or twenty pages, and what about entire books?"

The answer is that the principles remain the same, only the frequency with which we apply cue words must change.

If we wish to remember a book which has about three hundred pages, and perhaps from fifteen hundred to two thousand paragraphs, we obviously cannot form a chain consisting of from fifteen hundred to two thousand cue words. Not that it couldn't be done; but from a practical viewpoint it would take too much time, and since time is just what we wish to save, it does not seem feasible. Remembering every paragraph in every book is neither opportune nor desirable. In everyday life we are satisfied if we remember the contents of a book in such a way that we have a clear conception of the ideas it presents or the story it tells. That can be done by using a number of cue words approximately equivalent to its chapters. If some chapter headings are suitable for recalling their contents, these headings could be used as cue words provided that there is a possibility of linking them together and forming a chain. Unfortunately, the chapter headings do not always serve this purpose, but in such a case we should have no difficulty in finding one or two cue words for each chapter which will suffice to recall its contents and can be linked according to our need.

Whenever we have finished reading a book we should construct such a chain, which serves two good purposes at one and the same time. By selecting the cue words and by linking them together, we have an excellent test to check our knowledge and understanding of what we have just read. We cannot select cue words intelligently without such an understanding, and therefore the very fact that we are able to construct the chain is sufficient proof that we really grasped the ideas of the book. Furthermore, such a chain will be sufficient to recall the gist of the book at any time we wish. As long as we are not entirely familiar with this method, we should write down our chain and look at it after the lapse of a few days. Using these cue words, we should repeat the contents of the book, and we should have our written chain at hand in order to check whenever necessary. Having done this once or twice, we may be sure that the book has become our mental property for all times.

The principles which apply to books also apply to stage plays and movies. Over and over again you must have discovered, when the name of a picture was mentioned which you saw some time ago, that you have forgotten everything but the title and perhaps the name of the star. Not all pictures are worth remembering, but the rules which apply are again: cue words and chain. To select cue words for plays and movies is more difficult than for books because we have no chapter headings to guide us and we cannot turn back the pages if we are not sure of which words to select. But it is just this difficulty which makes it better training.

The thing to do is to sit down as soon as possible after having seen a play or motion picture and to think over the plot. Recalling the plot is easy if we do it right after coming home. It is much more difficult if we wait one or two days. If we do it immediately, the scenes will still be foremost in our minds. We can treat them like chapters in a book, and we can select our cue words and form a chain. It is a good test for your memory to use this chain a few days later in order to recall the entire story, and it is still better to try to tell it to somebody else, using your cue words like a spool to unwind the story.

CHAPTER 11

How to Construct and Remember a Speech

Have you ever had that awful feeling of anxiety in the middle of a speech when you did not know how to continue? There you were, in front of your audience, and all of a sudden your mind went blank. You felt as if the ground was giving way under you. As a matter of fact, in those moments you wished that it would happen, so that you could vanish from the scene and no longer have to face all those people.

If only you had known how to use a "chain" for your speech you could not have had such a blackout and you would not have had to undergo such an ordeal. Using the Chain Method, you would have been confident throughout your speech from beginning to end, always 100 per cent sure of knowing how to continue.

Of course, you can write out your speech, word for word, and then read your manuscript. However, a speech which is read can hardly be called a speech. You may as well hand out mimeographed copies so that everyone in the audience can read along with you. Actually you would not even have to go through the motions of reading your "speech." The desired effect is lost anyhow.

A speaker needs contact, or rapport, with his audience. This rapport is established not only through the voice but just as much, if not more so, through the eye. A speaker should not merely face his listeners but also look at them, and look at them in such a way that every member of his audience feels that he is personally addressed. Such a feeling cannot be created if the speaker's eyes are fixed on a manuscript.

A good speech is like a conversation between speaker and listener, even though the latter is perforce silent. After all, even if the listener does not say anything, his eyes, his facial expression, the way he slumps in his chair, or his restlessness may "speak" just as clearly. It is for this reason that the speaker must watch his audience so that he can sense their response and be guided accordingly. If he doesn't, his speech becomes a monologue, or just the opposite of a conversation.

The eyes of the listeners may express that something the speaker is trying to explain is not clear to them, or even that they do not agree with him. An alert speaker will recognize these signs and realize that he should rephrase a statement and give a clearer definition or add some stronger arguments and examples of what he intends to bring out. Or he may notice from their facial expressions and other symptoms that his listeners are getting tired. Then he should know that he had better cut his talk short and omit unnecessary elaboration.

But all this a speaker can do only if he masters his topic and his language sufficiently well to add or omit thoughts at will *and* if he watches his audience in order to *see* the reactions which he cannot *hear*. Both are impossible if his words are immutably fixed in advance and if he keeps his eyes glued to his script.

Speaking without a manuscript is by no means the same thing as speaking without preparation. Any fool may be able to *read* a speech, if the manuscript has been written by someone else. But in order to speak effectively without a script, not only must one have perfect command of topic and language, but one must also have made careful preparation. There is no magic formula for speeches. A political speech, in which you try to convince your audience that Mr. Smith is the only possible candidate, cannot follow the same pattern as a travelogue on a polar expedition. But all speeches have this much in common:

We must gather and we must review our material.

We must classify this material, and we must choose what to use for the introduction, for the body of the speech, and for the conclusion.

We must form a chain which keeps all the important thoughts together and in proper sequence, so that we can dispense with the manuscript and still be sure that we will not forget anything of importance.

In order to construct such a chain it is not necessary to write down the whole speech. Writing it down exposes us to the danger of learning it by heart. Aside from that, written sentences are usually longer and more complicated than those which we form while speaking. Therefore, the listener will immediately sense whether the speaker has memorized a speech verbatim or whether he is creating it as he goes along.

Suppose we have gathered our material, made an outline, and classified all the facts and ideas at our disposal. We have also made notes, so that we have the skeleton of the speech on paper. The next step, then, must be to select cue words, which may actually consist of one word or several words or even sentences. In choosing these cue words, we keep the fact constantly in mind that they must serve a twofold purpose. They must recall the thought for which they were selected, and they must fit together so that they can easily be linked to form a chain. Since our speech consists of connected thoughts, we will not face any difficulty in finding these links.

Before we go further, we make sure to master this chain—we make sure that each cue word comes easily to mind whenever we think of the preceding one. A few repetitions usually assure us. Nothing in this part of our preparation should be left to mechanical memorizing, but we should always be fully aware of the associations and the links between the cue words in sequence.

When we have finished this work, we write down the cue words in such a way that each one is clearly visible at a distance of approximately two or three feet. This is usually the distance between our eyes and the desk or table before us. Beginners in public speaking should take this cue sheet along for the speech. Even if we have mastered our cue words, it gives us a feeling of sureness and security to know that if anything happens to interrupt the flow of our thoughts we can see at a glance the spot where we left off and from which we have to continue. For this reason it is important to write the cue sheet, not at the last moment before the speech, but hours or even days ahead of time, and to use it several times in advance to run through the speech mentally. In this way we become familiar with the cue sheet and with the position of each cue word. This point cannot be over-emphasized, for too many speakers fumble through their notes in search of a certain item, thus producing a painful interruption of the speech. It is by far the best for you to have the chain so firmly anchored in your mind that you will not need a cue sheet at all, but as an emergency aid this sheet should be so familiar and so clearly visible that a glance of a split second, which is hardly noticeable to anyone in the audience, should be sufficient to bring you back to the point where your trend of thought was halted.

As an example of a speech let us choose a rather difficult topic, the Declaration of Independence, which is reprinted in the Appendix to this book. The Declaration of Independence is divided into three parts: the preface, the main body, and the conclusion. The chain for the preface looks about like this:

Cue Words	Linking Thoughts
When in the course of human events . . . one people dissolves political bands . . .	
	Why?
Declare the causes: All men are created equal	
	Equality means
Inalienable rights	
	They consist of
Life, liberty, and the pursuit of happiness	
	Who has to secure these rights?
The government	
	If it does not?
It is the right of the people to alter the government	
	Will this be done lightly?

Cue Words	Linking Thoughts
Governments long established will not be changed for light causes	
	What is the contrast to light causes?
A long train of abuse	
	What is the consequence of such abuse?
It is the right of the people to throw off such government	
	What happened in the Colonies?
The history of the present King is a history of injuries and usurpations	

(Your cue sheet should contain only the words on the left-hand side of the page, since those on the right-hand are only the linking thoughts and are not needed on paper).

The second part, the main body of the Declaration, is without doubt more difficult since it consists of all the various grievances, the enumeration of all the "injuries and usurpations" mentioned at the end of the preface. But, again, proper classification will help us to overcome these difficulties. Looking over the complaints, we find that those injuries committed by the King alone are introduced by the words "He has," whereas those committed by King and Parliament (which is not mentioned by name) are introduced by "for quartering," "for protecting," "for cutting off," etc. However, since commentators* on the Declaration agree that this does not involve a differentiation in principle, it is not necessary to complicate our classification by any such distinction.

* Friedenwald, *The Declaration of Independence* (New York: The Macmillan Co.); Carl Becker, *The Declaration of Independence* (New York: Harcourt, Brace & Co.).

We can classify the grievances into those concerning: law—legislature—judges and justice—army—military men—crime—office—trade—taxes. From this we can form the following chain:

Cue Words	Linking Thoughts
Law	
	Who makes the law?
Legislature	
	Who enforces legislation?
Judges and justice	
	Right—might
Army	
	An army consists of military men
Military men	
	Murder (This association is made easier if you observe that the last complaint concerning the military men ends with the word "murder," as you will see in the following pages)
Crime	
	Town (One of the crimes is "burnt our towns")
Office	
	Business
Trade	
	Profit
Taxes	

To repeat: for a cue sheet the words on the left-hand side should be sufficient. Make sure that you master this chain before you proceed.

When you have mastered it, read the main part of the Declaration again and give some thought to which injuries are covered by each cue word. Then you will arrive at the following story, which contains the grievances in detail and which makes it much easier to repeat the main part of the Declaration.

CONTENT

1. LAW

He (George III) has refused his assent to laws
and has refused to pass laws

He has forbidden his governors to pass laws

He took away our charter, abolishing our most
valuable laws

Who makes the
laws?

2. LEGISLATURE

He has dissolved representative houses repeatedly and has refused to cause others to be
elected

He has suspended our own legislatures

He has called together legislative bodies at unusual places

Who enforces
legislation?

3. JUDGES AND JUSTICE

He has made judges dependent upon his will
alone

He has obstructed the administration of justice

He has combined with others to subject us to a
restriction foreign to our constitution

He has deprived us in many cases of the right
of trial by jury

Right—might

4. ARMY

He has kept among us in times of peace standing armies

He has conscripted our fellow citizens into his
armies

He is at this time transporting large armies to
our country

Army consists of
military men

5. MILITARY MEN

He has rendered the military independent of
civil power

He has quartered large bodies of armed troops
among us

He has protected these bodies from punishment
  for murder

                                    Murder is a crime

6. CRIME
He has plundered our seas, ravaged our coasts,
  burnt our towns

                                    Town—office

7. OFFICE
He has erected a multitude of new offices

                                    Business

8. TRADE
He has cut off our trade with all parts of the
  world
He has obstructed the laws for the naturalization of foreigners

                                    Profit

9. TAXES
He has imposed taxes upon us without our
  consent

The third part, the conclusion, is not difficult at all. Whereas
the second part dealt with the deeds of the British King and
Parliament, the third part deals with the reaction of the colonists.
All we have to remember is an almost natural sequence:

Cue Words   *Linking Thoughts*

We have petitioned

                                    When that did not
                                      help

We have warned them

                                    Several times

We have reminded them

                                    Last appeal

We have appealed to their native justice

                                    What was the
                                      effect?

To that, too, they have been deaf

                                    Conclusion?

We, the representatives of the United States of
America, declare that these United Colonies
are free and independent States

                                    What does this
                                      mean?

Cue Words	Linking Thoughts
Cue Words	*Linking Thoughts*

They have full power to levy war, conclude peace, and do all other things which independent States may do

How to support this?

We mutually pledge to each other our lives, our fortunes, and our sacred honor

We suggest that you prepare a cue sheet consisting of the cue words on the left-hand side of all three parts. Then follow the instructions as given above and see whether you can recite in your own words the gist of the entire Declaration of Independence. If you are ambitious, you may add sundry remarks to your speech, perhaps the fact that the Declaration was removed from Philadelphia four times during the years. Try it this way:

REMOVAL OF THE DECLARATION OF INDEPENDENCE FROM PHILADELPHIA

The document containing the Declaration of Independence was removed from Philadelphia four times.

1. The British threatened Philadelphia after the capture of Newark and New Brunswick in 1776.

2. The British threatened Philadelphia after the capture of Germantown in 1777.

3. The British threatened Philadelphia after the capture of Washington, D.C., in 1814.

4. The document was buried in the vaults of Fort Knox when Germany and Japan declared war on the United States in 1941.

Three times it was the British who threatened Philadelphia. The first two years are easy to remember because the first was the year in which the Declaration was written; the second, the following year.

1814 and 1941 are easy to remember because the last two digits are reversed. Another way of remembering these two dates would be to substitute "veteran" for (1)814, a veteran being easy to associate with Washington; and "buried" for (1)941 because the document was buried at Fort Knox.

(How to remember historical dates by the use of the Number Code is explained in Chapter 20.)

You realize, of course, that this entire task is somewhat more difficult than recalling a speech created by yourself. If you compose your own speech and the supporting chain, you will know it much better because it is your own brain child; and if you write your own cue sheet, it will be more familiar to you than a paper prepared by someone else. Don't forget that being a good speaker entails practice, and don't expect a perfect speech at your first attempt. But in this chapter you have been given all the tools you need; and if you use them properly you may rest assured that you will be able to speak on your own whenever and wherever the opportunity arises.

Some of our former students will explain in later chapters how they use the Chain Method in order to remember sermons, law cases, sales talks, and stage roles.

CHAPTER 12

How to Remember Verbatim

PROSE AND POETRY

In the two preceding chapters we made a strong case against remembering verbatim where stories, books, and speeches are concerned, and for good reasons. There are, however, occasions in which it is imperative that we recite certain material word for word, exactly as it was originally written. For actors it is a basic requirement that they know their roles verbally, and the same holds for singers. Then there are clergymen who want to cite certain passages from the Scriptures, judges and attorneys who need to quote articles of law or important decisions. Actually every public speaker has occasion at one time or another to quote literally from a document or other source in order to substantiate or illustrate a point.

In all such instances it is not enough to know the gist of the material. The omission of a phrase or even a single word can be detrimental, yes, fatal, and defeat the very purpose it was meant to serve. In reciting prose or poetry a slight deviation from the text can also greatly reduce the effect and spoil the beauty of style and phraseology imparted by the author.

The method by which most people memorize their lines is still the primitive rote system, mechanically repeating line after line. It is time-consuming and a drudge at the same time. By extending our Chain Method we can do away forever with this so-called system of endless parrotlike repetition and avoid wasting precious hours which could be put to better use.

We have already experienced the value of cue words, linked into a chain, for remembering the gist of reading material. The cue words guide us from paragraph to paragraph, enabling us to recall and retell a story in all its details. In memorizing verbatim we go one step further. We again avail ourselves of cue words, except that we use more of them, so that we can weave a much finer mesh.

A cue word may be one word, two words, or a short phrase, whatever appears appropriate. However, we cannot allow ourselves the freedom to choose a word that is not in the text. For memorizing verbatim we must take the cue words from the text only.

Before we start selecting our cue words we must read the entire text so that we have a clear idea of its contents. Every author has his own style and it is important that we capture the meaning of *what* he says and *how* he says it.

We then must decide, especially if the text covers numerous pages, how much of it we can safely handle at one time. This is a highly individual matter and usually is found by trial and error. It does not take long before one knows his own limitations in this respect. It seems advisable not to take too large a segment in the beginning and to lengthen the span gradually until a certain optimum is reached. For a first attempt, limit yourself to a piece of roughly one hundred words.

After reading through the entire text as recommended above, turn to the first segment and read that part again before selecting cue words. A good way to select cue words is first to pick out those words which are the primary points, and later fill in secondary ones.

When assembling our cue words we must make sure that no important thought is left out. Whether we underline the cue words or write them on separate sheets of paper makes no difference. The main thing is that by touching upon each cue word the thoughts of the author should come to our mind. The question is here: "Do the cue words link?" There is no doubt about it that the thoughts of the author formed a continuous chain for him. Very often we will have no problem in following his thoughts, but this may not always be the case. Occasionally in prose, more often in poems, the continuity of thought escapes us. In such event we have to make an "artificial" association, one which works for us, if not in a logical sense, then in an illogical way. In such cases we resort to imaginative associations. In order to test yourself whether the cue words come back to your mind, try recalling them without looking at them, and then check to see whether you skipped any of them and reinforce your associations in any weak spots.

At this point you are ready for the final phase, which consists of rereading your text with due attention to the wording in between the cue words. Do this a few times, then put the text aside and recite the entire segment from memory. You will find that your recall is amazingly accurate. As a beginner you may have to refer back to the text in a few instances, but that should not discourage you. Many famous actors, who had considerable trouble recalling their lines, have applied this system with great success.

Learning in this fashion is a far cry from the boring and monotonous rote system. And it is at the same time much more effective because in selecting cue words we engage our thinking processes and sense the continuity of thoughts and the messages or ideas the author conveys to the reader.

Let us apply this method to a few literary pieces. First a piece of prose. The following is a statement made by President Franklin D. Roosevelt* in 1941 which has become known as:

THE FOUR FREEDOMS

In the future days, which we seek to make secure, we look forward for a world founded upon four essential human freedoms.

The first is freedom of speech and expression—everywhere in the world.

The second is freedom of every person to worship God in his own way—everywhere in the world.

The third is freedom from want—which, translated into world terms, means economic understandings which will secure to every nation a healthy peaceful life for its inhabitants—everywhere in the world.

The fourth is freedom from fear—which, translated into world terms, means a worldwide reduction of armaments to such a point and in such a thorough fashion that no nation will be in a position to commit an act of aggression against any neighbor—anywhere in the world.

* President Franklin D. Roosevelt, Message to Congress, January 6, 1941.

The primary cue words, which represent the most important words, have been underlined with solid lines; the secondary cue words, which serve to round out the continuity of the statements, have been underlined with broken lines.

It is good to notice certain patterns in any piece of literature such as this one. President Roosevelt was a master of oratory. When he used a word or a phrase more than once in a speech, it was not by accident but for a definite purpose. Every word was selected for optimal effect.

Notice the framework of the statements:

1. Freedom of speech
2. Freedom of worship
3. Freedom from want
4. Freedom from fear

Notice also that the first two freedoms apply to man as an individual, the last two to nations, accentuated by the addition of the phrase—*"which, translated into world terms, means."*

Three times the concluding phrase is *"everywhere in the world";* once, at the end of the last statement, this becomes *"anywhere in the world."*

After reading the primary cue words a few times add the secondary cue words and read them too a few times. Then put the book aside and repeat them from memory. Check back with the text whether you skipped any. Next, read again the entire text, not leaving out a single word. You may have to do this as a beginner two or three times and then recite the entire piece out loud without looking at the text. We suggest you do this slowly because these are weighty statements which lose their magistral quality when uttered at a fast pace.

As a second exercise let's take the poem by Robert Frost entitled:

STOPPING BY WOODS ON A SNOWY EVENING*

Whose woods these are I think I know.
His house is in the village, though;
He will not see me stopping here
To watch his woods fill up with snow.

My little horse must think it queer
To stop without a farmhouse near
Between the woods and frozen lake
The darkest evening of the year.

He gives his harness bells a shake
To ask if there is some mistake.
The only other sound's the sweep
Of easy wind and downy flake.

The woods are lovely, dark and deep,
But I have promises to keep,
And miles to go before I sleep,
And miles to go before I sleep.

We have to approach memorizing poetry with an appropriate attitude. There is no point in reciting a poem, even if we do not miss a single word, without sensing its underlying feeling and expressing that by the tone of our voice, as well as by proper emphasis and phrasing. To get this underlying feeling we need to observe the details delicately described by the poet. All the elements of observation which we discussed earlier in this book come into play. What applies to observing a picture or a scene is equally applicable to observing the image which the poet is drawing for our mental eye. Visualization is also here the most effective aid to our memory.

After reading the above poem of Robert Frost, one is filled with a feeling of stillness. Actually, this feeling is only expressed in so many words in the following three lines:

* From *Complete Poems of Robert Frost* (New York: Henry Holt & Company, Inc., 1949).

> The only other sound's the sweep
> Of easy wind and downy flake.
> The woods are lovely, dark and deep . . .

But notice how all the other lines deepen the aspects of the mood of the poem:

The first two lines impart remoteness from the world (village).

The following two lines impart solitude.

The following six lines impart strangeness of action (stopping).

The last three lines impart distance again and a call for return to reality (duties).

All the physical attributes which are involved in this poem should each make a distinctive detail in your visualization of the scene; the woods, the owner's house in the village, the stopping of the horse, the wagon (which is not mentioned in the poem), the snow piling up, the nearby lake, the dark sky, the harness bells, the sound of the wind and the snowflakes.

Once we *"see"* this picture evolving in front of our eyes it becomes so much easier to follow the poet's words. But they are his words and they will not become our mental property unless we make an effort to link them in the order in which he wrote them.

Which words you select as cue words is again a matter of individual preference.

The following is an example:

Whose woods—his house—the village—me stopping—his woods fill up with snow—my little horse—queer—without a farmhouse near—woods and frozen lake—darkest evening—harness bells—some mistake—only other sound—easy wind and downy flake—the woods—deep—promises to keep—miles to go—sleep.

Whatever your cue words are, go over them in your mind, follow the mood of the author at every turn, then go back to the text and phrase the lines exactly as the author wrote them, word for word. After doing so two or three times, repeat them out loud in slow tempo. It may surprise you how little time it takes to recite a beautiful poem like this without omitting one single word.

If at any time, when reciting either prose or poetry, you fail to recall a line or phrase, or even a single word, there is an indication that you need to go back to the text. Not merely to look up the words you did not remember but for the express purpose of finding a stronger connection from the point where you stumbled to the next line or phrase. It means that you have either to reinforce your association or to find a new and maybe entirely different association that links from one line to the other, or rather from one thought to the next.

Many students have expressed their relief after applying the Chain Method to prose and poetry and declared that it has given them an opportunity they never had before to enjoy reading and reciting pieces of literature which stirred their senses and imagination. It gives them a measure of enchantment to have such beautiful works of art stored in their memory, upon which they can draw at will any time they feel so inclined and re-enjoy the splendor of the written word.

Memorizing verbatim remains the same whether it concerns long pieces or short ones. Longer ones can be split up into manageable portions. An excellent exercise in this respect is to memorize the Declaration of Independence. You find the complete text in the Appendix to this book.

As a first step you might go back to the preceding chapter. We divided the entire Declaration into three main parts and selected our primary cue words. For verbatim remembering you can now add the connecting cue words. It provides you not only with a made-to-order exercise but also with an opportunity to make this document of national and historical significance your personal mental property.

The Hook Method

HOW TO REMEMBER ANYTHING CONNECTED WITH NUMBERS

CHAPTER 13

The Number Code

We live in the "number" age. More and more we are becoming deluged with numbers. Automation and computerization require that almost anything and everything be expressed in numbers. And since numbers in themselves have no meaning we sense a certain loss of identity in all this.

The old telephone numbers had exchange letters which were the first two letters of the name of the exchange area, so that there was at least some identification of the area or neighborhood. Now we have all-digit numbers, and besides the area code has been added, which results in a ten-digit number.

Your charge account cards and credit cards show your name, but the computer on which the records of all your transactions are kept could not care less about your name. It is the number that counts.

The Social Security number has become more important. The armed forces use it instead of the old serial number. The Internal Revenue Service uses it to keep track of all your sources of income, which in turn makes it mandatory for employers, banks, and others who report any payments of salary, interest, dividends, etc., to use your Social Security number in reporting these payments to the tax authorities.

We could go on and on. Numbers are all around us: highway numbers, license numbers, zip code numbers, etc. How can we remember all these numbers? Numbers have no meaning in themselves. Words do have a meaning and that's why they are easier to remember.

It follows, then, that if we find a way to transpose numbers into words we are well on our way to solving the problem. Through the centuries many scholars found devices and techniques for memorizing numbers, but it was not until the nineteenth century that the "Number Code," as we know it today, became generally accepted.

The principle of the Number Code is the substitution of letters for numerals. This code is very easy to memorize if you use the following suggestions:

1=*t* Notice the similarity: both have one downstroke.

2=*n* The letter *n* has two downstrokes.

3=*m* The letter *m* has three downstrokes.

4=*r* The word four has *four* letters, the fourth letter is *r;* besides, the *r* is the emphatic consonant in the word *four.*

5=*l* Think of the Roman capital letter *L* which stands for 50, or stretch out your *L*eft hand so that your *five* fingers form the letter *L.*

6=*j* If you turn 6 around, you practically have *j.* A handwritten 6 reflected in a mirror shows similarity to a *j.*

6 = J

7=*k* Visualize the capital letter *K* written as two 7's leaning against each other.

7 = K

8=*f* The small written *f* has two loops similar to the figure 8.

8 = f

9=*p* If you turn 9 around, you have a *p.* A 9 reflected in a mirror appears like a *p.*

9 = P

0=*z* The last numeral 0 represents the last letter in the alphabet *z.* Also *zero* begins with *z.*

As you see at first glance, this code system is extremely simple to understand. We now have the following:

1	2	3	4	5	6	7	8	9	0
t	n	m	r	l	j	k	f	p	z

You will observe that we use only consonants. The reason is that we wish to transpose numbers into words and, by doing so, we want to be free to use the vowels as we please in order to get words.

If we translate the word *net* into numbers, we mentally cross out the vowel *e* and arrive at *n*=2 and *t*=1, thus *net* is translated into 21.

In the same manner, crossing out the vowels, you can readily translate the following words into numbers:

man	=	32	park	=	947
map	=	39	paper	=	994
rat	=	41	panorama	=	9243
tree	=	14	monopoly	=	3295
lamp	=	539	Furst	=	8401

Still our Number Code would not be complete if we used only the 10 consonants shown above. Somehow we have to find numbers for the remaining consonants of the alphabet.

Suppose *you* had to invent such a method. What way would you choose to bring the rest of the consonants into this system? You are aware of the fact that we have only ten digits at our disposal and that therefore some kind of duplication is necessary. What is the easiest way to bring about such a duplication? In thinking it over, you will agree that the *sound* of the letters provides the best means. While there are very few consonants which sound exactly alike, such as *f* and *ph* in *Filipino* and *Philippines,* there are many which are similar, and we can use this similarity for building up the entire Number Code in the following way:

For the digit 1: Use *d* or *th,* as well as *t,* since all three are similar in sound.

For the digit 6: Similar to the sound of *j* are the sounds of *ch* and *sh,* as, for instance, in the words *chair* and *ship.* In addition, *g* when it has a soft sound as in *George, germ,* or *giant.*

For the digit 7: Hard g goes with the *k* sound, because in such words as *garden, game, guest,* the sound is similar. In this group, also, belongs the hard *c,* as in *calm, call, Cambridge.* The *q* obviously belongs in this group.

For the digit 8: Similar to the sound of *f* is the consonant *v,* and also *ph* in such words as *pharmacy, phone, phase.*

For the digit 9: *p* sounds like *b,* for it also is a labial.

For the digit 0: *z* is phonetically like *s,* as is also soft *c,* in such words as *cipher, civic, cigar.*

This completes the system of numerals and gives us the following:

1	2	3	4	5	6	7	8	9	0
t	n	m	r	l	j	k	f	p	z
d					sh	hard g	v	b	s
th					ch	hard c	ph		soft c
					soft g	ng			
					tch, dg	q			

You will notice that the letters *h, w,* and *y* are missing. These letters have no number value. They are sometimes referred to as half vowels. It may help you to remember these three letters by rearranging their sequence and thus spelling out the word "why."

The letter *x* is also missing because it sounds like a combination of two letters, *k* and *s,* in words like *fix, mix,* etc., or like *hard g* and *z,* as in *exaggerate* or *exam.* In these cases the translation of *x* is 70.

Only in a few words, when they start with *x,* like *xylophone* and *Xavier,* is the *x* pronounced as a *z* and it is then translated into 0.

The *ng* sound, as in words like ri*ng,* maki*ng,* is classified as 7 in order to avoid disagreement as to whether we hear one sound or two.

The same goes for sounds such as *tch* (as in wa*tch*) and *dg* (as in lo*dg*e), which are both classified as 6.

Since our system is purely phonetic, we go by sound only, not by the spelling. Therefore, double consonants count as single consonants. For instance:

$$\begin{aligned}
\text{coffee} \quad &= \quad 78 \\
\text{better} \quad &= \quad 914 \\
\text{Fillmore} \quad &= \quad 8534
\end{aligned}$$

Also letters which are not pronounced are disregarded and thus:

$$
\left.
\begin{array}{lcl}
\text{knee} & = & 2 \\
\text{knife} & = & 28
\end{array}
\right\} \quad k \text{ is not sounded}
$$

$$
\left.
\begin{array}{lcl}
\text{gnash} & = & 26 \\
\text{gnaw} & = & 2
\end{array}
\right\} \quad g \text{ is not sounded}
$$

pseudonym	=	0123	p is not sounded
psalm	=	03	p and l are not sounded

Now try for yourself. Translate the following cities in the United States into numbers, always remembering that the sound and not the spelling is decisive. These cities are:

New York	Cleveland
Chicago	Baltimore
Philadelphia	Tulsa
Detroit	Boston
Denver	Washington

The correct numbers are found below.

It is important that you become thoroughly familiar with the translation of words into numbers, and for that reason you should translate as many words as possible. Use any spare moment to do this exercise; take any word that comes to your mind, always going by the sound, not by the spelling.

New York	247	Cleveland	758521
Chicago	677	Baltimore	95134
Philadelphia	85158	Tulsa	150
Detroit	1141	Boston	9012
Denver	1284	Washington	6712

CHAPTER 14

The Principles of Basic List and Hook Method

In the preceding chapter we saw that numbers can be translated into meaningful words, which makes it much easier to remember them. If we wish to recall a number, all we have to do is to retranslate the word back into the proper number. For instance, the number 247 can be translated among other possibilities into the words New York, and when we want to recall that number, we translate the words "New York" back into 247. We shall find numerous applications later on for this simple technique that gives such amazing results when we deal with telephone numbers, price lists, and all kinds of numerical data.

For the moment, however, we want to draw your attention to a different feature of the Number Code, which you can put to work for you as a mental filing system. This feature is called the Basic List of key words for the numbers from 1 to 100.

In order to have these key words at our fingertips any time we need them, it is necessary to select one key word for each number. Just as we want to be able to put our hands on a specific file from our filing cabinet, we want to be able to recall the same key word of our Basic List any time we want to use it.

The question is now: how can we arrive at key words that bring back to our mind, immediately and automatically, the numbers they stand for? For each number we have to make a choice, once and for all, out of several possible words which all translate into the same number. For instance, number 71 can be translated into:

> kit—kite—kid—kowtow—Kate
> God—good—gait—goat—get—guide
> quit—quiet—quite—quote—quota
> cat—cod—coat—cot—code, etc.

Since all these words represent the number 71, how can we manage to agree on one of them in such a way as to be sure to find it again without delay tomorrow, next week, next month, or many years hence?

The same question applies to each and every one of the 100 key words. We therefore have to apply a set of rules by which we arrive for each number at an acceptable word that will be the same for all of us. First of all, since these words are going to be used for making associations, we shall limit our choice of words to nouns only, preferably nouns representing tangible objects, persons, or animals. We then limit the use of consonants as well as vowels, as follows:

1. *Consonants*

The numbers in the twenties, thirties, forties, and fifties present no problem since they start with the number 2, 3, 4, and 5, which leave no alternatives in the translation, $2=n$, $3=m$, $4=r$, and $5=l$.

For the numbers in the teens, sixties, seventies, eighties, and nineties, we have a choice of consonants, but we select for the starting numbers 1, 6, 7, 8, and 9 the letters which are most frequently used in our language. Therefore, in principle, we use for the words which stand for the numbers:

> from 10 to 19, only words starting with *t*
> from 60 to 69, only words starting with *ch*
> from 70 to 79, only words starting with *c*
> from 80 to 89, only words starting with *f*
> from 90 to 99, only words starting with *b*

Exceptions to these rules should be made only as a last resort. If you now look back at all the words listed for 71 (page 115), you will notice that this procedure eliminates the first three lines—the words beginning with *k*, hard *g*, and *q*—and thus leaves only the fourth line from which to make our final choice, words starting with the hard *c*.

2. *Vowels*

We are all accustomed to the sequence in which the vowels appear in the alphabet; that is, *a, e, i, o, u, y*. If we make it a point to use them in the same sequence and to stop as soon as we have found a word, or better, an object, which lends itself to association, our problem is solved.

In our search for key words we proceed in the following way: for example,

13 consists of 1 and 3, or **t-m.** Inserting the first vowel, *a,* we find the word **tam** (short for tam-o'-shanter).

14 consists of 1 and 4, or **t-r.** Inserting the first vowel, *a,* we find the word **tar.**

15 consists of 1 and 5, or **t-l.** Inserting *a* and adding a mute *e* at the end would give us **tale.** Although this is an acceptable word, it is rather abstract and not easy to use for associations. Therefore, we prefer to insert *ai* instead, and then get the word **tail,** which meets all requirements; it is a noun and an object, and therefore lends itself readily for associations. **Tall** would be another possibility for 15, since the double *l* translates into 5 and not 55. However, "tall" is an adjective and can therefore not be used for association.

If the insertion of the vowel *a* does not lead to an appropriate word, we proceed to other vowels, always following the sequence of the alphabet.

For instance:

21 consists of 2 and 1, or **n-t.** If we insert the vowel *a,* we have **nat,** which is not a meaningful word. Therefore, we go on to insert the next vowel, *e,* and find the word **net,** which is satisfactory.

22 translates into **n-n.** We see that **nan, nen,** and **nin** are not meaningful words. By doubling the vowel *o,* we would get **noon,** which is a noun, but rather abstract. Thus, we insert the next vowel, which is, *u,* and find **nun,** which is satisfactory.

From all the words listed for 71 in the beginning of this chapter, only one can be correct. Inserting the vowel *a* between **c-t,** we find **cat,** which satisfies all requirements.

If we follow this procedure and keep in mind to accept only nouns which are easy to associate with other items, we all must arrive at approximately the same list of words. "Approximately," because we may have a different opinion in a few cases as to whether or not a certain word should be used.

We have, for example, avoided words like *knave, light, lamb* for 28, 51, 53 respectively. These words contain consonants which do not count in our code because they are silent. Theoretically, *knave* should have preference over *navy; light* over *lot;* and *lamb* over *lime.* However, we prefer *navy, lot,* and *lime* because experience has shown that some students become confused if the pronunciation deviates from the spelling. An exception here is *comb* for 73. Initially we used *cam* for this number, but because most people did not seem to be familiar with that word, we found that *comb* was more readily accepted notwithstanding the silent *b*.

Thus we arrive at the following Basic List:

1. tea	35. mail	69. chip
2. Noah	36. match	70. case
3. May	37. mike	71. cat
4. ray	38. muff	72. can
5. law	39. map	73. comb
6. jaw	40. race	74. car
7. key	41. rat	75. coal
8. fee	42. rain	76. cash
9. pea	43. ram	77. cake
10. toes	44. rear	78. cuff
11. tot	45. rail	79. cap
12. tan	46. rash	80. face
13. tam	47. rake	81. fat
14. tar	48. reef	82. fan
15. tail	49. rope	83. fame
16. tissue	50. lace	84. fare
17. tack	51. lot	85. file
18. taffy	52. lane	86. fish
19. tap	53. lime	87. fig
20. nose	54. lair	88. fife
21. net	55. lily	89. fob
22. nun	56. lash	90. base
23. name	57. lake	91. bat
24. Nero	58. leaf	92. bean
25. nail	59. lap	93. beam
26. niche	60. cheese	94. bar
27. neck	61. chat	95. ball
28. navy	62. chain	96. badge
29. nap	63. chime	97. back
30. mass	64. chair	98. beef
31. mat	65. jail	99. baby
32. man	66. judge	(100. thesis)
33. mama	67. check	
34. mare	68. chef	

Note that the word *tissue* for 16 is no exception, since the double *s* is pronounced like *sh* and therefore translated by 6.

Unavoidable exceptions are *jail* for 65 and *judge* for 66 because there are no suitable words that start with *ch*.

For the one-digit numbers from 1 to 9 it is impossible to find words containing just one consonant and one vowel; we had to resort to double vowels. In order to make things easier we chose words which rhyme, such as *May—ray; law—jaw; key—fee—pea.*

We suggest that you construct your own list of words from 1 to 99, following the principles which we have just developed. Then compare your list with the list in this book. If there is a deviation, please compare your word and ours and decide which one you prefer. It is not absolutely necessary for you to have exactly the same word list that we use, but it will be helpful in future exercises. And it is necessary that you stick, once and for all, to any chosen word. That means no harm is done if you prefer *light* to *lot* for 51 or *touch* to *tissue* for 16; but once you have made your choice, you must stick to it. You cannot use *light* today, *lot* tomorrow, and *light* again next week.

Make sure that you memorize this list in a few weeks, and at least half of the list before you go on to the next chapter.

Take twenty or twenty-five numbers at a time and see whether the words come back to your mind. If you are uncertain about any of them, before looking them up in your book try to reconstruct them. The beauty of the system is that the key words have not been chosen haphazardly but by following definite rules. By following these rules you will always be able to arrive at the correct word.

We shall use these words for associations and therefore they must be represented by pictures; and these pictures must be very clear in your mind.

On the pages which follow, you will find pictures for all the key words. They are only examples, just in case you would like some help. Actually, we much prefer that you select your own. We further suggest that, whenever possible, you give them a personal touch, especially when the key word can be pictured in various ways. It is important, however, that you have one particular picture for each word and that you never change it.

This picture must be so clear in your mind that you see it mentally at the very moment you think of the word; or, better still, when you think of the number.

Therefore, it is not good to picture just a key, any key, for number 7, but a particular key, maybe your house key, preferably a key that is a little different from others.

For 11—*tot,* not just any child will do; select one particular one and keep that picture forever. The same goes for other words, especially those which otherwise might be vague. For 31—*mat,* think of a particular mat in your home or in front of your door, one which you can immediately identify. For 32—*man,* choose a certain man, one for whom you have great affection or admiration.

As stated in the chapter on association, we can remember a new idea only by connecting it with something we already know. The numbers—or, better, the word pictures—represent the things we already know, and therefore they must be firmly established in our mind. Any number between 1 and 100 should always, and promptly, recall the same picture so that there is no room for doubt.

Since we shall use these numbers, words, and pictures like hooks on which to hang the items we wish to remember in any special case, we call this method the Hook Method, as distinguished from the Chain Method, which we discussed earlier.

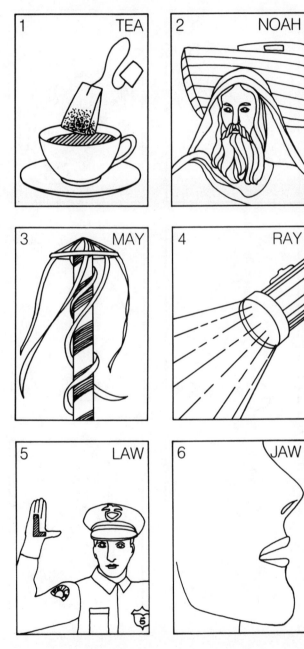

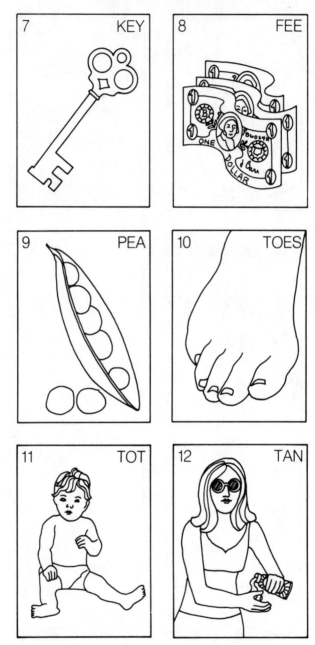

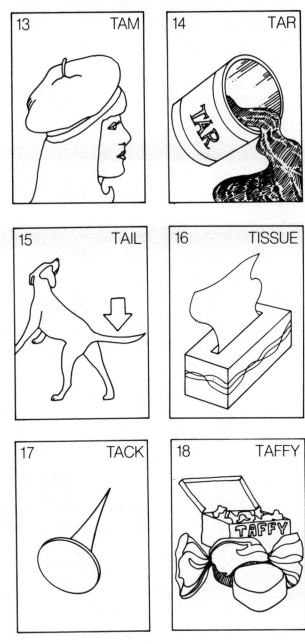

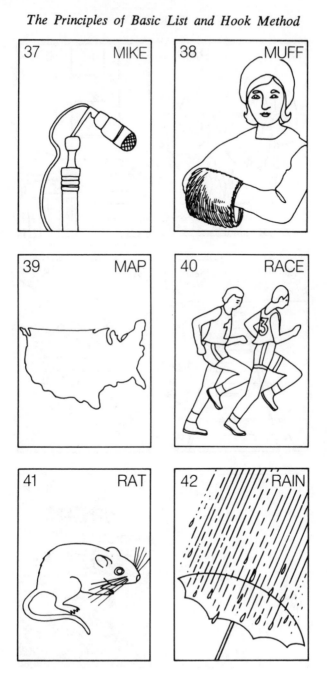

43 RAM

44 REAR

45 RAIL

46 RASH

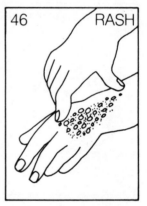

47 RAKE

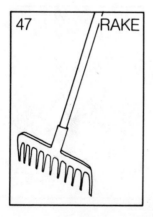

48 REEF

49   ROPE

50   LACE

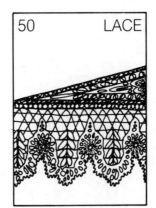

51   LOT

52   LANE

53   LIME

54   LAIR

55 LILY

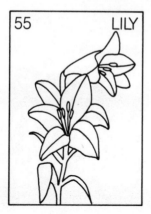

56 LASH

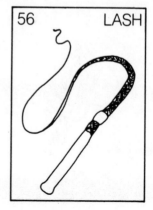

57 LAKE

58 LEAF

59 LAP

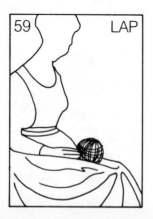

60 CHEESE

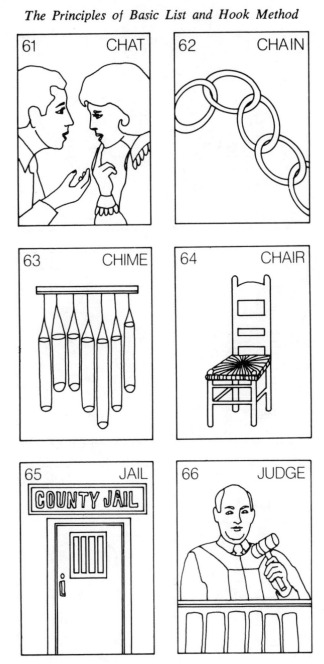

79   CAP
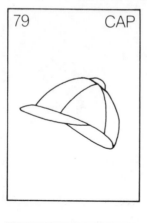

80   FACE

81   FAT
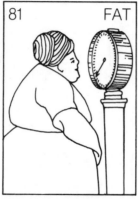

82   FAN
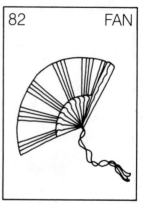

83   FAME

84   FARE
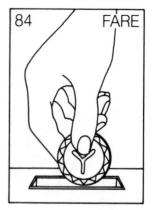

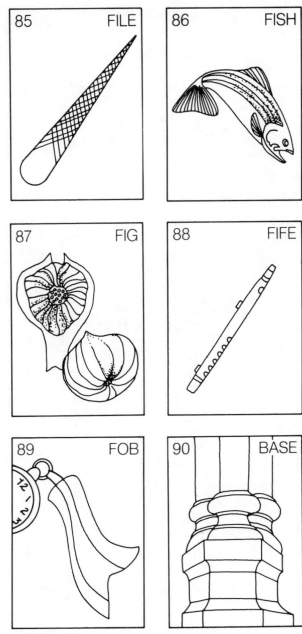

85 FILE

86 FISH

87 FIG

88 FIFE

89 FOB

90 BASE

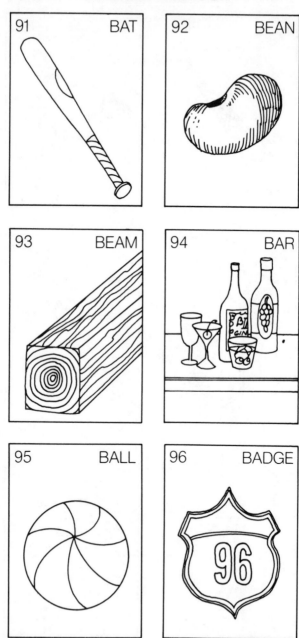

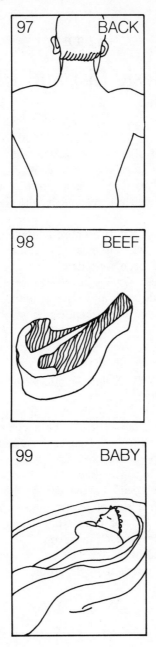

CHAPTER 15

The Basic List and Errands

The applications of the Number Code and the Basic List are many. At this early stage we can already give you some idea of how to make it work. As a first exercise we have chosen a shopping list which you will remember with the help of the Basic List.

The practical value of this exercise is obvious. Ask anyone who ever went shopping what it means to come home and discover that some item had been forgotten.

There are other less obvious benefits however. You must realize that whenever you do such an exercise—either this one or others which will follow—you are strengthening your memory power in general.

In addition, since you are going to connect items on an errand list with key words of the Basic List, you are increasing your powers of imagination, which is so indispensable for making effective associations.

Furthermore, the Basic List, as you will see, is an excellent tool for remembering all kinds of items. To become adept at handling this tool, practice is the best teacher, as usual.

Now, let us suppose that you are going to give a party tomorrow night and that you have to buy twenty items for this party. Of course, it would be the easiest thing in the world to write them down on a slip of paper; but, aside from the danger of losing that slip, by not using your "memory muscles," you would not be doing yourself a favor. Therefore we prefer to *remember* the items. With the use of our Basic List we make sure that we won't forget a single errand.

The items in question are:

1. frankfurters
2. wine
3. cigars
4. film for camera
5. firecrackers
6. nuts
7. sugar
8. pastry
9. Coca-Cola
10. dance records
11. ice cream
12. chairs
13. flowers
14. coffee
15. pretzels
16. gifts
17. cheese
18. candy
19. beer
20. napkins

Now try to remember these twenty items by connecting them with the first twenty words of our Basic List. Make sure that you only form an association between the particular basic word and the item you wish to buy; do not connect one errand with the other. Below, you will find some suggestions, but it is definitely better if you first try to form your own associations.

Here are our suggestions:

1. tea—frankfurters	Imagine yourself stirring your tea with a frankfurter.
2. Noah—wine	Use your imagination and visualize old man Noah with a bottle of wine.
3. May—cigars	See big cigars hanging on a maypole.
4. ray—film for camera	Visualize yourself using a flashlight in your search for a roll of film.
5. law—firecrackers	See yourself setting off a firecracker in front of a policeman.
6. jaw—nuts	Think of the movement of your jaw to crack the nuts.
7. key—sugar	Imagine you drop your key in the sugar bowl.
8. fee—pastry	You are paying a fee by placing dollar bills on the pastry.
9. pea—Coca-Cola	See peas floating in a Coca-Cola bottle.
10. toes—dance records	Visualize yourself sticking your big toe through the hole in a record.
11. tot—ice cream	Picture your little tot licking ice cream from a cone.
12. tan—chairs	You accidentally drop some suntan oil on a chair.

13. tam—flowers	Imagine that you stick some flowers into your tam-o'-shanter.
14. tar—coffee	See a can of coffee falling into the tar on the road.
15. tail—pretzels	Hang the pretzels on the dog's tail.
16. tissue—gifts	See yourself wrapping the gifts in tissue paper.
17. tack—cheese	Picture yourself using a tack (instead of a toothpick) to pick up the cheese bits.
18. taffy—candy	You mix some saltwater taffy with your chocolates or bonbons.
19. tap—beer	Imagine you turn on your water tap and out comes beer.
20. nose—napkins	Instead of a hanky you use a napkin to wipe your nose.

The pictures on the following pages show you how the associations suggested above can be visualized.

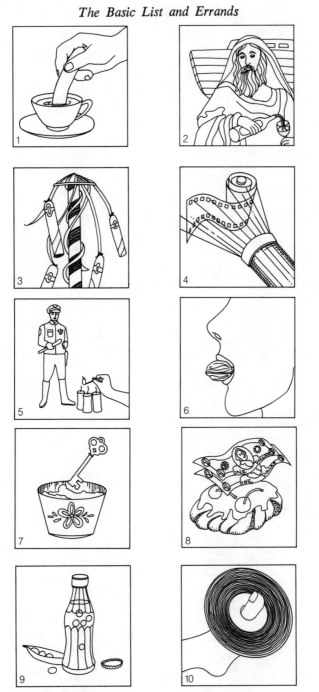

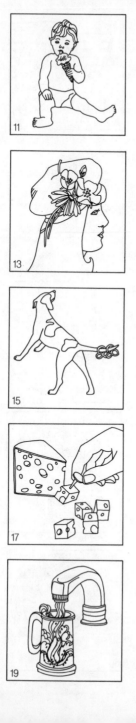
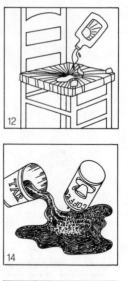

When you have finished forming these associations, you must be able to recall all twenty items by thinking of the first twenty words of the Basic List. You can enumerate these twenty items not only in sequence but also out of sequence. If asked what is item number 15, you know that 15 is *tail* in the Basic List and that you connected pretzels with it. If you made good associations and visualized them clearly, you will have no problem enumerating them even backward. Test yourself and see how effective the system is.

You may have thought that the easiest associations were those where there was an obvious similarity, such as 18. *taffy—* candy. Taffy is a kind of candy. You might even conclude that it would help to arrange the items in such a way that they have a closer relation to the Basic List words. It won't work that way.

First of all, you do not normally make a shopping list in that manner. Whatever comes first to your mind should be the first item on your (mental) list without giving thought to how it can be associated with the Basic List word. Anything can be associated with any word of the Basic List. Logical or natural associations are not easier to recall. To the contrary. As you will soon experience, the more far-fetched and ludicrous or bizarre your associations are, the more readily they will come back to your mind. Whenever the association is obvious because of some similarity or otherwise, be sure to exaggerate at least part of the picture you are trying to visualize or make the picture an unusual one. For instance, if the first item should be "sugar," you should not see yourself putting some sugar in your tea; you should rather picture yourself emptying your teacup into the sugar bowl!

Unusual, imaginative associations are much easier to recall.

The uses of the Basic List are many. We shall have occasion to discuss the various applications in practical life later on. For the time being, the best thing for you is to do some exercises.

Simply ask someone to give you twenty or thirty items at random. Ask for objects, tangible things. Abstract items should come later.

If you find that the associations you had made previously interfere with the new ones, use other parts of the Basic List.

Use the numbers from 20 to 40 on one day, 40 to 60 the next day, and so on. By doing so, you will also gradually master the entire Basic List so that it becomes your mental property.

CHAPTER 16

The Distinction between the Hook Method and the Chain Method

At this point you should give some thought to the question: "What is the distinction between the Hook Method and the Chain Method?"

There are several important distinctions in construction as well as in application.

In order to illustrate the difference in construction we have drawn a diagram of both methods as we applied them to the errand list in the previous chapter and the Intrepid Airman story, discussed in Chapter 10.

Errand List	Intrepid Airman Story
tea – frankfurters	dentist chair
	/
Noah – wine	terminal
	/
May – cigars	airport bus
	/
ray – film	airport

As you notice, the above diagrams do not cover the entire errand list or the entire Intrepid Airman story. It is not necessary, because from the few items listed above you get already a clear picture of the distinction in the construction of the two methods. You realize that in the first method (Hook) the words of the Basic List are used to form the associations. These words— which never vary—must be in our mind before we can start. But in the second method (Chain) the words we wish to remember are linked together without any help from outside.

When the construction of both methods is clear in your mind, try to decide when and where in practical life you would apply the Hook Method and when and where you would apply the

Chain Method. If you think this through, you will be able to find at least three distinctions as far as the application of either method is concerned.

I. In order to find the first distinction, ask yourself the following question: What is the difference between the items which I remembered for the party and the cue words which I remembered for the story about the airman?

The answer is that there is a logical connection between the cue words in the story, while such a connection is lacking as far as the party items are concerned. It does not matter whether we use visual images or the laws of association. At any rate, the cue words of the story are logically connected. However, the *wine* is not logically connected with the *cigars,* and the *cigars* are not logically connected with the *film.* They are all bought for the same purpose, the party, but one has nothing to do with the other.

Then ask yourself whether the fact that the items are logically connected is more important for the use of the Chain Method or the Hook Method. It is immediately clear that such a connection is very important if you use the Chain Method, because here one item is linked to the other, and each preceding item is supposed to recall the following item to your mind. And evidently such a connection is of no consequence if you use the Hook Method, by which *Noah* has to recall the *wine,* and *May* has to recall the *cigars.*

Thus we see that *we use the Chain Method whenever we have to remember connected items or thoughts,* such as we find in speeches, newspaper and magazine articles, entire books, and the like. *We use the Hook Method whenever no such connection exists,* as for instance in party items, pages of magazines, playing cards, and the like.

II. In order to make it easier for you to find the second distinction, consider the following. Suppose you remember the items at the beginning of this chapter for a party that you are going to give tonight, and you intend to have another party tomorrow. You have to buy twenty new items tomorrow, and in order to remember them you will use the same words of the Basic List. What will happen to the items which you have remembered for tonight?

The answer is that they will disappear from your memory because they will be replaced by tomorrow's items, which are connected with the same words. It will now be easy for you to find the second important distinction between the Hook Method and the Chain Method: that is, the fact that *we can use the Hook Method only for things which we have to remember for a short time.* As soon as we try to remember something else by using the same Basic List, the previous items disappear.

For everything that we wish to remember for a long time or permanently the Chain Method must be used. Since each chain covers a different subject and starts with a different word, it is possible to have hundreds of chains in our minds, and one will not interfere with the other. That is the reason why the Chain Method enables us to keep hundreds of different speeches in mind or to remember hundreds of magazine or newspaper articles, books, etc. We shall talk about the details later on. For the moment it is enough if you merely understand the principle of this second distinction.

III. In order to find the third distinction between these two methods, think back to our party items and try to recall which objects were connected with the numbers 14, 7, and 18.

You probably have no difficulty in giving the correct answer without referring to the preceding pages. However, if you were asked what was the eighth or the fourth word to be remembered in the story, it will be difficult for you to give the right answer without counting from *dentist chair,* number 1; *terminal* number 2; etc.

You have thus found the answer for the third distinction. It is the fact that the *Hook Method enables us to remember any item out of sequence,* whereas in the Chain Method we would have to start counting from the beginning to locate any one item we want to know. Therefore we must use the Hook Method whenever it is necessary to know a certain item out of sequence; for instance, the sixteenth President of the United States, the Thirteenth Amendment, and the like.

Before reading further, make sure that you know these three distinctions between the Hook and the Chain Methods and that they are perfectly clear to you.

Of course, in everyday life the distinction is not always so obvious as it sounds in theory. It may very well happen that we wish to know something out of sequence but for a long time to come. If that is the case, we must combine the two methods.

The Practical Application of the Number Code and Hook Method

CHAPTER 17

How to Memorize a Magazine and a Series of Anecdotes

An excellent way to strengthen your powers of imagination and observation is to do the magazine exercise.

The Hook Method is the tool by which we memorize page by page, connecting the contents of a page with the word of the Basic List that corresponds to the number of the page in question. This can be done with a newspaper as well as with magazines. Pictures lend themselves better for association, and that's why we have chosen ten to show you how the Hook Method can be applied.

We have numbered these ten pictures from 21 to 30 as if they appeared on those pages in a magazine. We proceed in the following way:

First we translate the page number into the Basic List word. Then we select one particular item on the page which we associate with this basic word. When there are several items on the page to choose from, the item we select does not necessarily have to be the most important one on the page. It should be an item that can most effectively be associated with your basic word picture. Apply this procedure to the "magazine" pages one by one and make your selections and your associations. At this point we abstain from giving you examples because there is nothing better for your progress in memory training than to do them on your own. Gradually, you should become less and less dependent on ready-made solutions. You will retain and recall associations which you have formed on your own much better.

Now go through the following ten pages. First look at the page number, think of your basic word picture for that number, select the item on that page which is readily associative with the basic word. At this moment take only *one* item or feature per page. Do not write anything down at this point.

Here are the ten pages:

21

22

23

25

26

27

28

29

30

After you have gone through these ten pages and made your associations, take a piece of paper, think of your basic words from 21 to 30 and write down next to each number the one item you associated with that page number.

Before we discuss the subject a little further, compare your associations with those given below:

Page	Contents	Basic Word	Association
21	Deep-sea diving operations	NET	The diver brings his "catch" to the surface in a net.
22	Slicing of bread	NUN	You can visualize a nun cutting the bread.
23	Employee suggestion box	NAME	You print your name in bold letters on the suggestion blank.
24	The White House	NERO	See Nero standing on the portico with the President of the United States.
25	Automobile races	NAIL	A large nail punctured one of the tires.
26	Moon shot	NICHE	See your niche in the nose cone of the spacecraft.
27	German shepherd	NECK	The dog nudges up to your neck.
28	Statue of Liberty	NAVY	Picture a navy ship passing the Statue of Liberty.
29	Living room	NAP	Imagine yourself taking a nap on the couch.
30	Opera house	MASS	Association is obvious.

No doubt for some of the pages you may have chosen different items for your associations. Even if yours are all different, it does not matter. No two minds think exactly alike. Even if we choose the same item on a page for our initial association, the picture that we mentally draw in combining the basic word with that item can still be vastly different.

Look at the first of the ten pages, page 21. You can connect the *net* with the diver, as we did. You could also have connected it with the man who handles the hose, or with one of the other men in the picture, with the boat itself, with the diver's helmet, or a number of other features.

Even if two persons take the same item from a page as an orientation point, as for instance the diver on page 21, they can still come up with entirely different pictures in connecting it with the basic word; in this case *net*. We thought of the diver using a net to scoop up things from the bottom of the ocean and bringing them to the surface in this net. One might also picture the diver himself being hauled aboard in a net, or seeing the diver casting a net to the men, or latching it onto any of the structures on deck. The beauty of this way of associating is that there are so many possibilities and that each of these possibilities can work so effectively as a stimulant to our memory power.

If you are ambitious you will not be satisfied with remembering just one item on each page. You will try to give as many details as possible.

When you wrote down your connecting items, you must have been surprised to discover that you remembered already quite a bit more than just one item per page.

At this point, turn back to any one of the pages and recall your connecting item or feature for that page. Now look over the rest of the picture and observe more details, adding them to your memory storage without much effort. Some pictures, of course, contain more details than others. Take page 24 for example: The association of Nero meeting the President on the White House portico brings automatically to mind the picture as you saw it at first: the White House blazing in the sunlight, overlooking the front lawn. When you look again, you may notice the beautiful trees, the fountains—there are eight of them visible, the flag hanging limply from the pole—there's no wind, the various structures on the roof, the steps leading to the portico, the limousine in the driveway to the right, two men (secret service agents?) standing near one of the lower entrances to the left, another person just barely visible next to the third fountain from the right. You can go on and find many more details.

Proceed in a similar fashion in observing the other nine pages. Then close your book and see in how much detail you can recall each page, going mentally through your Basic List words from 21 to 30.

This kind of exercise is one of the most effective means of improving your powers of observation. You are induced, in a pleasant way, to increase your concentration almost without realizing it. If you are impressed with your prowess in recall—as you undoubtedly will be—pick up a current magazine, preferably one with many illustrations, and apply this method to, say fifty pages, or as many as you feel you can handle. After you have made your associations and reviewed the pages for details, test yourself, and if you feel prepared, hand the magazine to some friends of yours and let them ask you for the contents of any of the pages which you have memorized. Give them the description of the page they call out in as much detail as you can about items, persons, animals, colors, or what have you. Then let them ask for another page, and so on. You will sense a pride of accomplishment, and rightly so; in addition, you will enjoy the admiration of your friends.

The thought might have occurred to you that the ten magazine pages were easy to remember for the reason that the Basic List words for the page numbers 21 to 30 just happen to be suitable for making associations with the pictures on these pages. In other words, would the system work just as effectively if these pictures had appeared on other pages?

You can find the answer by going back to (magazine) page 21 and asking yourself: "If this picture had been on page 22, could I have associated it with the basic word for 22—*nun?*" Of course you could have. You would "see" a *nun* as the diver or standing at the ship's railing. Had the picture been on page 23, you would have had no difficulty bringing your *name* into the picture. You would "see" your name in gold letters on the bow of the ship for instance. Had the page number been 24, it would have been just as easy to picture *Nero* standing on the ship's deck viewing the operations.

By proceeding in this manner throughout the entire Basic List you would find that this system works all the way.

You may now realize why we made it a definite requirement in constructing the Basic List that the key words should represent objects or persons, because they lend themselves perfectly to any kind of association.

It takes only a few exercises to convince yourself of what we stated before: anything and everything can be associated with the words of the Basic List. As a result—since the basic words stand for numbers—we have put meaning into meaningless numbers and thus made remembering a joy instead of a drudge.

HOW TO REMEMBER A SERIES OF ANECDOTES

An exercise which is closely related to remembering magazine or newspaper pages is to remember a series of short stories or anecdotes. Below you will find twelve anecdotes. Try to remember them by using the Basic List, and you will find that this experiment is very similar to the magazine exercise. Instead of choosing a picture or part of a picture, choose a cue word that will recall the anecdote.*

Anecdotes

1

WAITRESS: "Do you wish coffee?"
CUSTOMER: "Yes, coffee, without cream."
WAITRESS: "You'll have to take it without milk. We have no cream."

2

As the boat was sinking, the captain lifted up his voice to ask: "Does anybody know how to pray?"

One man spoke confidently in answer: "Yes, Captain, I do."

"That's all right then," he declared. "You go ahead and pray. The rest of us will put on life belts. They're one short."

3

A soldier went to his colonel and asked for leave to go home to help his wife with the spring housecleaning.

"I don't like to refuse you," said the colonel, "but I've just received a letter from your wife saying that you are no use around the house."

The soldier saluted and turned to go. At the door he stopped: "Colonel, there are two persons in this regiment who handle the truth loosely, and I'm one of them. I'm not married."

4

The man of the house finally took all the disabled umbrellas to the repairer's. Two days later, on his way to his office, when he got up

---

* These anecdotes are chosen from *10,000 Jokes, Toasts and Stories*, edited by Lewis and Faye Copeland, published by Doubleday & Company, Inc.

to leave the streetcar, he absentmindedly laid hold of the umbrella belonging to a woman beside him, for he was in the habit of carrying one. The woman cried, "Stop thief," rescued her umbrella and covered the man with shame and confusion.

That same day he stopped at the repairer's and received all eight of his umbrellas repaired. As he entered a streetcar, with the unwrapped umbrellas tucked under his arm, he was horrified to behold glaring at him the lady of his morning's adventure. Her voice came to him charged with a withering scorn:

"Huh! Had a good day, didn't you!"

5

The lawyer for the defense was cross-examining a witness in a robbery case.

"When did the robbery take place?" demanded the counsel in a bullying tone.

"I think—" began the witness, but the lawyer interrupted him. "We don't care what you think, sir. We want to know what you know."

"Then if you don't want to know what I think," said the witness quietly, "I may as well leave the box. I can't talk without thinking— I'm not a lawyer."

6

A Londoner went into a bird store to buy a parrot and was offered one at a price of 45 pounds. "That's pretty steep for a parrot," said the man.

"Well, it's a very special bird—speaks six languages."

"I'm not interested in that," countered the purchaser. "All I want to know is—is it tender?"

7

A young couple who had received many valuable wedding presents established their home in a suburb. One morning they received in the mail two tickets for a popular show in the city, with a single line:

"Guess who sent them."

The pair had much amusement in trying to identify the donor but failed in the effort. They duly attended the theater and had a delightful time. On their return home late at night, they found the house stripped of every article of value. And on the bare table in the dining room was a piece of paper on which was written in the same hand as the enclosure with the tickets:

"Now you know!"

8

After considerable effort the freshman finally finished his examination paper, and then at the end wrote:

"Dear Professor, if you sell any of my answers to the funny papers, I expect you to split fifty-fifty with me."

9

"Waiter."

"Yes, sir."

"What's this?"

"It's bean soup, sir."

"No matter what it's been. What is it now?"

10

"No," growled the quartermaster, "you can't have a new pair of shoes. The pair you have are not worn out."

"Not worn out," cried the recruit. "Why, if I step on a dime, I can feel if it's heads or tails."

11

"Mother, how much do people pay a pound for babies?"

"Babies are not sold by the pound, darling."

"Then why do they always weigh them as soon as they are born?"

12

Pullman passenger to porter: "What is the matter? I find one black and one brown shoe under my berth."

Porter: "I cannot understand, but it is the second time this morning that this has happened."

You certainly will have no difficulty in forming your own associations for memorizing these twelve anecdotes. As you will again realize, we can choose various cue words for each anecdote, as we did in the magazine exercise. And naturally we choose the cue word which is the easiest to associate with the corresponding word of the Basic List. For instance, to recall the third anecdote, we could choose as cue words *soldier* or *colonel* or *spring* or *housecleaning* or *lie* or *not married*. Each of these cue words would be enough to recall the anecdote to mind, but since it is the third anecdote and the cue word has to be connected with *May, spring* may be the easiest to associate with *May*.

Here are the cue words and associations which serve the purpose:

1.	tea	milk (or coffee)
2.	Noah	sinking boat (ark)
3.	May	spring (housecleaning)
4.	ray	umbrella (sunshine)
5.	law	lawyer
6.	jaw	parrot (tender)
7.	key	thief (passkey)
8.	fee	paid by funny paper
9.	pea	bean soup
10.	toes	worn out
11.	tot	baby on scale
12.	tan	brown shoe

We realize that these associations, like everything else for which we use the Hook Method, will stay with us for only a short time. If we wish to remember anecdotes for a long time we must switch to the Chain Method and link the cue words together without using the Basic List. In order to construct a chain which is easy to remember, it may be necessary to change the sequence; and it may even be necessary to change some cue words.

There are numerous ways to construct a chain out of the above twelve cue words. To give you an example, try to visualize the following events in sequence:

Cue Words	*Linking Thoughts*
Thief	climbs aboard
(sinking) boat	which is owned by a
Lawyer	who had just done the
Spring cleaning.	Looking around, he saw a
Parrot	eating
Bean soup,	and a
Baby on a scale	drinking
Milk.	He also found a
Brown shoe	for which he had no use because it was
Worn out	so he only took an
Umbrella	and wrapped it in the
Funny papers.	

The same cue words can be woven into a story like this:

After doing his *spring cleaning,* a *lawyer* wearing *worn out brown shoes* sits on his *boat* under an *umbrella,* eating *bean soup* and drinking *milk,* while reading the *funny papers;* his *parrot* keeps screaming: "A *thief* is stealing your *baby on a scale."*

We can keep numerous chains in our memory. However, if someone should want or need to remember hundreds of anecdotes, it would be better to classify them first into main subjects and subdivisions, and then chain the series in the last subdivisions.

CHAPTER 18

How to Remember a Schedule for a Day and for a Week

Once in a while it must have happened that you forgot an appointment or something that you intended to do during the day or during the week. Perhaps that was even one of the reasons why you took up memory training. It will not happen again if you follow the rules laid down in this chapter.

As far as the current day is concerned, there is no difficulty at all in applying our system since the Basic List easily provides everything we need. If you have to see your dentist at eight o'clock, all you have to do is associate him with *fee* (which stands for 8) and picture yourself paying the fee for his professional services. If you have to remember that you must telephone Mrs. Green at five o'clock, you associate her with *law,* visualizing her being arrested by a policeman.

However, our task becomes somewhat more difficult when it comes to remembering appointments for the entire week rather than for one day. Especially if the appointments and assignments vary from day to day, the person with an untrained memory faces two alternatives: either he forgets half the things he planned to do and as a result suffers the consequences in misunderstandings, disputes, and the like in business and personal life, or he jots down each item in his appointment book in detailed copybook style. By doing so, it is true, he manages to keep close track of his appointments; yet he is thereby damaging his memory, for, as we know by this time, reliance upon putting everything down in black on white has a decidedly harmful effect upon systematic memory training. Also, as soon and as long as he is away from his desk and does not carry his appointment book on his person, he is facing trouble, because he depends entirely on this book.

How can we apply our system to a schedule that comprises

activities for an entire week? By this time we have had enough experience to know that we must link up this problem in some way or another with our basic series of key words. We start with numbering the days of the week as follows:

Sunday	1
Monday	2
Tuesday	3
Wednesday	4
Thursday	5
Friday	6
Saturday	7

After we have identified the days of the week with the numbers 1 through 7 in this fashion, we add to them the particular hours of the day which are to be remembered. Here are some examples:

Since Sunday is 1, we think of 2 o'clock on Sunday as 12
3 o'clock on Sunday as 13
4 o'clock on Sunday as 14, etc.

So we arrive at:

Wednesday —	3 o'clock equals 43 or	*ram*
Monday —	7 o'clock equals 27 or	*neck*
Friday —	5 o'clock equals 65 or	*jail*
Thursday —	2 o'clock equals 52 or	*lane*

Then the association with the assignment which you are to undertake is made in the usual manner. Below are ten appointments, which purposely have not been listed in chronological order. This is because in everyday life we do not, of course, make an appointment first for Sunday, then for Monday, next for Tuesday, etc.; rather, we must accept and memorize the appointments as they occur and still be able to recall them in chronological sequence so that no appointment will be overlooked.

Here is how the method works: Suppose you have an appointment with your insurance broker for Monday at four. Monday at four is translated into 24 or *Nero*. The association between Nero and an insurance broker is not difficult because Nero reminds us of the burning of Rome, a fact easy to connect with fire insurance.

In this manner we arrive at the following associations for remembering these appointments:

Monday at 4:   appointment with insurance broker.
     association: *Nero*—fire—fire insurance.

Tuesday at 7:   invitation to the mayor's office.
     association: *mike*—the mayor delivers a speech over the microphone.

Friday at 7:   buying a birthday gift after office hours.
     association: *check*—paying for the gift by check.

Saturday at 4:   appointment to go swimming.
     association: *car*—using the car to go to the beach.

Friday at 9:   appointment with stockbroker.
     association: *chip*—trying to win at the stock market "game."

Wednesday at 5:   meeting friend who comes from New Rochelle.
     association: *rail*—he rides in the train between New Rochelle and New York.

Saturday at 1:   take the children to the zoo.
     association: *cat*—zoo.

Thursday at 7:   appointment for a sailing trip.
     association: *lake*—sailboat.

Tuesday at 5:   appointment at your lawyer's office.
     association: *mail*—lawyer reading his mail. (Or visualize yourself writing a letter to your lawyer.)

Wednesday at 2:   tennis appointment.
     association: *rain* (It's a ludicrous picture if you visualize yourself playing tennis in the rain. But don't form the association that you are *not* playing tennis because it is raining, for the reason that negative thoughts cannot be visualized.)

You can test yourself best as to whether you have understood and remembered these examples by writing down on a sheet of paper the ten words of the Basic List which we used. Then see whether these words bring back the appointments in question to your memory. But do not be satisfied with this test alone. Try the opposite: write down the appointments on a separate sheet of paper and see whether you recall the basic words in question, the time of day, and the day of the week. And finally, still working with the same examples, ask yourself what appointments you have for a specific day—for instance, Tuesday. In order to answer this question, mentally run through the basic words for Tuesday, that is, through numbers 31–39 (*mat* through *map*). You will not find it difficult to recall that only *mail* and *mike* were used, and thus you know that on Tuesday you have appointments for five and seven o'clock. No other words in the series for Tuesday were used in the examples; therefore all your time except the hours of five and seven is free.

Three more questions remain to be answered:

(1) How do we differentiate between day and night?

(2) How shall we treat ten, eleven, and twelve o'clock?

(3) What shall we do with appointments on the half hours or in between?

As far as day and night are concerned, you will agree that distinguishing between them is more theoretical than practical. Generally, our appointments and assignments for the day are so completely different from those for the evening or night that mistaking one for the other is hardly possible in practice. If you insist upon making an extra distinction, you might enter the moon into the picture which you visualized to make your associations for any appointment which falls during the nighttime hours.

As to the second question—How shall we treat ten, eleven, and twelve o'clock?—the answer is that ten o'clock causes no difficulty at all if we treat 10 as 0.

Monday	10 o'clock is	*nose*
Tuesday	10 o'clock is	*mass*
Wednesday	10 o'clock is	*race*. And so on.

However, eleven o'clock and twelve o'clock cannot be treated in this manner, as we would come in conflict with one and two o'clock. For them we must use figures of three digits. Since there are no three-digit figures in the basic series, we shall have to construct them for our purpose. For instance, Tuesday at twelve o'clock is 312. For this number we can substitute a word like *mutiny*.

In order to eliminate the task of looking up such words in a dictionary, here are some examples for the hours of eleven and twelve for all the days of the week:

Sunday:	111: attitude, dotted, deadwood, teetotaler
	112: Titan, tighten, deadend
Monday:	211: entity, united, nudity, want ad
	212: Indian, intense, antenna, Anthony
Tuesday:	311: method, imitate, humidity, matador
	312: matinee, mutiny, maiden, home town
Wednesday:	411: rotate, radiate, redhead, hardwood
	412: retina, redneck, warden
Thursday:	511: latitude, altitude, hold out, low tide
	512: Latin, lightning, litany, lowdown
Friday:	611: agitate, cheated, shoot-out, jaded
	612: jitney, shut in, sheath knife, chutney
Saturday:	711: cadet, cathedral, cathode, cutout
	712: cotton, cadence, codeine, gideon

As to the third question, what we do with appointments which are not exactly on the hour, but on the half hour or in between, we handle them as follows:

First of all, if an appointment is for 4:50 or 4:55, it may not do any harm to fix it in your mind at 4:45. If you have to make a plane leaving at 7:37, no problem will arise if you arbitrarily make it 7:30. In this way we can advance any appointment that is not exactly at the full, half, or quarter hour to the nearest preceding quarter hour.

For every quarter of the hour, except the full hour, we add a touch of color, going by the sequence of the colors of the U.S. flag: red, white, and blue.

For every appointment at a quarter after the hour, we add the color red, at the half hour, the color white—or silvery, at a quarter off the hour, the color blue.

In other words, if you have to meet someone arriving by train at

5:18, you substitute 5:15 and picture him or her in your mind as arriving in a red train.

Similarly, if the arrival time were at 5:39, you would substitute 5:30, and color the train white, and if the arrival time were 5:51, you would advance it to 5:45 and picture the train blue.

Advancing appointments by a few minutes can hardly be detrimental. In fact in most cases it may have a decided benefit in that we avoid being too late.

Of course, if one works in an airline or railroad office and it is of paramount importance to remember arrival and departure times to the exact minute, the solution lies in the use of our "Secondary List," which we shall discuss in the next chapter.

CHAPTER 19

The Secondary List

Up to this point we have translated numbers into appropriate words by using the Number Code, drawing upon our own vocabulary and, when needed, with the help of a dictionary.

However, there are occasions when we simply do not have enough time at our disposal to make a meaningful sentence out of a series of numerals.

You are familiar with such situations. Someone gives you his phone number when you meet him on the street. At a social gathering or a sports event, a car may be blocking yours, or you may see that the parking lights are burning or the radiator is leaking. The only way to trace the owner is by the license number.

You are asked to meet someone at the airport and have to remember a flight number plus the exact time of arrival.

There is not much time to make a lasting association, neither is it necessary to remember the numbers for a long time. We need a quick association for a short time.

Let us go back to the person who asked you to call him up. When you hear the number, you should repeat the number aloud to make sure that the other person corrects you if you had it wrong. Assume it is 321-3957. You start thinking of a way to translate the first three digits, and undoubtedly some words like *minute, mind, month, mountain, Monday* or others come to your mind. Next, you want to translate the four-digit number 3957. You could split the number in two two-digit numbers and use the Basic List, giving you *map* for *39* and *lake* for *57*. Combining the words you now have, you arrive at:

> *month* — *map* — *lake*
> or *mind* — *map* — *lake*
> or *mountain* — *map* — *lake*
>
> etc.

You select the association that most appeals to you and go on your way. But by the time you want to dial that number you could recall the words in the following order:

mountain — lake — map
instead of *mountain — map — lake*

and get a wrong connection.

There was no confusion about the first three digits because you know that you used a word with at least three consonants (not a basic word) for the first three digits. But the Basic List words used for the four-digit number can easily be interchanged since there is no fixed sequence in the order of the Basic List words. Neither do pictures have a fixed sequence. The picture of a lake on a map can easily be substituted for a map on a lake.

The same can happen with prices of merchandise. If we intended to remember $31.24 (*mat—Nero*), we might later recall *Nero—mat,* which is $24.31. The arrival time of 10:12 (*toes —tan*) may come back to us as *tan—toes,* which makes it 12:10. All kinds of complications and embarrassments can result from such confusion.

However, there is a remedy.

We know that each thought in our mind produces other thoughts, and each word recalls other words. For instance, what is the first thing that comes to your mind when you think of the word *tea?* You might say, "Coffee." It might be another word, but remarkably enough, no matter what word it is, chances are that the same word will again first come to your mind when you are asked the same question a week, a month, or a year from now. As this amazing feature can be put to good use, first go through your Basic List and write down for yourself next to each basic word the word that first comes to your mind, like *tea—coffee, Noah—ark,* and so on. Allow yourself half a minute to think of a word that fits. Be careful to take only words that are concrete nouns—things that are visible or tangible—because we need them for associations, and you know that abstract nouns, verbs, or adjectives are not suitable for association. Of course, you cannot use any word of the Basic List. Make sure that you establish your own Secondary List before looking at ours. Also, once you have selected your Secondary List words, do not deviate from those words, but always use the same secondary word for the same number.

It will take you about an hour to construct your own Secondary List. For the purpose of illustration and later use in practical applications, you will find our Secondary List below.

1. tea – coffee
2. Noah – ark
3. May – calendar
4. ray – lamp
5. law – summons
6. jaw – tooth
7. key – ring
8. fee – bill
9. pea – soup
10. toes – shoe
11. tot – toy
12. tan – make-up
13. tam – ribbon
14. tar – feathers
15. tail – donkey
16. tissue – box
17. tack – thumb
18. taffy – candy
19. tap – beer
20. nose – handker-
    chief
21. net – veil
22. nun – church
23. name – credit
    card
24. Nero – fiddle
25. nail – hammer
26. niche – statue
27. neck – tie
28. navy – ship
29. nap – pillow
30. mass – candle
31. mat – rug
32. man – cigar

33. mama – jewelry
34. mare – stable
35. mail – stamp
36. match – ashtray
37. mike – stage
38. muff – glove
39. map – flag
40. race – trophy
41. rat – bread
42. rain – umbrella
43. ram – wool
44. rear – door
45. rail – train
46. rash – medicine
47. rake – spade
48. reef – stone
49. rope – cowboy
50. lace – needle
51. lot – grass
52. lane – tree
53. lime – soda
54. lair – lion
55. lily – vase
56. lash – horse
57. lake – sailboat
58. leaf – flower
59. lap – basket
60. cheese – crackers
61. chat – telephone
62. chain – necklace
63. chime – bell
64. chair – table
65. jail – guard
66. judge – gavel

67. check – pen
68. chef – menu
69. chip – game
70. case – wood
71. cat – milk
72. can – opener
73. comb – brush
74. car – gasoline
75. coal – miner
76. cash – register
77. cake – ice cream
78. cuff – collar
79. cap – gown
80. face – mirror
81. fat – butter
82. fan – air condi-
    tioner
83. fame – medal
84. fare – ticket
85. file – scissors
86. fish – fork
87. fig – olive
88. fife – drum
89. fob – watch
90. base – pillar
91. bat – stadium
92. bean – carrot
93. beam – house
94. bar – glass
95. ball – racket
96. badge – button
97. back – knapsack
98. beef – knife
99. baby – cradle

Please bear in mind that the new words have nothing to do with the Number Code. If we deal with four-digit numbers, we shall always use a Basic List word for the first two digits and a Secondary List word for the last two digits.

For example:

> 3957 becomes *map — sailboat*
> 4028 becomes *race — ship*
> 9025 becomes *base — hammer*
> 3603 becomes *match — calendar*

You will realize that confusion of the first two digits with the last two digits is now eliminated. *3957* is *map—sailboat.* Even if you recall the words in reverse order, it does not matter; you immediately rearrange them, because you know that *sailboat,* not being a basic word, must come in second place.

Check for yourself whether your Secondary List is firmly ingrained in your mind. Write down as many four-digit numbers and the Basic and Secondary List words as you need to familiarize yourself with this procedure.

You will see that the Secondary List extends our Basic List not just to 2×100 words, but to almost 10,000 combinations; 9999 to be exact. In this and in later chapters you will find additional applications for the Secondary List, partly for serious work and partly for fun.

A good example of the advantage of the Secondary List presents itself when we have to remember dollars and cents. We use the Basic List for the dollars, the Secondary List for the cents. We can also use it when we have to remember the exact time of arrival (or departure) of planes, trains, buses, etc. The Basic List words are used for the hours and the Secondary List words for the minutes.

> $25.65 would be *nail — guard*
> $67.42 would be *check — umbrella*
> The time 11:20 is *tot — handkerchief*
> The time 2:09 is *Noah — soup*
>
> etc.

Another very practical application of the Secondary List can be found in remembering birthdays, when we want to remember not only the day and the month but also the year of birth. We use the Basic List for the day, the Secondary List for the year, and add an adjective for the month.

For instance, assume you want to remember the date August 5, 1964, which in numbers is usually written as 8.5.64. You first find a picture for the combination of the Basic List word for 5—*law,* and the Secondary List word for 64—*table* (secondary for *chair*). If your basic picture for 5 (*law*) is a policeman, you can picture the policeman sitting at your table. You may want to make it more unusual—which is always recommended—and see the policeman standing on top of the table or crawling under the table, or carrying a table. Now you add an adjective of which you translate only the first consonant. Since the number is 8, you can use any adjective that starts with an *f* or *v* sound, like: *fiery, fatherly, flabby, faithful, famous, factual, fierce, flamboyant, flouncing, foreign, formidable, frustrated, full-dress, valiant, venerable, veteran, vigilant, visiting, phlegmatic, efficient, off duty, overpowering,* and many more.

The complete picture depends on your preferences. The components may be:

> <u>f</u>atherly policeman (sitting at) table
>
> or
>
> <u>f</u>ull-dress policeman (standing on) table

or any other combination; it will always spell 8.5.64.

The only thing left to be done is to associate the person whose birthday you want to remember with the picture. The selection of your adjective may well be influenced by your regard for that person. You hardly need any suggestion as to how to accomplish that. It is that simple and obvious. The number of different pictures you can (mentally) draw depends only on your imagination.

In order to assist you in your search for adjectives, here are a few for each month.

1 for January: tall, true, timely, timid, tolerant, thick
2 for February: naive, narrow, neat, naked, noted, annual, honest
3 for March: mad, main, manly, mean, merry, mild, human
4 for April: raw, real, reluctant, rich, ripe, rough, regal
5 for May: lame, late, lawless, low, loyal, ill, old
6 for June: jolly, joyful, just, showy, shy, aged

7 for July: gay, coy, great, grand, cozy, keen, kind, calm, good
8 for August: fair, fake, false, fat, few, fearful, free, fine, full
9 for September: bad, bright, big, peaceful, proud, happy, openly

For October, November, and December we must make sure that we do not confuse the adjectives with those for January. For that reason we use only adjectives starting with *t* or *th* for January, and choose adjectives starting with *d* for October (10), November (11), and December (12) as follows:

10 for October: decent, distant, distinct, dusty, desperate
11 for November: dated, determined, deadly, dedicated
12 for December: dense, dental, dainty, dynamic, down

If all these words do not satisfy your needs, just open up any dictionary and you will find dozens more to choose from.

CHAPTER 20

How to Remember Numerical Data

HISTORY DATES, GEOGRAPHICAL DATA, PRICES, AREA CODES, TELEPHONE NUMBERS, POPULATION FIGURES, ETC.

One would think that it is easy to remember numbers of a few digits, certainly one-digit numbers, without the help of a memory system. Apparently not for the man who gets off a turnpike at exit 9 only to discover to his chagrin that he should have turned off two exits earlier. This can mean a detour of dozens of miles and result in being late for an appointment, a wedding, or a graduation. The embarrassment and aggravation are worse than the loss of time.

Other motorists can be seen stopping on the side of the highway to check their maps. They may finally decide to pull up at the next gas station to ask for directions. One always gets where one wants to go in the end, but the waste of time could have been avoided by memorizing the entire route beforehand. The highway numbers can be translated into words, and the words linked together into some kind of a chain. Since there is no logical sequence, this chain will hardly make much sense to the uninitiated, but as long as we think in word pictures and make full use of our powers of imagination the entire route will be sufficiently ingrained in our memory so that we never have to doubt about which turn to take and where.

The applications of the Number Code and Hook Method in everyday life are numerous. Numbers of one, two, or three digits show up everywhere. You may have to remember a street and house number, the number of a bus line and the platform number at the bus terminal, a hotel room or hospital room number, an air flight number, to name only a few.

Imagine you live in New York City and you are invited to visit a friend of yours who just moved to a new apartment in New Jersey. You have the following information: At the bus terminal on 8th Avenue between 40th and 41st Streets, you go to platform 64, take bus 99, get off at the 18th Street stop in Union City, New Jersey, and walk east toward 380 Mountain Road; the building is called Troy Towers.

Now let us assume that you wanted to make a little chain out of this "itinerary." Most likely you would use only Basic List words to translate the numbers you want to remember, since that's exactly what most students do in the beginning. Let us try that for the moment and see how we can construct such a chain.

The bus terminal is on 8th Avenue between 40th and 41st Streets.

8 = fee⎫ You can choose either 40th or 41st Street, you do not
40 = race⎬ need both.
41 = rat ⎭ Picture yourself getting the **fee** (bus fare) ready while you **race** to the terminal.

If you insist on using both 40 and 41, you can picture the **rat race** in the bus terminal.

You have to find platform *64,* where you sit on a **chair,** while waiting for the bus. You do not board a bus until the bus number *99* reminds you of the word **baby,** either visualizing a baby in the bus or on top of it, or driving it!

While en route, you keep in mind that you want to get off where you can buy some **taffy** (18th Street) for the baby. There you look *east* toward the *mountain.* You notice a building consisting of two towers, which look like **muffs** standing on end.

The Basic List really helped us all the way, even when we translated the number 380 as the plural of the word for 38— **muff.**

For all practical purposes, however, you should not limit yourself to the words of the Basic List, but avail yourself of any word that fits the purpose.

Taking the same "itinerary" again as an example, you have a wide choice of words for each of the numbers involved, and you might construct a story as follows:

You go with your wife (8th Ave.) for a ride (41st) to Jersey (platform 64). The bus is chauffeured by a bobby (99) who wants to *stop* to watch TV (18th Street stop), but you take him east to a moviehouse (380) on the *mountain* (road) to see a film starring Helen of *Troy* (Troy Towers).

The two "stories" or chains have been given just to show you how to go about it. Maybe you prefer other words for certain numbers. For 99 we chose *bobby,* a London policeman, which presents a graphic picture. But if you prefer *papa,* or *baby,* or *puppy,* or any other word that translates into 99, that's quite all right—and this goes also for any one of the other numbers. You should by all means select words that appeal to *you,* because you remember a story of your own creation much better than one suggested by someone else. Only, make sure that you picture in your mind's eye the events which you are stringing together like beads on a thread. Translating alone is not enough. It is the visualization that strengthens the recall when and where you need it.

As far as your choice of words is concerned, you can allow yourself many more liberties, within the framework of the rules. Let us develop them step by step.

You may have noticed that we used the word Jersey for the number 64, while this word actually translates into 640. There is no risk of confusion here, since there is no bus with such a high number. Also, you will experience that any word that you have selected yourself comes back to your mind exactly with the message you intended it to convey.

Let us assume that you want to remember that a pair of shoes cost $26. You may think of the word niche and picture those shoes standing in your "niche." But you can also use any of the following words or combinations of words: enjoyment, unusual, new shoes, no shape, etc., without any risk that you would translate more than two digits, because you know very well that the price of a pair of shoes could not be in the $260 range.

Another way to widen your choice of words for certain numbers is to use words that start with an *s* sound, starting either with the letter *s,* soft *c,* or *z.* For instance, we can use *salad, solid,* or *salt* for 51 and disregard the zero. We have to bear in mind, however, that we can only do so if we are dealing with the kind of numbers that cannot possibly start with a zero, such as house numbers, page numbers, prices, etc. If we are dealing with telephone numbers, zip code numbers, and the like, numbers which may have a zero as the first digit, we cannot indiscriminately disregard the starting *s* sound because in such numbers we must distinguish between 51 and 051.

In order to make it still easier for you to find meaningful words, we make it a rule that we translate never more than the first three consonants of any word. For instance, theoretically the word *telegram* is 15743; in practice, however, we translate it into 157. The reason for this rule is that, while it is easy to find words for numbers of one, two, or three digits, it is rather difficult and sometimes impossible to find words for numbers of four or more digits.

This means that when we wish to translate three-digit numbers we are not limited to words with three consonants. We can use any word that has three or more consonants, but we translate only the first three and disregard the others. For the number 143 we can use words like: *term, tram, trim, dream, drum,* but in accordance with the rule that we only translate (at most) the first three consonants, we can also use words like: *terminal, thermometer, trombone, turmoil,* and many more. As you notice, because of this three-consonant rule, your choice of words is considerably expanded.

Let us now see how we can apply the system to prices of merchandise. Suppose you wish to remember that the price of a certain diamond ring is $742. To translate the number 742, we have a choice of words like:

carnation, carnival, chronic, corn, corner, cornet, cornice, corona, coronation, coronet, crane, crank, crown, currant, current, garnet, garnish, grain, granary, grand, granite, grant, granular, green, grin, grind, ground, guarantee, kernel, acorn, quarantine, aggrandize, scorn

Which of the above listed words you prefer as a good association with a diamond ring is a personal matter. Several of them can serve the purpose, such as: *coronet, coronation, crown, garnet, grand.* Choose *one;* not more than one. Trying to remember more than one would defeat the purpose.

Following is a list of articles and their prices with suggested word associations. Feel free to select another word whenever you so prefer; again, it is easier to recall a word you choose yourself than one that someone else suggests. Give each association some thought and, more importantly, try to visualize the association between article and word. You will be surprised how well the system works. Spend at least ten minutes on the entire list:

article	price	word associations
electric blanket	$ 29	nap or knapsack
room air conditioner	$205	noiseless
power mower	$121	dandelion
refrigerator	$270	snacks
color TV set	$625	channels
electric knife	$ 19	deep or dip
washing machine	$251	unload
outboard motor	$783	gay family
indoor jogger	$ 60	chase
sheepskin car coat	$140	dressy
diamond ring	$742	crown
used car	$875	vehicle
golf clubs	$120	woodens
surfboard	$ 80	waves
binoculars	$ 80	views
cosmetic case	$ 70	cosmetics or case
skis	$ 76	ski shoes
violin	$470	orchestra
typewriter	$173	document
living room set	$945	parlor

Now turn to Chapter 1, Test No. 3, page 5, where you will find an identical list of items and prices, only without the suggested word associations. Cover the dollar amounts so that only the names of the articles are visible, and write down on a piece of paper the price of each item. Upon completion give yourself one point for each correct price. Then compare your total score with the score you had when you took the same test at the time you read Chapter 1.

There may still be one question on your mind. You may find it easy to associate the word substitutes for the given prices with the merchandise in question, but it may take you quite some time (with or without the help of an ordinary dictionary) to find such words on your own and to select the one that is most apt for association. Continuous practice will no doubt make you more proficient in this respect. But for those who still like some help in finding good words, we have compiled a *Number Dictionary* which covers the numbers from 0 to 1000. This little booklet has proven to be very helpful and timesaving in translating numbers into words. The *Number Dictionary* offers a choice of words for each number. It makes it much easier to select a word which best fits the occasion for which you need it.*

Let us now see how the same technique can be applied to historical dates. The examples given below represent events which are not too well known to the average reader. They were selected exactly for that reason. If we were to use dates like the year of the discovery of America, or the start of World War I, there would be no point in making associations since everybody would know the answers already.

If you were asked when the Gregorian calendar was introduced in England and its colonies, you might or might not know the answer, which is 1752. But if you associate the year 1752 with the word **ca**_len_dar, you would hardly be able to forget it. True, the exact translation of the word calendar gives us 752, not 1752. However, since it is hardly possible to be mistaken by a thousand years, we do not need to translate the first digit; we disregard the millennium.

Here is a list of historical dates with suggested associative words. Most associations are so obvious that no further explanation is required. These historical events are not listed in chronological order. This has been done on purpose, since events are to be associated individually with the years in question, and not with the events preceding or following.

First Congress met in Philadelphia	1774	**Qua**_ker_ (Philadelphia is called the "Quaker City")
Discovery of the Philippines	1521	is_lands_
Pilgrims' landing at Plymouth	1620	_ch_an_ce_ (the Pilgrims took a chance when landing on foreign soil)

* Printed in pocket size form. You can order it by writing to Mrs. Bruno Furst, 7300 Sun Island Drive, South, Apartment 1502, South Pasadena, FL, 33707 and enclosing $2.00. The *Number Dictionary* is not available in bookstores.

First telegraph in the U.S.	1843	**form** (new form of communication)
Biggest earthquake in Japan	1703	**cosmic** or **chasm**
First passenger railroad in the U.S.	1830	**fumes**
Death of Napoleon	1821	**fainted**
Invention of the cannon	1340	**Mars** (Mars is the Roman God of war)
The great Chicago fire	1871	**victims**
Founding of Washington, D.C.	1791	**capital** or **capitol**
First English Parliament	1295	**nobility**
First printing machine introduced in England	1474	**record**
Death of Franklin D. Roosevelt	1945	**burial**
First college degree for women	1841	**freedom** or **overdue**
Birth of Benedict Arnold	1741	**coward**
Purchase of Florida	1819	**fat buy**
Joan of Arc burned at the stake	1431	**harmed** or **warmed**
Lindbergh's flight across the Atlantic	1927	**opening** (of transatlantic air travel)
Inauguration of the Marshall Plan	1947	**break** (for Western Europe)
Introduction of the Gregorian calendar in England and her colonies	1752	**calendar**

Take approximately half a minute for each date to think about each of these associations and to visualize them. You will see that you have little or no trouble recalling them. If you wish to test yourself on this material, turn to Chapter 1, Test No. 5, page 10, and cover the years so that you can read only the historical events. Then write on a separate piece of paper the answers that come back to your mind by translating the associative words into numbers. Compare your score with the one you had when you read Chapter 1, before you learned how to apply the system. Your progress must be impressive. If not, it means that you need to make stronger associations between events and associative words, or that you should take more time for each of them to get the desired result. No doubt you are convinced by now that it is a much easier and better system for learning historical dates than the rote-learning system you probably used when you were in school.

You may now also realize that this system of memorizing numbers and figures has still many more applications.

Area codes, Social Security numbers, license numbers, zip code numbers, telephone numbers, etc., can all be easily translated and therefore easily remembered.

As we have seen before, not just any translation will do. If at all possible, we should give meaning to the word or the little sentence we are constructing.

In the case of telephone numbers it is of utmost importance that we come up with a line that applies to the person whose number we want to put to memory. The same holds true for stores or companies. If we can let some characteristic factor come through in our translation, its meaning will impress itself so much deeper in our memory. As a result, at the moment we want to place a phone call to the person or company in question, the picture that we visualized when we originally formed our little sentence comes immediately to mind and we can dial the proper number by automatically translating the words into numbers.

We shall cover the seven-digit telephone numbers later in this chapter. First we shall deal with the three-digit area code numbers. It is better not to associate them with the individual person or corporation, but with the area, state, city, or other geographical entity to which they belong.

Here are a few examples of area code numbers and suggested associations:

New York City	212	**U.N. town**
Wisconsin (Madison area)	608	**Cheese factories**
Nevada	702	**Casino**

If you find it easier to use one word for each digit, counting only the first consonant of each word, do not hesitate to do so. Whatever comes easier to you is the best solution for you.

For the above area code numbers using the latter method, you could form the following associations:

New York City	212	national television networks
Wisconsin (Madison area)	608	cheese Wisconsin's fame
Nevada	702	gambling state Nevada

You will have noticed that we made use of characteristic features of the areas in question. In cases where you are not familiar with any characteristics and do not know any landmarks in the area, you can still make an association, albeit an artificial one. For instance, the area code of Alaska is 907. Suppose the word **bicycle** comes to your mind. Can you associate this word with Alaska? Not logically. But with a bit of imagination you could see yourself traveling on your bicycle through or to Alaska! Ludicrous? Yes, but very effective as you will find out.

So far we have dealt only with numbers of one, two, and three digits, but the procedures already outlined give you the wherewithal to handle any number, no matter of how many digits it may consist. "Long" numbers crop up everywhere. Everyone faces them in everyday life. Students, for instance, could certainly save themselves considerable time, and at the same time attain better grades at exams, if they used the tools provided by this system. It goes without saying that what we can do with historical dates we can also do with geographical data such as heights of mountains, depths of oceans, length of rivers, etc.

Here are a few examples of possible associations:

Highest peak in North America:		
Mount McKinley, Alaska	20,300 ft.	**Highness amazes**
Highest peak in California:		
Mount Whitney	14,494 ft.	**Tree arbor**
Highest peak in Europe:		
Mont Blanc	15,781 ft.	**Tall gift**

It depends a great deal on the degree of accuracy you require or desire, whether you translate a "long" number to the last digit. In the above examples of mountains, for instance, you may be satisfied having a rough idea of their heights. In that case you need only translate the first two digits which give you for Mount McKinley—**highness,** for Mount Whitney—**tree,** and for Mont Blanc—**tall.** There is no need to translate the zeros once you have decided for yourself that you only want to remember approximately how many thousand feet high these mountains are. Of course, you may select entirely different words for the numbers 20, 14, and 15 to suit your own associations.

Examples of still "longer" numbers can be found in the population figures of cities, states, or countries. Here again, it depends on how accurate you want to be, or need to be, in recalling these data.

The following examples are based on population figures according to the 1970 census:

Miami's population is 334,859. Miami area translates into 334 giving you the approximate population in thousands. To cover the exact figure of 334,859 you might construct a little sentence like: Miami's main resource, fine long beaches. Using one word for each digit, whereby only the first consonant in each word counts, is often the easiest way to form sentences.

New Orleans has a population of 593,471. The word album gives you 593, the population in thousands. The association is very appropriate if we think of a record album and New Orleans as the birthplace of Dixieland jazz. Album ragtime would give you the exact figure of 593,471. Using the one-word one-digit method you may come up with a line like:

Louisiana's prime musical recording companies' town

or

Lake Pontchartrain Mississippi River come (or get) together.

As you see, no matter which method is used for the translation of the digits, there is always ample opportunity to bring some characteristic feature into the words or sentences. The more you know about a certain city, the more choice you have in forming a sentence. You may avail yourself of any associative thought that appeals to you, for instance, a relative who lives in a particular city, or a baseball, football, basketball, or other team, even one of the players on a team, or a corporation, a college, a monument, a hotel, restaurant, or any other establishment that has some particular significance to you. The importance of the associative subject or object in general is of no concern as long as it does have a specific meaning for you. That is the reason why ten people may arrive at ten different associative sentences for the same number.

Also, you can be very flexible in using the various methods of translation. You might translate the population figure of Phoenix, Arizona, 581,562 into **lofty legen**d, thinking of the legendary bird Phoenix that is consumed by fire every five or six hundred years and arises from its own ashes. For Boston, population 641,071, you may find: We **cheer tossing t**ea (associating it with the Boston Tea Party) or: **Shrewd scout** (thinking of Paul Revere). In such lines you make every consonant count, which is an ideal application. However, you need not be too rigid in the way you translate numbers without having to worry whether you will remember later on which method you applied. The examples given above for the population of New Orleans present a clear illustration of what we mean. No matter whether you remember 593,471 by two words or by a line of six words, both methods are effective. For that matter you can use two words for one 6-digit number and six words for another 6-digit number. You will find that when you recall the words or sentences you created, you will automatically translate them in the correct manner.

Apparently, most students are inclined to prefer the one digit-one word method. However, their first question is always: How do I find the words to fit the numbers? Since a little guidance goes a long way, we shall now show you that it is rather easy.

When you look at a number and know what it stands for, some associative words come promptly to your mind. At that point you check whether any of these words start with a sound that, translated into a number, corresponds with one of the digits in the number. Often you will find that more than one word fits the same digit and also that several words fit several digits. The next thing to do is to weave a sentence to cover the remaining digits which is usually no problem at all.

Let us apply this approach to some practical examples.

Washington, D.C., has a population of 756,510. Thinking of Washington, numerous words come to your mind: Government, Congress, Capital, Capitol, Executive, guide, and others, all of which can serve as the first word since the first consonant of all these words translate into 7. You do not necessarily have to go in sequence. By glancing over the number 756,510, words come to your mind such as: Senate, security, center, system, U.S., house, for the *0* at the end; democracy, department, defense, head, diplomacy, authority, for the digit *1;* justice, judiciary, surety, agency, for the *6;* law, election, legation, legislation, alliance, illustrious, for the *5.* No doubt you can think of many more and different words. The thing to do now is to select a few that appeal to you most and start stringing them together in a line.

For instance, you may notice that the three branches of government are represented in the words: Executive, legislative and judiciary, which happen to fit exactly the first three digits of the population figure, 756. This may be enough for you if you want to remember that the population of Washington, D.C., is roughly 756,000. If you go for the exact figure, you will not have much trouble in finishing the sentence one way or another. For instance:

Executive, legislative, judiciary illustrate democratic system
Or you might, by using other words, arrive at:

Guides will show whole White House
The possibilities are many and varied. Looking at the population figure of Columbus, Ohio, 539,677, it will not be difficult to spot the name of Christopher Columbus as fitting the two 7s, the last two digits, and America or Americans for the 3. From there you start developing your sentence. For instance:

All Americans praise (or applaud) Genoa's Christopher Columbus
Similarly you will promptly recognize the characteristic elements in the following sentences for some more population figures:

New York City: 7,867,760

Gotham features ships cruising Caribbean shiny seas
or

Capital of shopping (or shipping), culinary cuisine, show-business center

Pittsburgh, Pa.: 520,117

Leading in steel, thanks to Carnegie

Omaha, Nebr.: 347,328

Omaha area converts most Nebraska's farmproducts

Louisville, Ky.: 361,471
  <u>M</u>agnificent <u>Ch</u>urchill <u>D</u>owns <u>r</u>uns <u>K</u>entucky <u>D</u>erby

Las Vegas, Nev.: 125,787
  <u>Th</u>roughout <u>N</u>evada <u>l</u>uxurious <u>c</u>asinos <u>f</u>eature <u>g</u>ambling

Milwaukee, Wis.: 717,099
  <u>C</u>ome <u>t</u>o <u>q</u>uaff (or <u>g</u>et) <u>Wis</u>consin's <u>p</u>erfect (or <u>b</u>ock) <u>b</u>eer

Los Angeles, Calif.: 2,816,061
  <u>In</u> <u>f</u>amous <u>D</u>isneyland <u>sh</u>ows <u>s</u>een <u>sh</u>ot <u>d</u>aily

Then there are our "long," seven-digit telephone numbers. The old type of phone number with two exchange letters is still around. However, the new all-numeral telephone numbers are in common use to such an extent that we can eliminate the exchange letters, the more so since numerals can be substituted for them anyway. There are various ways of handling telephone numbers. It is largely a matter of what comes easiest to you.

For instance, you might select one word for the first three digits. The remaining four digits can then be split into two sets of two digits, selecting two words of which only the first two consonants are translated. A few examples will show how this works:

The telephone number of the Barbizon Plaza Hotel in New York is 247-7000. The first three digits can be translated into <u>N</u>ew <u>Yo<u>rk</u></u>. Dividing the last four digits (7000) into 70 and 00 we can use two words, of which only the first two consonants count, such as:

and   <u>c</u>ozy, <u>c</u>osmopolitan, <u>g</u>ue<u>s</u>t or <u>g</u>a<u>s</u>tronomic for 70,
          oasis, houses, size for 00.

<u>N</u>ew <u>Yo<u>rk</u></u>.—<u>g</u>ue<u>s</u>t oa<u>s</u>i<u>s</u> is one line that would fit the numbers as well as the association with the hotel. You can arrange other combinations to your own liking.

The telephone number of Dr. Dintenfass, who wrote the article entitled "Memory and Anatomy—The Human Skeleton" in this book, is 265-2150, which can very aptly be translated into: <u>un</u>u<u>s</u>ua<u>l</u> a<u>n</u>a<u>t</u>omy <u>l</u>e<u>ss</u>ons. Some more examples follow. These numbers have been taken from the New York City telephone directory.

Brooklyn College (Adult Education)	780-5184	g̲i̲ves a l̲o̲t̲ f̲r̲ee
N. Y. Football Giants	582-7272	el̲e̲v̲e̲n̲ c̲o̲ntinue c̲o̲n̲quest
Passport Bureau	971-5581	p̲o̲ck̲e̲t̲ loyalty aff̲i̲davit
Immigration & Naturalization Service	264-1880	n̲a̲t̲u̲ralization d̲i̲v̲ision off̲i̲ce
N.Y.C. Towaways	757-1533	k̲i̲ll̲i̲ng̲ d̲e̲lightful m̲e̲m̲ories

Again, if you find it easier to use one word for each digit, counting only the first consonant of each word, feel free to follow your own preference.

How this method can result in meaningful sentences for the above telephone numbers is shown in the examples below:

Brooklyn College (Adult Education)	780-5184	C̲ollege f̲eatures s̲pecial l̲ectures a̲t̲ e̲v̲ening hou̲r̲s̲
N. Y. Football Giants	582-7272	E̲leven f̲ound n̲ew q̲uarters i̲n̲ G̲otham's n̲eighborhood
Passport Bureau	971-5581	P̲assport g̲ives t̲raveling l̲andsman l̲egal, off̲icial d̲ocumentation (or i̲dentification)
Immigration & Naturalization Service	264-1880	U̲niformed a̲g̲ents r̲eg̲ister t̲ravelers f̲rom f̲oreign s̲tates
N.Y.C. Towaways	757-1533	C̲ops hau̲l̲ c̲ars t̲o a̲ll̲ow m̲ore m̲ovement

Try your hand at some numbers you want to remember, and apply both methods to find for yourself which of these methods comes most natural to you.

Names and Faces

CHAPTER 21

How to Remember Faces

All these situations are familiar to you:

One of your friends gives a party. About twenty people are invited, and you are introduced to each one of them. But during dinner you remember only five or six of them. And the next day you can recall not more than two or three.

Or you may attend a business meeting. The project under discussion is extremely important to you. There are about thirty people there, representing different corporations from different areas of the country. Each has his own viewpoint and you would very much like to refer to them by name when you state your own opinion. But you do not remember the names of all those who have spoken.

Suppose you are a professional man—a university professor, a physician, or a lawyer. You have met a student, a patient, or a client several times, but when he greets you in the street you cannot remember his name; you are unable to introduce him to your wife, your friend, or whoever is with you. You feel acutely embarrassed. But that is not the worst. You also feel that the person, whose face and name you cannot remember, instinctively draws the conclusion that you are not much interested in him as a person. "How can he remember my case if he does not even remember my name?" That is exactly what your patient or client thinks; you feel it and you are afraid of losing him.

These are only a few examples taken from everyday life; no doubt you have heard about similar cases rather frequently.

Let us discuss the remedies step by step.

Remembering faces is quite different from remembering names. There are people who may meet you today and talk with you for an hour and yet, when they meet you again six weeks hence, do not remember at all that they have ever seen you before.

When you address them by name, you can sense that they are ill at ease. Their look of helplessness expresses better than words that they have not the slightest idea when and where they met you. This type of person is in the minority. The majority of people do not have as much trouble with faces as they have with names. Most people will recognize you after a moderate lapse of time, depending, of course, on what we mean by "recognize." It may mean that they know instantly that they met you on a cruise ship in the Caribbean, or that they were introduced to you at your friend's dinner party. Or it may mean that they only know they have seen you before without being able to determine the place and the time. In any case, however, they may not remember your name.

No matter to which category you belong, with proper training you can overcome your handicap as thousands of our students have done.

In more than thirty-five years of experience we have formulated some sound techniques, based on the application of the principles of observation, association, and classification. Not that everybody can learn how to remember fifteen to twenty thousand people, as it is said James Farley can. There are indeed a few people who are well known for their natural prodigious memories for names and faces. This, actually, goes far beyond the needs of the average person. Most of us are satisfied if we can keep a few thousand persons in mind, remembering, of course, both their faces and their names. Needless to say, the exercises which are necessary for someone who has difficulty with *faces* are different from those which strengthen the memory for *names;* therefore our goal is twofold: to recognize people *and* to be able to address them correctly without hesitation or evasion.

At a class session in which we talked about this topic, one of the students remarked, "How can I ever remember a person's face since everyone has two eyes, a nose, and a mouth?" He may or may not have been in earnest, but he certainly was not alone in his predicament of not being able to recognize people whom he met only once or twice. The old-fashioned admonition "You must observe a face very closely" is not a satisfactory answer. To cure this failing, it is necessary to be specific about *what* to observe. Of course, this "what" changes with every person one looks at, but let us start with some general rules. Looking at a person's face, you should select outstanding features, preferably those which cannot change. If everybody had such a distinctive mark as Jimmy Durante's nose you would not need much advice. However, there are always certain principal characteristics which make it possible to distinguish Mr. Green from Mr. Brown. You may discover that the person you look at has very large ears which look even longer because of very long earlobes. A good example you find in the ears of our former President Lyndon Johnson.

L. B. JOHNSON

On the contrary, you may find that another person has very tiny ears; the ears may be flaring, or they may be very close to the head; their shape can, for instance, be triangular or round.

Ears in general can be very striking, especially on men, since their ears are usually not covered up by hair, as ladies' ears often are.

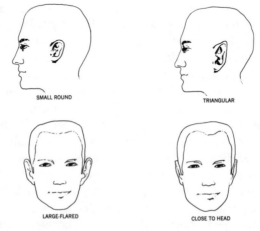

SMALL ROUND   TRIANGULAR

LARGE-FLARED   CLOSE TO HEAD

The forehead may be low or high, wide or narrow.

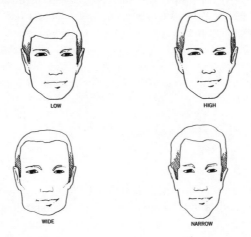

As to noses, the variation is not only in the size—large or small—but also in the shape, such as straight or convex, sharply pointed as compared to the pug nose. The size and shape of the nostrils can be so prominent as to be outstanding features by themselves.

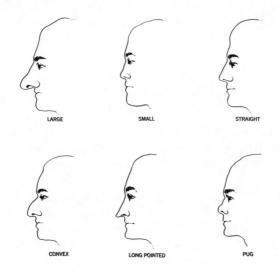

Another feature to look at are lips. Not only will you find very full or very thin lips, but one lip may be protruding while the other one is very thin, one lip may be curved while the other one is straight.

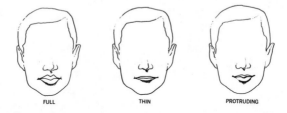

The chin may be round or pointed, jutting or receding. A double chin and a cleft chin are usually outstanding features.

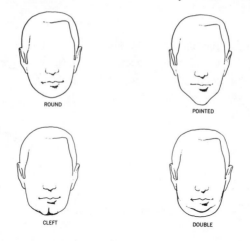

Be careful with hair-dos, beards, or mustaches because they change as rapidly as the fashions. The same holds true for eyeglasses. Some people wear glasses for reading only, or—speaking of the ladies—they may have different types of glasses or colors of frames, matching their wearing apparel. Never rely on these things because they may change and thus be misleading.

Of course, you should discover special marks, such as dimples, birthmarks, moles, burns, scars, or deep wrinkles on the forehead or going from nose to mouth.

Naturally, there are many other features to observe, especially if you find a person with beautiful blue, green, or brown eyes. Eyebrows may be very distinctive, especially if they are bushy, or like a pencil line; they may be so pronounced that the two sides almost meet midway above the nose.

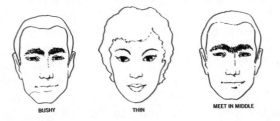

BUSHY   THIN   MEET IN MIDDLE

The eyes themselves can be the dominant feature of the entire face. Aside from their shape, they are more expressive than anything else of the character or feelings of a person. They may be lively or dull, searching, inquisitive or indifferent, happy or sad.

The position of the eyes may be deep-set or protruding, wide-set or close together.

The shape may be large or small, round or almond-shaped.

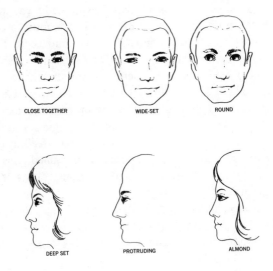

CLOSE TOGETHER   WIDE-SET   ROUND

DEEP SET   PROTRUDING   ALMOND

All this does not necessarily mean that the observation should be made of the face only. Take the entire appearance of a person and you may find outstanding features in the way a person walks, the way he talks, the way he carries himself, etc. Maybe he is extremely tall or unusually short. He may remind you of another person you know, or he may look like an actor you know, or a famous television personality.

If you belong to those who have difficulty in recognizing people's faces, try this observation exercise in order to find so-called "outstanding features." After all, the fact that some people have such an uncanny memory for other people's faces means mostly keen observation, and even if nature has not bestowed this gift on you, you can still accomplish your goal by applying our proven techniques.

The next step is to exaggerate in your mind these outstanding features much like a caricature, because you know what exaggeration does for your memory. Isn't it amazing how a caricaturist can draw a face in a few lines and bring out the most outstanding features so brilliantly that everyone immediately identifies the person? Well, what you are doing from now on is practically the same thing. Except that you do not make an actual drawing. But you readily see that, before putting his pencil to the paper, the caricaturist has already caught in his mind's eye the lines and the features that are most pronounced in his "victim's" face and mannerisms. To find these lines is a matter of practice. Fortunately, no two faces are exactly alike, and fortunately again, in our practice we do not have to search for subjects. There is a multitude of faces all around us.

However, there is one more element in caricatures which we should not overlook. The artist not only depicts the salient features of a face, he also attributes a certain feeling or mood or personality trait to it. Whether real or imagined, this is what gives his caricature its meaning, and by exaggerating it he gets his message over to the public.

You may say at this point that you already have trouble enough looking for striking features in a face and now you also have to find out a person's feelings, his mood and so on.

And all that while there is often little time to get acquainted anyhow.

Don't be alarmed; it actually is a short cut. Little do you realize that you have in fact always been doing this, but not consciously. From now on, do not suppress your intuition but give it free rein. The adjectives that can be used in describing a person's character—and there are many—can equally be applied to describing his facial expressions.

When you meet someone new to you, try to capture something that comes through in the way he or she greets you, in the smile, the eyes, the tilting of the head. Since you are going to pay more attention to the faces of people, notice that the face is not a static thing. Far from it. Just in order to speak, numerous facial muscles have to come into action; the entire face becomes a moving picture. See how the lips, the eyelids, the eyebrows, and even the nose take on shapes and lines that tell you something.

Your sixth sense may detect or imagine arrogance or humbleness, severity or mildness, morbidness or cheerfulness, phoniness or sincerity, secretiveness or openness. There is a host of traits and sentiments which can be conveyed by facial features and expressions. Whether they are real or imagined—intuition can deceive us—is not important at this point. The main thing is that it helps to strengthen your association. This aspect of recognizing people becomes even more important when we associate the name with the face, which we shall discuss later on.

Of course, you know that we all "see" people in a different way. What impresses you most may not mean a thing to someone else. Therefore, "study" as many persons as possible to get experience in picking out characteristics. The more you practice, the quicker it will go. Always make sure that you select at least two—better, three—outstanding features to hold onto. Should one change, at least the other two will help you to recall the person.

Let us now apply the above rules to a few photographs which you will find on the following pages. Of course, you are aware of the fact that a description from photographs is more difficult than a description of living persons, in whom it is easier to observe details which are not clearly visible in print. Nevertheless, let us try a description of the first six photographs:

1

2

3

4

5

6

7

8

9

10

11

12

No. 1

Age: 35–40
Face: square, full
Hair: straight, short sideburns
Nose: broad
Ears: close to the head
Mouth: full lips, protruding
  lower lip
Impression: contented, attentive

No. 2

Age: 20–25
Face: egg-shaped
Cheeks: dimpled
Eyes: almond-shaped
Forehead: high
Chin: pointed
Teeth: large, regular
Impression: cheerful, sporty

No. 3

Age: about 65
Face: round, full
Hair: wavy, white
Eyes: deep-set, bags under eyes
Deep lines from nose to mouth
Double chin
Impression: happy, generous

No. 4

Age: 25–30
Face: rectangular
Hair: wavy, parted on left
Forehead: wide, wrinkled
Eyebrows: widely separated
Ears: square-lobed
Lips: thin upper, full lower lip
Chin: square, cleft
Impression: serious, dreamy

No. 5

Age: 20–25
Face: oval, prominent cheek-
bones
Hair: parted on right side
Eyes: rather large
Eyebrows: thick, arched
Mouth: full lips, perfect teeth
Cheeks: deeply dimpled
Impression: studious, serene

No. 6

Age: 40–45
Face: triangular down
Hair: heavy
Forehead: low, deep horizontal
lines
Eyebrows: heavy, not symmet-
rical
Ears: standing away from the
head
Mouth: slanted
Deep lines from nose to mouth
Impression: sophisticated, pen-
sive

Compare the photographs with the descriptions. See whether you agree with the descriptions of the features and whether you can add some observations of your own. At any rate, try your own descriptions of photographs No. 7 through 12 and, later on, of living persons. Don't pay any attention to the lack of names on the photographs or to the names of the persons you are going to describe. We shall deal with names later on. Your main task now is to discover two or three outstanding or unusual features which distinguish one particular person from others.

The importance of the ability to observe faces and to recognize them afterward goes far beyond our professional or business needs. It knocks at the door of justice. Only too often the judge depends upon the more or less reliable memory of witnesses in identifying persons to distinguish the innocent from the guilty.

When I was practicing law I made it a point to test the memory for faces of every witness who claimed to recognize a defendant. Often enough my questioning proved that a witness, who seemed so sure of himself with regard to a person whom he saw only occasionally and perhaps quite some time back, was unable to describe somebody who had been in the court-room for hours and who had left only a few minutes before.

The cases of mistaken identity run into the thousands. But only a few of them have stirred up as much excitement as the case of Bertram M. Campbell, who was convicted of second-degree forgery on June 3, 1938, in the Court of General Sessions on charges of having passed two forged checks totaling $7576. He was sentenced to serve a term of five to ten years in Sing Sing by Judge Charles C. Nott, Jr.

Witnesses at the trial charged that, posing as a securities dealer named George Workmaster, he had opened an account in the Trust Company of North America, that he had deposited the two forged checks in that account, and that he had made two withdrawals totaling $4150. Mr. Campbell was identified at the trial by five witnesses, all of them employees of the bank. Each of them testified he was absolutely sure that Campbell was the man who withdrew the money. Campbell pleaded innocent and his attorney, James E. Wilkinson, ended his defense speech with these remarkable words:

"I only hope and pray to God that someday these malefactors that have been promoting this nefarious scheme into operation will be brought to justice. My client is innocent."

Campbell spent three years and two months in jail before he was paroled. The break in the case came on July 28, 1945, with the arrest of Alexander D. L. Thiel, a notorious narcotics addict with previous convictions for the sale of narcotics and for forgery. Thiel, who bore some resemblance to Campbell, was brought to New York from Lexington, Kentucky, for trial on a charge of forging a $4000 check on a Boston bank. Astute government agents and city detectives noticed his resemblance to Campbell, and under questioning by Detective Archie J. Woods, who originally helped convict Campbell, Thiel confessed commission of the Workmaster forgeries. Thomas E. Dewey, then governor of New York State, called for a report from the State Parole Board, which came to the conclusion that Campbell was innocent. In granting a full pardon, Dewey declared on August 28, 1945: "I have changed the recitals of the ancient form for pardon by eliminating the words 'he was represented unto us as a fit object of our mercy' and substituted for them 'he being represented unto us as innocent of the crime for which he was convicted.'"

On June 17 of that year the State Court of Claims had awarded Campbell $115,000 as compensation for more than three years spent unjustly in prison. But Campbell had little time to enjoy his fortune. He died on September 7 of the same year, and his physician, Dr. Rudolph Joseph, said the years of imprisonment had taken their toll.

This is only one of thousands of cases of mistaken identity. It shows how much injustice and misery could be avoided if people had better training in how to remember faces.

Recognizing a face is one important step, but the most important is still to come. We have to form an *association* between the person—his appearance, his features—and his name.

CHAPTER 22

How to Remember Names

For most of us, names are more difficult to remember than faces, and the reasons are easy to understand. Earlier we established that most people are predominantly eye-minded and remember best what they see. Since we *see* the face and *hear* the name, the face immediately has one advantage over the name. Furthermore, in speaking to a person, we look at him off and on, and thereby the image is constantly repeated, while the name was given only once upon introduction, and so the very important element of repetition is lacking. Another reason is this: it is much easier to recognize a picture that we have seen before than it is to draw the same picture from memory. It is much easier to recognize a melody we have heard before than it is to sing or whistle the tune ourselves. The face, stature, and general appearance of a person are offered to us the moment we meet him again. His name, however, has to be reproduced by our own memory. If, when meeting Allen Gordon for the second time, a heavenly voice were to whisper to us, "Is this Mr. Hines or Mr. Gober or Mr. Gordon?" we would have no difficulty in selecting the right name. But there is no such heavenly voice to come to the rescue, and we have to produce the name with no assistance from without.

To solve the problem, here are some basic rules for remembering people's names:

First of all: Get the name clearly and distinctly. That sounds very simple, almost elementary, and still this rule is ignored more often than all the others combined. The next time you are introduced to someone, notice how this person's name and your own are pronounced, and you will agree that in ninety out of a hundred cases the names are mumbled, muttered, or slurred. The person who introduces you just does not take enough time, but hurries over the names as if they were insignificant.

So it is up to you to make it clear to him or her, and—what's more important—to your new acquaintance, that the name *is* important to you and that you have an earnest desire to remember it in the future. If we don't get the name clearly and accurately, we cannot even speak of remembering or forgetting. We can neither remember nor forget something we never knew. Therefore, our first step must be to get the name in such a way that there's no doubt as to its pronunciation or spelling.

Don't hesitate to ask for both. Nobody feels offended if you say, "I did not get your name" or "How do you spell your name?" On the contrary, a person feels flattered because your question shows him that his name—and therefore his person—means something to you. If you were not interested you would not ask such a question; and just as success creates success, so interest creates interest. The person who senses your interest in him will become interested in you, and you may win a friend instead of a mere nodding acquaintance.

WOULD YOU MIND REPEATING THE NAME?

Reprinted by permission of the *Rotarian*, Chicago, and Don Herold, New York.

The next important rule is: Repeat the name immediately after the introduction and as often as possible during the conversation. In doing so, you make sure—first of all—that you understood the name correctly. Even if you repeat the name incorrectly, saying for instance: "Glad to meet you, Mr. Austin," though his name is Alston, he will correct you and thus enable you to get it right.

In repeating the name frequently during the conversation it will become more firmly ingrained in your mind. We know what repetition does for our memory, and if we know the name it is just as easy to say; "I agree with you, Mr. Mahony," as saying; "I agree," without using the name.

It is a generally accepted rule that in order to add a new word to our vocabulary we should use it at least four or five times. The same applies to names which are unusual or difficult to pronounce, and consequently the repetition of such names in conversation is the more essential. Gradually it becomes a habit and a pleasant one at that. It takes almost no effort on our part and every repetition fixes the name better and better in our mind, especially because in the meantime we can't help thinking about its sound, meaning, origin, association, and the person we are talking to.

This brings us to the next rule: See whether or not the name has a meaning in itself. This meaning may not tell anything about the person, but it definitely helps us to recall the name later on. Fortunately many names do have a meaning. Just think of the names of your friends and acquaintances, or glance through your telephone directory and you will find many names that have a meaning, such as names of:

cities or countries: Paris, York, London, Holland, France, Jordan
animals: Lamb, Wolf, Fox, Dolphin, Swan, Beaver
occupations: Smith, Taylor, Carpenter, Cooper, Cook, Barber
metals: Gold, Silver, Steel, Brass, Copper
adjectives or colors: Strong, Rich, Long, White, Black, Green, Brown
flowers, trees, or fruits: Rose, Lily, Hawthorne, Palm, Pine, Cherry,
    Berry, Lemon
famous persons: Caruso, Shaw, Edison, Morse, Ford, Churchill
objects: Buttons, Toy, Case, Block, Ball, Page, Bolt, Hammer

All such names and many more tend to project an immediate image in your mind, and so will names which are composed of two parts, when both are meaningful, such as: Armstrong, Blackstone, Goldsmith, Chessman, Silverman, Greenfield.

Then there are names which have no direct meaning but are so close in sound to meaningful words that we can put them in the same category, such as: Golden (*gold*), Parker (*park*), Clark (*clerk*), Faulkes (*folks*), Scotto (*Scot*), Rosa (*rose*), etc.

Originally all names had a meaning. When the growing population of villages and towns made it necessary to add a second name to the given name in order to distinguish among the hundreds of Johns and Bills and Toms, a second name was added, descriptive of a trade or place of origin or person or whatever John or Bill or Tom liked. However, in the course of the centuries, spelling and pronunciation changed. Sometimes they changed slightly, so that the origin is still clearly visible or audible. Very often, however, the changes were so radical that the origins of the names have become unrecognizable. In these cases we are dealing, for all practical purposes, with names that have no meaning—at least, no meaning for us.

What to do? We know that we can associate only things which furnish pictures or which at least make sense to us. For that reason we go by the following rule: If the name has no meaning, we substitute a meaningful word that comes as close as possible in sound to the name in question. When looking for a substitute, we try to keep the beginning of the name unchanged. The sound of the first two or, better, three letters should be preserved whenever possible in order to avoid mistakes.

Here are some examples of such substitutes for names without a meaning. These names have been gleaned from class lists of former students:

> Dubin: duping, Dublin, dub, dubious
> Fitchett: fidget, fish it, fit, fetch it
> Weissman: wise man
> Kirton: curtain, kirtle, curtail
> Hutchinson: hut, hutching, Hudson
> Mattern: matter, Matterhorn, maternal, material
> Valery: valley, valor, valerian
> Krohn: crown, crone, crony, crow
> Nahigian: nagging, Nahum, naked

To find meaningful words as substitutes for names is a simple matter if you use a dictionary. But you don't carry a dictionary around when you attend parties or business meetings. Therefore it is necessary to find meaningful words without a dictionary, and to find them quickly; you don't have much time at the moment of introduction. This requires practice, and the best way to practice is to look through a telephone directory or any other book that contains names of people, select those which have no meaning, and try to find substitutes. If you find it difficult, use a dictionary in the beginning. In a little while you will get so used to doing it that your mind will work faster without the dictionary. After practicing at home with names selected from the phone book, try to practice with actual people whenever you are introduced to them, regardless of how difficult their names may sound.

Another factor should be added. Very often it is helpful, in remembering a name, to realize to which nationality it belongs. We all know that Mac indicates a Scottish name; that O'Connor, O'Donnell, O'Rourke are Irish; and that Schneider, Braun, and Schulz are of German origin. Provinciano and Di Prinzio are Italian; and Shabazian and Bedrosian are Armenian; Roosevelt and Vandenberg are Dutch.

Names are not always so obvious in origin as those just cited; but if we gradually increase our knowledge of the origin of names we will gain another helpful means for remembering them. At the same time we may secure a clue for starting a conversation that will please our new acquaintance and again show him we are interested in his name and person.

Needless to say, the dividing lines between names which have a meaning, names which are close to a meaning, and names which have no meaning are flexible, depending upon our own background, our education, and, last but not least, upon the languages we speak. The names of Schneidermann and Trachtenberg are meaningful and easy if you know German; they are meaningless and difficult if you don't. Schneidermann is "a man who tailors"; Trachtenberg is "a costume worn on a mountain." Whenever we are introduced to a person with a foreign-language name, we should ask for the meaning of the name. It will help us to remember it, and it is interesting in itself.

Another example: We are introduced to Mr. Brearley. His name is difficult unless we know that it is the name of the inventor of stainless steel. Mergenthaler is still more difficult, except for those who know that it was a Mergenthaler who invented the linotype machine. These examples show how much difference our background and education make in the ease (or difficulty) with which we recall certain names.

We should give the same consideration to every name in our business and social circles as we do to the names of these inventors and other famous people. The most unusual and difficult name becomes easy if we know somebody else with the same name, regardless of whether or not there is a family relationship. The name Nahigian may seem rather difficult when you encounter it for the first time, but when you meet another person with that name the sound is already familiar. All the foregoing means that the more people you know, the easier new names will register in your mind. Even if the new name is not exactly the same as the familiar one, as long as it is similar, such similarity in itself is a big help. Bergamasco sounds difficult in itself, but it is easier if you already know a Mr. Bergamo or Bergamini; if you so prefer, you could even associate it with (Ingrid) Bergman.

Again, don't be misled by thinking of the brain as a storehouse with room for only a certain amount of knowledge. Just the contrary holds true. The more names we know, the easier it becomes to add new ones and to compare them with those we already know.

Finally, write down the name. Of course, not in the presence of the person, but as soon as possible afterward. Writing in itself helps the motor-minded person; seeing the name in writing helps the eye-minded person, and most of us are eye-minded. Furthermore, writing forces us to think not only of the pronunciation but also of the spelling, and to get a more accurate conception of the name. It is especially important when we happen to meet many persons at the same time, and we shall therefore discuss it in connection with meetings and parties in a later chapter.

THE ASSOCIATION BETWEEN NAME AND FACE

So far we have examined names and faces as isolated features, but we are fully aware of the fact that neither of them is complete as long as they remain separated in our mind. In order to address Mrs. Waters correctly whenever we meet her, we must connect her name with her person in such a way that one will recall the other automatically and without any effort. This result can be attained only by association. There is no other way. If a certain face produces a certain name in our mind, it is evident that our brains connect both in one way or another. Otherwise, the same face could produce any other name just as well. Therefore we can only repeat what we said in the introduction: if a person recognizes people and remembers their names, it is *not* a question of whether or not he has formed associations; it is merely a question of whether he has formed these associations *consciously* or *subconsciously*. If his mind forms them subconsciously and yet reliably, he will not have much difficulty.

If you have difficulties, as most people do, you must link the name consciously to the person to whom it belongs. Since we are already accustomed to forming associations of all kinds, this is no longer a problem.

On the one hand, we have the name, its meaning or its substitute; on the other hand, we have the person, his appearance, his face, any outstanding features. Sometimes we have even more: we may know and use for association his profession, his occupation, his hobby, his domicile—in short, anything we know about him.

You'll realize how important it is to give your imagination free rein and that all the previous exercises in association stand you in good stead when we apply them to connecting names with persons, their appearance, habits, mannerisms, etc.

We have already learned to create pictures in our mind of things that are not even there. Our imagination has been strengthened and has become livelier. When we are introduced to a lawyer whose name is Carpenter we have no trouble picturing him in the role of a carpenter; merely seeing him holding or using a hammer, chisel, plane, or any one of the other carpenter's tools is enough to anchor that picture in our mind.

It is not too far fetched at all when meeting Mr. Carrasquillo to visualize him driving a *car* that *squeals,* or to see Miss Dashinsky *dash in* on *skis.* Mr. Emmenegger may make you think of *ham and eggs,* which is not hard to associate with something in his face or appearance. Garzone should make you think of a *garrison* or a *garcon,* although he may have nothing to do with either. You can just see him either as the head of a garrison or as a waiter in a French restaurant. Fortunately, we never have to divulge to anybody how we make our associations.

But we must make a definite association. This means that you have to draw mentally the picture of the person together with whatever attribute you want to add. It is not enough to find something that sounds like the name. That's only the start. Often you can find some point, especially if it is an outstanding feature in the face. Try in your mind's eye to hang things on a person's ears, lips, chin, eyebrows, nose, teeth, etc. It is extremely effective.

The name Duivenboden means carrier pigeons. If you know that, you can picture these birds doing any of a number of things to or for this gentleman. If you do not know its derivation, you can see the man *diving* under a *boat* or *diving* to the *bottom* (of a lake for instance). The action picture is better than the still picture at any time.

It is no exaggeration when we state from experience that the names which seemingly are so difficult actually become the easiest to handle.

Let us try some exercises with the names of the persons whose photographs were shown in the preceding chapter. Their names are:

No. 1 Mr. Lipton	No. 7 Mr. Ashford
No. 2 Miss Almond	No. 8 Mrs. Baldini
No. 3 Mrs. Fulton	No. 9 Mr. Schneider
No. 4 Mr. Waverly	No. 10 Miss Teixeira
No. 5 Miss Dimpson	No. 11 Mr. Holley
No. 6 Mr. Villanova	No. 12 Mrs. Goldsmith

Of course, you realize that the task of remembering these names is somewhat more difficult than is the task of remembering the names of persons we meet in actual life, because we don't know anything about the people pictured in the book except their facial appearances. But in spite of this handicap, our system should work.

No. 1 is Mr. Lipton.

Lipton in itself has no meaning. We could substitute *lip,* connecting his name with his rather protruding lower lip. Or we can see him sipping a cup of Lipton tea. Combining the two, we could see a Lipton tea bag hanging from his protruding lower lip.

No. 2 is Miss Almond.

Almond is a meaningful name. Looking at the face, it is not difficult to associate the name with her almond-shaped eyes.

No. 3 is Mrs. Fulton.

To many readers the name suggests Robert Fulton and his early steamboat on the Hudson. We could picture this lady sailing on such a steamer. But, taking our cue from the first three letters of her name, we could substitute *full,* which is easy to connect with her round, full face.

No. 4 is Mr. Waverly.

We could see him swimming through the waves or dining with a "Wave," or substitute *wavy* for Waverly and connect the name with his hair.

No. 5 is Miss Dimpson.

Substitutes may be *dim, dimwit, dimple.* She does not give the impression of being a dimwit. The rather pronounced dimples in her cheeks make it easier to associate with her name.

No. 6 is Mr. Villanova.

This gentleman could be the owner of a villa, preferably one on the Italian Riviera, since that picture would remind us of the Italian derivation and spelling of the name. An obvious substitute would be *villain.* Even if his appearance does not create the image of a villain, we might still in our mind put him in that category, but if you so prefer, you might see him arresting a villain.

From here on you are on your own. Construct your own associations between the names of the remaining six persons, their faces, and their appearance, and see how the system works.

You realize, of course, that these pictures are only a preliminary step. The real test comes when you meet living people. But if the system works with photographs, you can rest assured that it will work even better in actual life.

For practical purposes get into the habit of checking every evening whom you met that day. What was the name of the person, what did the person look like, his or her outstanding features, and how did you connect name and features? Do not allow one day to go by without having done this repetition. You will find that after a while it becomes a habit and you do not have to remind yourself any more that this has to be done regularly. However, one repetition is still not enough to make it last forever. A second repetition after a few days or a week is necessary. It is therefore recommended that you keep a little notebook and enter every night the names of visitors, acquaintances, or customers you met during the day. The next day—before you meet new people—go over the ones you met the day before, recall their images and the associations you made with regard to their names, and then add the new ones. After a week you should glance through your notebook and check whether you recall the images of all the people you were introduced to during the week. This is like meeting them again, and it will reinforce the associations you formed with each one individually.

You will realize that the associations which you form must work in two directions. If you look at the name of a certain person you should ask yourself, "What do I have to expect if I meet Mr. ———?" By doing this, the "outstanding" features should come to your mind and recall the image of the person. On the other hand, if you look at certain pictures of persons, their features must form a bridge to their name. In other words, a forceful and reliable association works two ways.

If you return at this point to pages 8–9 and go through Test No. 4, you can then compare your present score with the one you had at the time you read Chapter 1.

CHAPTER 23

How to Remember Persons and Facts
and
How to Remember First Names

The ability to address people correctly by name is an important asset in business as well as in social life. Obviously, whenever we are introduced to someone, there is a specific reason for the occasion. The reason may be very important, such as to discuss business matters, or it may be a rather casual one, such as when you drop in on a friend or neighbor and meet one of his relatives or acquaintances who happens to be visiting him.

In either case, during the ensuing conversation you are bound to learn something or other about the person you meet. Whatever it is, you will want to remember it so that you will recall it if and when you meet the same person again, which may happen under entirely different circumstances and in a different environment.

The remarkable fact is, as you will experience yourself, that the additional facts about a person, which you want to remember, do not put a burden on your memory. To the contrary, they are a great help in remembering the person and his name. Of course, it calls for additional associations. But since they are all connected with one and the same person, the one association is likely to recall the other, so that the more we know about a person the easier it becomes to remember him and his name.

Should we then try to string all these personal data together according to a strict procedure for fear that we may forget any one of them? Not at all. It is enough to recall one particular item that made the deepest impression upon us. In the most casual chat we still get to learn something about a person. It may be the place where he lives or where he was born, his occupation or profession, his relation with the person who introduces him to us, something about his family, a special interest in sports, travel, literature, music, theater, social matters, a hobby, or some recent experience.

Even the briefest reference to any of these subjects can furnish us with a sidelight on his personality. We then add this facet of his personality, character, or attitude to the association we had already made with either his name or his appearance.

To give you an illustration of how this works, let us go back to the photographs in Chapter 21 and assume that we wish to remember certain facts in connection with some of these persons.

1. The first picture is that of *Mr. Lipton.* When you look at this photograph, the association you made between his name and his appearance comes immediately to your mind.

If you were now told that he is a plywood manufacturer, you could easily picture him dunking a Lipton tea bag in his teacup sitting on top of a stack of plywood. If he was a banker, you could visualize him doing the same thing while cashing your check and handing you a wad of dollar bills in the bank where he works. If he were a salesman, no matter in what line, you would not have much of a problem seeing him packing some boxes of Lipton tea bags with whatever product he is selling. Actually, since you have acquired the ability to associate imaginatively, there is no occupation or profession that he might have in which you could not in some way or other make an association with the name Lipton.

The same goes for other facts you may learn about this person. Whether it be his hobby, interest in sports, art, or any other activity, you can easily apply the same approach. But the connection between person and fact does not necessarily have to be made with the name. Since we normally first associate the name with the face (appearance), the face or a facial feature can just as well, and sometimes better, serve as a point of connection with these personal facts.

When we discussed the facial features of Mr. Lipton we pointed out that his protruding lower lip is a very useful feature for making associations. As you may have surmised, we deliberately chose as our first example a case in which the name and one of the outstanding facial features can be easily associated: Lipton—lip. Giving your imagination free rein, you can "hang" almost anything on Mr. Lipton's protruding lower lip. When you hear that he is fond of tennis, you use a tennis ball or tennis racket to form your association. In the same vein you could find ways to connect any type of sports equipment or other kinds of paraphernalia with a person, depending on whatever sport, hobby, or artistic activity he pursues.

Taking our cue again from Mr. Lipton's protruding lower lip, we can find still other ways of association. It does not require a great deal of effort to push your lower lip out so that it projects itself forward, almost covering your upper lip. If you do so—try it for just a moment—you will intuitively notice that it conjures up a certain feeling. It brings with it a sense of contemplation, and if you looked in a mirror you would see that it gives you a kind of questioning, critical look as if you were showing disbelief or disapproval of something or somebody.

For Mr. Lipton this is not an incidental facial expression, it is a permanent feature. This gives us again new and different opportunities of association, with persons he deals with, or with things, circumstances that are connected with his business or social life. No matter how brief a reference is made in our first meeting to any one of these areas of personal interest and environment, it is not difficult to bring in this real or imagined aspect of his personality since it is a feature that lends itself to adaptation in any and all kinds of background information we may happen to hear about.

We have purposely spent some extra time on the association of personal data and the name and face in this first example. You may discover still other possibilities for association. No two minds think alike and we all look at things in a different way and see different aspects of the things we look at.

2. As we turn now to the second photograph, that of *Miss Almond,* we do not have to go into such an elaborate discussion as we know now what approach to take.

Your initial association may have been with Miss Almond's almond-shaped eyes; you may have pictured her with an almond between her teeth; you may have "seen" her blanching almonds. No need to resort to substitute words like *alms, Alamo, alimony, almanac, allemande, almandine,* although you are free to avail yourself of such substitutes if you so desire.

For the moment we assume that an almond is part of your association. Let us further assume that, after exchanging the usual pleasantries at the introduction, the conversation gets to what she does for a living. She may be a photographer, a statistician, an airline stewardess; whatever it is, you should not have much difficulty bringing an almond into the picture you form of her, working with the equipment that is essential to her job, such as the camera, the graph paper, the airplane galley. If she is a photographer, you might see the camera lens in the shape of an almond like her eyes. As a statistician you have her doodling almond-shaped figures on the graph paper; as an airline stewardess she nibbles on an almond every time she returns to the galley, or any other kind of visualization that strikes your fancy.

If instead the subject of the conversation were her fondness of cooking or baking, playing the violin, horseback riding, or field hockey, you would hardly need any suggestions on how to bring an almond into the picture. An oversized almond will fit in with whatever she cooks or bakes, the hockey ball in the shape of an almond is a rather odd but therefore graphic picture, and so is an almond-shaped violin or horse stable.

3. The lady in the third picture is *Mrs. Fulton.* Associative alternatives: *Fulton*—steamboat; *full*—facial image. Whatever topic is discussed upon meeting this lady, it is possible to avail ourselves of a Fulton steamboat (paddle steamer) as part of our associative pictures. She may talk about the old country, where she was born, about her prowess in the kitchen, her husband, children, or other relatives, or about her last vacation trip to a national forest. Any student who has by now acquired the ability to think in vivid, imaginative pictures can see her standing at the railing of the Fulton paddle steamer leaving her native country, or preparing the gourmet meals on board; her husband and other relatives can be seen navigating the ship. As for her vacation trip to a national forest, it is very picturesque, even though utterly impossible, to visualize her sailing on this Fulton boat to or through that forest.

If your association was connected with her *full* face and the cheerfulness it radiates, you can substitute this face for the steamboat in each event and obtain the same result. For some people this would be easier, for others not. It is the initial association between name and appearance that is decisive in this respect, and the very fact that you selected a particular feature for your association signifies that this feature is best for you, no matter what anyone else may prefer. It remains a highly individual matter. The main thing is that *your* associations work for *you*.

In the same manner, following the same procedure, we can put the persons in the remaining photographs against similar backgrounds and in similar circumstances. Always be sure that you first make a strong association between the name, or its substitute, and the face, or the appearance. The topics that come up during and after the introduction form the backdrop which adds meaning to your associations. Whenever possible, bring movement, action into your mental pictures. Such pictures are more likely to stick in your mind. We are all motor-minded to a certain degree, a fact which you may have discovered for yourself. When walking along a street, passing many store windows, you may go for several blocks without looking at any of them, until your attention is drawn by a window display that is in motion. It is quite natural for you to react that way. It proves that motion appeals to the imagination, which in turn strengthens the memory.

There is another very interesting application in practical life which we would now like to discuss with you.

No doubt, there have been occasions when you were given somebody's name without seeing him—for instance, when you called a store, or a company, to make inquiries about their products or services. When you have been connected with the appropriate department it pays to ask for the name of the person you are talking to, so that you do not have to go through all the preliminaries and explain in detail the purpose of your call for the second time when you call later on to follow up your request or order.

This kind of thing happens in everyday life and it can save a considerable amount of time and aggravation if you remember the name of the person you talked to earlier.

Since in these cases we cannot make any association with

the face or appearance, we depend all the more on the name. Actually we have two names to connect with each other: the name of the person and the name of the company or organization he or she works for.

If we call the telephone company to request the installation of an extra extension phone and we are talking to Mr. Carter, the thing to do is to associate: telephone company—Carter. For instance, you can see someone *carting* telephone sets, including your new extension, to the spot in your home where you want it installed.

It just may happen that, a few weeks later, when the promised delivery date has passed and nothing has happened, you have to call to find out the reason why. If you do not know the name of the man you talked to originally, you may tell your story to three or more people before you get someone who seems to understand what you are talking about and who can do something to correct the situation.

When seeking information by phone from the Public Library, make sure to ask for the name of the person with whom you are speaking. Upon hearing that the name is Genevieve Leniec, quickly substitute *lending* for the name Leniec and connect it with the library. Of course, library and lending are easily associated. Sometimes the name of a corporation does not indicate any more what it stands for, especially since the growing trend toward diversification in industry and trade has created conglomerates which are known only by a few initials. However, since there must be a reason why we want to contact them by phone, we must also be familiar with at least one of the products they handle.

If we talked to Mr. Sampson at G.A.F. Corporation about their latest sales campaign for floor coverings, we know this much about G.A.F.: that floor covering is one of their many products; and if we do not know that G.A.F. originated from General Aniline Film, it does not hinder us in making an association between the name of the person and the company's product. The biblical Samson comes to mind. In this instance you see him carrying an immense load of floor-covering material.

It should not be hard to apply this technique in your daily life. You will find many occasions to do so from day to day.

FIRST NAMES

First names can be viewed as an extension of "persons and facts." So far we have dealt only with last names, but in everyday life there are numerous occasions on which people address each other only by first names, especially young people. First names are much easier to handle than last names because they are limited. There are approximately 500 male and 500 female first names in common use and they are constantly repeated. If you happen to meet a person with the first name Bob, you most probably know already at least one other Bob. It does not necessarily have to be an acquaintance of yours, it may be a person well known from stage or screen—like Bob Hope—or a person known in politics, sports, literature, etc. All you have to do is to associate the new Bob with the one you already know, like seeing them together, maybe performing together, as in the example of Bob Hope. Since most first names repeat so often, it becomes very easy to put, for instance, all the "Bills" in line and add another one to that particular line when you are introduced to a new "Bill."

There are only a few outlandish first names which may be more difficult. Then you have to use the same procedure as we used for last names. To some people it seems to be helpful to know the meaning of the name. For instance:

Howard	means	"keeper of a stronghold"
Michael	means	"who is like God"
William	means	"defender"; "protector of many"; "shield"
Theodore	means	"divine gift"
Dorothy	means	"gift of God"
Helen	means	"light"; "bright as the dawn"
Joyce	means	"sportive"; "vivacious"
Margaret	means	"pearl"; "precious"

If you are interested in the derivation of the original first names, there are various little books or booklets—most of them are distributed free of charge by various companies that deal with baby products. Look up the meaning of the first name and add this meaning to your other associations which you formed with this particular person.

Now try it—and good luck!

CHAPTER 24

How to Remember Groups of People

Is there any difference whether we meet one person or several, say as many as twenty, thirty, or more, at one time?

Not in our rules. With each person you meet, you still go through the sequence of:

Getting the name clearly and correctly.

Repeating the name upon introduction.

Finding a meaning in the name or a substitute.

Observing the face and appearance.

Selecting some outstanding features.

Associating the name with the person.

Using the name in conversation.

The only difference between meeting a number of people in a comparatively short time and meeting one person individually is that we have much less time. Although the rules remain unchanged, we shall give you some sound advice on how to cope with that situation and how to be successful at it.

1. First of all, make sure that you have had enough practice at remembering people one at a time. If you have not gained the necessary experience, it will definitely be disappointing to try to apply your knowledge all of a sudden to a group of thirty or more people.

When you have noticed quite an improvement in your ability to remember and recognize people, it is still not advisable to take on too large a group all at once. Proceed gradually.

If you know beforehand that you will have an opportunity to meet a good number of persons at a certain meeting or social gathering, set yourself a limit. Be satisfied, at this first attempt, to remember say twelve or fifteen persons, no matter whether there are many more present. Once you have proved to yourself that you can handle twelve or fifteen easily, you can take on more the next time.

2. Our next advice is: be early. From experience you know that when the bulk of the guests arrive the host or hostess starts speeding up the introductions, the names are no longer clearly pronounced, and you become confused as to who is who. If you are one of the early ones, you have the advantage that the pace is not so hectic. Also, when other guests arrive, you not only hear their names, you also hear again some of the names of those who are already there and to whom you were introduced earlier.

3. As soon as you have reached your self-imposed limit, find a quiet corner and look around at all the people you have met. Check your impressions, recall their names. If you are not certain about one of them, join the little group of which he or she is a part and ask the person in question for the name again. The reaction will be pleasant. The sweetest sound to anyone is the sound of his own name and the interest you show in somebody's name is always appreciated.

4. For certain business meetings, seminars, and conferences, a list of the participants is mailed to those who will attend. The list may show the company affiliation, title, and sometimes the seating arrangement for luncheon or dinner. This gives you an excellent opportunity to familiarize yourself with the names prior to the event. You can go over the names and see whether they have a meaning. If not, you can find substitutes at your leisure, so that you have already done part of the work before meeting these people in person. All there is left for you to do is to associate the name or its substitute with the person at the time you are introduced to him or her.

5. Occasionally you will attend a meeting where everyone is identified by a badge bearing his or her name. Quite frankly, it is not a remedy against forgetting someone's name. It is meant as a convenience for strangers to be able to address each other by name. However, one depends so much on the fact that everyone carries his name on his person that it takes away the incentive of trying to remember the name. The result is in effect the opposite of what it was supposed to be. Most people are at a loss at the end of a day to remember whom they met a few hours before.

6. Since the purpose of our system is to be able to remember people's names days, months, and years after we met them, there is one more and most important step to be taken.

At the earliest opportunity, on the same day, you should take a few minutes and let your mind go back to the meeting or gathering you attended. When the persons you met come back to your mind, you should write down their names and concentrate for a while on their appearance, image, and preferably one or two distinctive features. A week or so later you should go over these names again and try to recall the persons. In this manner you anchor both the persons and their names indelibly in your memory.

If you follow these recommendations step by step you will notice that they offer you quick results in a very short time and in a twofold way.

You will derive great satisfaction from your ability to recognize people whenever and wherever you meet them again. Furthermore, you will be pleased with the remarkable improvement in your memory for names and faces.

Isolated Facts

CHAPTER 25

How Not to Forget Incidental Items and How to Overcome Absentmindedness

Since we have talked about classification and the Hook and Chain Methods as well as names and faces, one would think that we had covered almost every eventuality that may confront us in practical life. But that is not so.

We may not have any difficulty remembering a shopping list of, let's say, twenty items and we may be able to remember our daily schedule item by item but still forget completely to do one odd thing during the day when it is not fixed to a certain day or hour. You will soon see why we bring all such things under the heading "Isolated Facts."

These unpleasant and annoying experiences stem more from absentmindedness than from forgetfulness. Many people have the bad habit of doing something while they are thinking of something else. Our problem therefore is to educate ourselves to do things *consciously* and not to allow our thoughts to wander. This is not easy when we have sinned in this respect for so many years. However, with some willpower we can overcome.

Everyone is familiar with the problem in question. The busy housewife complains: "The bell was ringing, I had my eyeglasses (or my keys) in my hand, and I put them 'somewhere.' I opened the door, talked to the person outside, and afterward I wondered, 'Where did I leave my eyeglasses,' or 'What did I do with my keys?'" The proper thing to do would have been to put the eyeglasses or the keys on the desk, the table, or the piano *consciously,* and then go to the door. If you see yourself putting the keys on the table, you will not have any trouble finding them later.

Well, men are no better! A man may drive around in his car for quite a while looking for a parking space. He has an appointment somewhere and is almost desperate because he does not want to be late. Suddenly, he discovers a spot, parks the car, and runs. Afterward he asks: "Where in the world did I leave my car?" He walks around from block to block to find it. If people only realized how much time is wasted throughout the day by searching for things they misplaced, and how much could be accomplished in that valuable time! The man who parks his car must lock it when he gets out, and while he is doing that he could look around and ask himself: "Where am I?" He might notice, for instance, that he's close to a house with a green roof, or in front of a flower shop, or three houses from the corner of West End Avenue and 70th Street. If we only learn to observe for a split second where we are, there can be no doubt in our minds afterward where we parked the car.

Let us look at another example of a frequent happening. Suppose you had some time on your hands and wrote a letter to a friend. You put this letter in your pocket, but now you want to make sure that it does not remain in your pocket but that you mail it as soon as you pass the nearest mailbox. How can you be certain that you won't forget?

The remedy is obvious. Since there is no natural association, you must form an artificial one. You must connect such an item with something you are sure to observe. You might visualize the person to whom the letter is addressed sitting on top of a letter box. We all know a certain letter box in our neighborhood which we pass every single day. Now let us make it a habit to check this box every day in asking ourselves: "Who is sitting up there today?" If we get a picture of a certain person it means: "Mail the letter!" Most people are not very orderly, but by getting into such a habit of checking certain things or places regularly, we can train ourselves to become orderly. Just as we do not forget to brush our teeth in the morning, we can acquire a certain routine all through the day which makes us think and remember.

It may be beneficial to stop and check a few times during the day by asking ourselves: "What were the things I wanted to do today—telephone calls, appointments, pickups? How many of these things did I accomplish up to lunchtime, what can I do right after I come back from lunch, and what must I do on my way home?" Connect the things you want to do after lunch with the first thing you are going to work on, or—in the case of telephone calls—connect the persons you wish to call with the telephone on your desk. As soon as you see your telephone it will come back to you that you have to make these calls. We know that one part of the picture will recall the entire picture. However, let us assume that you see your telephone and the picture does come back to you, but one of your calls does not get through because the line is constantly busy. You do not want to waste your time and wait until that line is free. You continue your work, but how do you remember that you must make that call later on? The picture association which you formed with your phone is used up and may not work again. One suggestion might be to move your telephone from the spot where you are accustomed to finding it, maybe to the middle of your desk where it is in your way. Because it does not belong there, it will do what it is supposed to do: namely, remind you to repeat your call.

Now let us go one step further and assume that there are still a few more things to be done later on in the afternoon before you leave the office or on the way home. In order to cover this, stop and take stock of yourself every day around the same time, say before you sign the mail. Go mentally through your program and the assignments of your day and check what was accomplished and what is still left to be done. You may discover that you still have to make a few calls; plan for the next day or two; give instructions to someone if you are going to be away the next morning; take certain papers home, and numerous other things which should be done before you leave your place of work. Planning the day, and checking whether every detail has been done, makes all the difference in the world.

When you finally leave your office, think whether you are supposed to pick up something on the way home. If so, form an association with a landmark or something else you are sure to see before you get to the place where you are to buy something.

If you acquire the habit of planning and checking all through the day in this manner, you will enjoy the result of becoming more orderly and accomplishing a great deal more.

Now let's talk about something else which belongs in the same category of absentmindedness. Many people leave things like packages, umbrellas, etc., behind in restaurants, stores, buses, on trains or planes. For instance, because it was raining in the morning, you carried an umbrella, but during the day the sun came out and therefore, with no further need to think of the umbrella, you left it behind at one of your stops. The mistake actually was made at the time you put the umbrella down. At that moment you should have formed a picture, seeing the umbrella fall in your way, thus reminding you to take it along. If you happened to be in a department store you could for instance picture the umbrella blocking you when stepping into the elevator or onto the escalator.

Another solution to this problem which works very well is to count how many things you are taking with you when leaving your home. If you are a woman, you'll carry a handbag, perhaps a package, an umbrella and a magazine, say in total four items. You take a bus and read your magazine. You put your umbrella next to you. As soon as you get up to get off the bus, ask yourself: "Do I have the four things I had with me?" When you are in the first store where you want to buy something, you may put your package and your umbrella down to examine something the saleslady shows you. Once you make a decision what to take and move on to the cashier, make sure that you pick up what you put down, and from here on count to five in order to check that you do not leave anything behind. There is nothing more annoying than coming home and missing an item, not only because you have to go back to pick up what you left behind, but you may not recall in which store you left it behind. And it may very well be lost forever.

There is something else that belongs to the same topic of "Isolated Facts." Sometimes we wake up at night and a valuable thought or a great idea comes to our mind, but in the morning we rack our brains and cannot recall any more what it was. It is gone completely. What we should have done was to take something from the night table, put it on the floor, and form an association with it. When we wake up in the morning and see the object in a place where it does not belong the association with the thought will come back. It works!

Memory and Education

CHAPTER 26

How to Apply Memory Training in Teaching

The Means of Perception

Educators came to realize long ago that variations in under-standing, comprehension, association, co-ordination—briefly, the varieties of mind—are just as important as, or even more im-portant than, those of the body.

The modern school pays more and more attention to these variations and tries to develop the skill of the individual pupil in his particular field rather than force an "average standard" on the whole class. Such an average exists only in Shangri-la.

But even the modern school, which pays attention to individual abilities, skills, and interests, does not concern itself enough with the individual child's memory, especially his means of perception. This holds true in elementary grades as well as in high school.

There is ample room for improvement in this respect. The teacher should have a good knowledge of eye-, ear-, and motor-mindedness. He should give simple tests to his pupils at the earliest opportunity in order to determine to which type they be-long. Since the printed word can always be replaced by pictures, such a test is possible even before the child knows how to read. Testing for type as far as perception is concerned is of special importance for children who are below average in reading, writing, or spelling, because the help they need depends largely on the type to which they belong. Printing letters and words in an ex-aggeratedly large size may be good for the eye-minded pupil, but it is no help at all to the ear-minded child. Conversely, rhyme and rhythm may help the ear-minded child while it is of no advantage to the eye-minded.

Since the child has no means of adjusting his manner of per-ception to the "average," the teaching must be adjusted to him. If it is not, the child feels neglected and pushed aside and, as a result, develops a feeling of insecurity which breeds self-consciousness, anxiety, and fear.

The Object of Perception

The teacher must very soon observe that there are almost no two pupils in his class who remember the same objects with equal ease. He will find one little boy showing an astounding memory for numbers, another for maps or architecture, while a third amazes everybody by quoting long passages of prose or poetry by heart. There is no doubt that the type of memory each child possesses, as far as the *object* is concerned, gives strong hints as to his interests, inclinations, and abilities. Observing these factors may indicate the direction of his future vocation. Such observation should play a more dominant role in vocational-guidance tests.

Observation

Listening to a child as he describes an outing, a party, or a shopping trip offers important clues to his interests and his ability to observe. Suppose a little girl attended a party. Does she describe the games they played, or the conversation, or the ice cream, or the dresses of the other girls? We know that we observe most keenly the things we are interested in and that we neglect the others. Therefore such a description is closely connected with the child's interests. But the case should by no means rest with this statement. It is much easier to guide observation in any given direction in childhood than it is later on, and since play is the best means of learning, parents and teachers should invent party games which serve this particular purpose.

At a children's party, ask one child to leave the room for a few minutes while the others try to describe his or her face. Give a few prizes for the best descriptions. If this little game is repeated several times, you will notice improvement in the observation of faces, since every child likes to win prizes and will make an effort to do so. As time goes on, this conscious effort will gradually become less conscious but just as effective.

We can also develop keenness of observation with regard to faces by asking them questions about the features of people, children, or adults they have met for the first time. We can often hear parents ask their children questions about the topics of conversation or about the food served at a party, but very seldom about the appearance of persons. Yet these questions are surely much more important for their children's future lives.

Of course, all this guidance has to be done in a conversational way rather than in a pedagogic manner. Without any admonition, the child will feel the inadequacy of his answers and will try to do better next time. In school much more could be done in developing observation. Schoolbooks should contain a multitude of exercises in which small deviations among almost similar drawings have to be detected. Aside from this, almost every picture in every book can be used for an observation exercise. In the beginning, the teacher should ask questions about the details of a picture while the children are looking at it. Later on, these questions should be asked five minutes, thirty minutes, several hours after the book has been closed, thus steadily lengthening the interval between seeing and recalling.

The ear should not be neglected in favor of the eye. Music, choral speech, and pronunciation offer good exercises, but they are not sufficient. Wherever the school is located, various sounds will reach the ears of the pupils. The teacher should ask what kind of sounds they are. Outings and excursions provide an excellent opportunity for questions of this type. How many city children can distinguish one bird call from another? How many country children can distinguish the various noises heard on city streets? These noises may not be so pleasant as bird calls but they are just as suitable for an exercise in aural observation.

Association and Classification

A little girl will easily detect clothes for her doll in a shop-window. She has no difficulty in connecting the doll with her dress, hat, or carriage, although she has never heard of the laws of association and would not understand them if she had. The same little girl knows at an early age which dresses and other articles of wearing apparel belong to her, and she can distinguish them from her sister's or anyone else's. Soon she is able to answer questions as to what is needed for cooking, for setting the table, for going to school, or for planning an outing. Such knowledge is the beginning of association and classification, and exercises in this direction should be encouraged as much as possible.

Hook and Chain Methods

A good case can be made for the advisability of teaching the Hook and Chain Methods to students at an appropriate age. By the time their assignments include book reports they should be able to use the Chain Method to great advantage. There would be nothing wrong with introducing them to the rudiments of the Chain Method when they are starting their "show and tell" exercises.

As soon as the curriculum calls for the memorization of numerical data of whatever type, the Hook Method would prove an invaluable aid. In this connection we refer to previous chapters in this book, in particular the section entitled "The Practical Application of the Number Code and the Hook Method," in which we discussed the application to historical and geographical data.

Names and Faces

One of the topics generally neglected in our educational system is how to remember names and faces. Although teachers and members of boards of education must hear adults complain about their difficulty in remembering names and faces, little or nothing is done in school about this important problem. It should be realized that the lack of a good memory for names and faces is much easier to cure in childhood than it is at a more advanced age.

As far as faces are concerned, there are things that parents can and should do. They can extend the party games, suggested earlier under "Observation," to the facial features of other children. Similar exercises can be done in school with the help of pictures of persons which appear in schoolbooks or, better yet, with pictures specially enlarged for the purpose. In such specially prepared pictures small details in face and appearance are more clearly visible, and the teacher should point to the outstanding features of each personality. At a very early age children notice that somebody is blonde or brunette, tall or short; but when it comes to less obvious details they are at a loss without proper instruction.

For most adults, remembering names appears to be more difficult than remembering faces, and again nothing is done about it in school.

In the first place, the teacher himself should make a conscientious effort to know the names of his pupils on the second or third day of school. His example alone makes the pupils more name-conscious. The teacher should not leave it to time and chance for students to learn the names of their classmates. He should introduce them as soon as possible and, while clearly pronouncing each name, explain to the class how to remember it, using the rules laid down in Chapters 21–24.

The teacher does not have as many opportunities as the parents to ask questions about the names of strangers whom the children have met during the day or shortly before. Therefore the names of characters in the stories which were read in class or at home must replace the names of actual people, since they can serve the same purpose as long as a picture of the person exists in the pupil's mind and the examples are first used to explain the rules for remembering faces.

CHAPTER 27

Foreign Languages, Vocabulary Building, and Spelling

Our earth grows smaller day by day—smaller in the sense that we can circle it more and more quickly. No point on earth is farther than twenty-four hours from your home town! The easier it becomes to reach foreign countries the more desirable it is to be able to speak foreign languages. The manager and the head-waiter of the Hilton may speak English whether the hotel is located in Rome or in Rio de Janeiro, but we know how much more pleasure we can derive from a trip if we can converse with the people—understand the taxi driver, the salesgirls, the man in the street.

What affords us pleasure on vacation trips becomes a necessity when we travel on business. No translator, good as he may be, can ever act as substitute for our own knowledge of the language of the country we are traveling in. The salesman who speaks the language of his prospective customer has such an enormous advantage over a competitor who does not that there can hardly be any doubt about the comparative success of their respective business trips.

What is the easiest way to acquire a foreign language? Obviously, if we wish to speak French fluently, the best way is to go to Paris and live there for a year or two. But very few of us can afford to do so, and we must therefore find some method for studying at home.

The scientific way to approach a foreign language is through etymology. English words are largely derived from Old High German, Old Saxon, Old Gothic, or Latin. Since French, Italian, Spanish, and Portuguese are also derived from Latin, we can often find in all of these languages the same roots as we find in English words. But while some of them are so similar that we recognize the common root immediately, others have changed to such an extent that it takes a study in itself to discover their mutual source.

And in many more cases there is no such common source.

Etymology is an interesting study in itself, but the time it consumes makes it almost as impractical a way of learning a language as is a prolonged stay in a foreign country. However, it does show us the easiest way of learning foreign words by association. For example, the English *flesh* derives from the German *Fleisch*. The English *butcher* derives from the French *boucher*. We can readily remember the German word *Fleisch* because we associate it with *flesh,* and we can remember the French word *boucher* just as readily because we associate it with *butcher*. Whenever such a natural association is lacking, we must look for a linking word which comes as close as possible in *meaning* to the word in our own language and in *sound* to the foreign word that we wish to remember. For example, the French word *jeu* has no common root and no similarity with the English word *game*. But if we use *joy* as a link, we have found a word that is similar in meaning to *game* and similar in sound to the French *jeu*. Because of this similarity we are sure that the link is sufficient to recall the foreign word whenever we need it. Moreover, experience shows that after a while the linking word will vanish from our mind and the association between the word of the mother tongue and the foreign word will become so strong that we shall recall the other directly and without the help of the linking word. Here are some more examples:

English	*Linking Word*	*French*
railway station	guard	*gare*
sidewalk	trot	*trottoir*
depth	profound	*profondeur*
body	corporal	*corps*
knife	cut	*couteau*
foreigner	stranger	*étranger*
the back	dorsal	*le dos*
father	paternal	*père*
mother	maternal	*mère*
green	verdant	*vert*
	(Vermont— green mountains)	

English	Linking Word	French
horse	cavalry	*cheval*
flower	florist	*fleur*
hunter	chaser	*chasseur*
blacksmith	forger	*forgeron*
cattle	beasts	*bestiaux*
building	basement	*bâtiment*
tablecloth	napkin	*nappe*
to ring	sound	*sonner*
to give	donate	*donner*
calf	veal	*veau*

English	Linking Word	Spanish
barn	grain	*granero*
narrow	strait	*estrecho*
sea	marine	*mar*
desk	secretary	*escritorio*
book	library	*libro*
word	parley	*palabra*
ladder	scale	*escalera*
sky	ceiling	*cielo*
tree	arbor	*árbol*
cloud	nebulous	*nube*
world	mundane	*mundo*
stone	petrous	*piedra*
water	aqua	*agua*
silver	plate	*plata*
pretty	bonny	*bonito*
to drink	imbibe	*beber*
dinner	comedy	*comida*
priest	curate	*cura*

English	Linking Word	German
mirror	speak	*Spiegel*
medicine	arsenic	*Arznei*
miracle	wonder	*Wunder*
short	curt	*kurz*
black	swarthy	*schwarz*
girl	maid	*Mädchen*
chair	stool	*Stuhl*
piano	clavichord	*Klavier*

English	Linking Word	German
flour	meal	*Mehl*
desk	pulpit	*Pult*
river	fluid	*Fluss*
steam	damp	*Dampf*
string	cord	*Kordel*
glove	hand shoe	*Handschuh*
mob	people	*Pöbel*
sleeve	armhole	*Ärmel*

English	Linking Word	Latin
new	novel	*novus*
land	territory	*terra*
field	acre	*ager*
man	human	*homo*
war	belligerent	*bellum*
storm	tempest	*tempestas*
hand	manual	*manus*
head	cap	*caput*
punishment	penal	*poena*
love	amorous	*amor*

English	Linking Word	Italian
to travel	voyage	*viaggiare*
lively	vivacious	*vivace*
Sorry!	I'm displeased	*mi dispiace*
money	soldier	*soldi*
to think	pensive	*pensare*
to praise	laud	*lodare*
elderly	ancient	*anziano*
to dance	ball	*ballare*

As you may have noticed in some of the examples given above, we used different kinds of associations relating to the various laws of association which we discussed earlier in this book. The most important thing is to form a picture association which will give a strong link to the foreign word that we want to remember. To give you some examples:

The English word *tablecloth* is *nappe* in French. Thinking of tablecloth, see the napkin lying on it, and the word *napkin* comes very close in sound to *nappe*.

The English word *railway station* is *gare* in French. Picture a guard standing in front of a railway station. Again, *guard* comes close in sound to *gare*. These associations will work even better for you once you find your own links.

So far we have covered languages which are all related to English. But our system works just as well with languages which have not the slightest relationship with the English language. As an example you find below some words in Tagalog, the native language of the Philippines. They were sent to us by Dr. Robert Lynn, a former student, who applied this system successfully while he was serving in the Pacific as a captain in the U. S. Army during World War II:

English	Linking Word	Tagalog
far	Malaya—far from here	*malayo*
hand	Camay—for the hands	*kamay*
nose	long—a long nose	*ilong*
to throw	harpoon—formerly used for whales	*tapon*
to arrive	date—arrive for a date	*dating*
coast	bye-bye—wave good-bye from the coast	*baybay*
costly	Taj Mahal—India's costliest shrine	*mahal*
rich	Miami—resort for rich people	*mayaman*

Learning foreign words by links and associations is a definite asset, but we may go one step further to discover another time-saving device which is too often neglected. Most words do not stand alone but belong to word-families. A word-family is a series of words which are all derived from the same root. If a word-family in English implied a similar word-family in Latin, French, German, or any other language it would not be necessary to point out this significant fact. However, this is not the case. A word-family in English may consist of words which are entirely different in the foreign language and vice versa. Here is an example for German-English:

Landbau	agriculture
Landbauer	farmer
Landbriefbote	rural mailman
Landedelmann	squire
Landenge	isthmus
Landkarte	map
Landkutsche	stagecoach
Landlaeufig	customary
Landmacht	army
Landmann	peasant
Landmesser	surveyor
Landpartie	excursion, picnic
Landplage	national calamity
Landrecht	common law
Landreise	journey
Landschule	village school
Landstrasse	highway
Landstreicher	tramp
Landstreichertum	vagabondage
Landsturm	general levy

As you see, all these German words belong to one word-family since they are all based on the root *Land*. However, the English translations of these words are not based on one root and have no similarity among themselves. It goes without saying that learning these twenty words together takes by no means twenty times as much effort as learning one word of this family. Therefore it saves a great deal of time if we remember them together, instead of learning each one as it occurs more or less accidentally in our books, newspapers, or conversation.

If you look for the roots of words and are familiar with the various prefixes and suffixes, you will find numerous word-families which in turn greatly expand your vocabulary in a relatively short time.

Naturally, the same holds true for a foreigner who is learning the English language, and we know from many students, both Europeans and South Americans, how much time this method has saved them.

Since we are accustomed to speaking our mother tongue from infancy on, and since a child learns in quite a different way than an adult, we do not pay much attention to these word-families in our own language. But word-families exist in English just as they do in any other language. The examples below are based on the root *firm* and the root *set:*

> firm, firmness, firmament, affirm, affirmative, affirmation, confirm, confirmation, infirm

> set, onset, outset, seat, settee, setting, settle, settled, settler, settlement, unsettled

The rules which we apply to the vocabularies of foreign languages can likewise be applied to words in our own language which are unfamiliar to us. Theoretically speaking, it does not make much difference whether we hear a Spanish word or an English word for the first time. If we do not know this particular word, we must do something about it and we have already agreed that the best way to remember it is to find a linking word. Following are some examples. Again we ignore the question as to whether or not the new word and the linking word have the same etymological root:

Word	Meaning	Link
ablution	washing, cleansing	bluing, or lotion
helot	a slave	It's a *hell of a lot* to be a slave.
hedonism	self-indulgence, devotion to pleasure	plunging *head on* into pleasure
psoriasis	a skin disease	sores
litigant	one engaged in a lawsuit	little to gain
amanuensis	secretary	manuscript
monolith	a large block of stone	monument
hegemony	superiority of one nation over another	hedge (first over the hedge)
flagellate	to whip	flog
conversant	familiar	conversation
aver	to affirm positively	verify
apothegm	a brief statement of a recognized truth	apostle
exculpate	to clear from alleged fault or guilt	culprit

This system for increasing one's vocabulary can also be applied to spelling. There are very few logical rules for spelling in English, and where there are rules there are always many exceptions. So spelling in English is almost entirely a matter of memory, and memory aids should be given whenever possible. Norman Lewis* made the following list of words which are most often misspelled by students, and we shall give you some hints on how to avoid these mistakes. No one need misspell any of these words again after having read these simple memory aids. In the following examples (correctly spelled) the letter or letters which usually form the stumbling block are printed in boldface:

coolly:	Double the o, double the l, And **coolly** you will spell.
super**s**ede:	Supersede means set a**s**ide.
s**ur**prise:	He who is surprised **sur**renders.
disa**pp**ear: and disa**pp**oint:	**Two p**artners were disappointed and disappeared.
inimi**ta**ble:	The **table** at the party was set in an inimitable way.
reco**mm**end:	The **Comm**andant recommends **two m**ariners for promotion.
privi**lege**:	Every **leg**acy is a privilege.
inciden**tall**y:	Whether someone is **tall** or short is purely incidental.
ba**lloo**n:	The child played with his ba**ll** and his balloon **too**.
di**s**criminate:	Discriminate against men who are **dis**honest.
occu**rr**ence:	That the cu**rr**ent issue of a magazine is sold out is a frequent occurrence.
tru**ly**:	"I love you truly" does **not** always mean for **e**ternity.
assistant:	Nobody wants an **ass** as assistant.
compa**ra**tive:	Compared to **ra**ts, mice are small.
o**cc**asion:	For the occasion, **C**oca-**C**ola was served.
ne**c**essary:	If you listen **c**arefully, it will not be necessary to say something twice.
gram**mar**:	Don't m**ar** your speech by using poor grammar.
princi**pal**:	If you obey school rules, the principal will be your **pal**.
drunke**nn**ess:	The drunkenness of **two n**obs lasted **two n**ights.
sacri**leg**ious:	What is sacrilegious is also i**lleg**al.

* Author of *How to Read Better and Faster.*

repetition:	To have one **pet**, then another pet, and again another pet, that is repetition.
parallel:	**Two** lines run a long way together.
precede:	Precede is related to precedent.
proceed:	Proceed with speed.
pronunciation:	**Nuncios and nuns** must have good pronunciation.
seizure:	Seizure of enemy installations.
receive:	Receive exclusive information.
conscience:	Justices of the Supreme Court must have good consciences.
embarrassed:	**Two robbers** were embarrassed when they found themselves in Sing-Sing.
friend:	**End** comes at the end.

It is often difficult for students to remember letters that are not pronounced. Since these letters are silent in pronunciation it is helpful to use a memory aid, such as:

neighbor:	Be good and helpful to your neighbor.
debt:	Pay your bills and avoid debt.
listen:	Listen to the tune.

These examples should be sufficient to show you how to handle any word you have trouble spelling. If you find that you are in doubt as to whether a word is spelled with *ei* or *ie,* whether with an *s* or a *c,* all you have to do is form an association similar to those in the examples just given.

Memory and Entertainment

CHAPTER 28

Playing Cards

Playing cards provide an excellent means of training our memory and our powers of concentration. This chapter will deal with playing cards for that purpose and does not relate to any card game. In addition, there is a decidedly entertaining aspect connected with the card exercises.

If you think of playing cards as training material and not in connection with games or gambling, it is apparent that each reshuffling results in a new sequence and thus a new exercise. Besides, since cards are small, you can carry a deck with you and practice in your spare time.

It makes no difference whether or not you are interested in card games. Some students have stated that the exercises improved their card sense and their bridge games. However, people who never played cards in their lives can derive definite benefits if they practice the exercises described in this chapter. The only requirement to do them with the desired effect is that you master the Basic List.

Let us give you first the basics for all card exercises.

A deck of cards consists of 52 cards, divided into 4 suits of 13 cards each.

We number the suits in alphabetical order:

clubs = 1
diamonds = 2
hearts = 3
spades = 4

We distinguish between number cards (1–10) and picture cards (or face cards), and first connect the number cards with the suit number. For instance:

club 2
(or the 2 of clubs)   is 1 and 2, or 12
diamond 9
(or the 9 of diamonds)   is 2 and 9, or 29
heart 4
(or the 4 of hearts)   is 3 and 4, or 34
spade 7
(or the 7 of spades)   is 4 and 7, or 47

The ace counts as 1 in each suit:

spade ace
(or the ace of spades)   is 4 and 1, or 41
club ace
(or the ace of clubs)   is 1 and 1, or 11

The 10 of each suit is substituted by 0; consequently

club 10
(or the 10 of clubs)   is 1 and 0, or 10
heart 10
(or the 10 of hearts)   is 3 and 0, or 30

Using this method, we arrive at numbers of two digits, which can be translated into the key words of our Basic List. For example, Basic List words would be substituted for the cards listed above, as follows:

The 2 of clubs is 12, or *tan*
The 9 of diamonds is 29, or *nap*
The 4 of hearts is 34, or *mare*
The 7 of spades is 47, or *rake*
The ace of spades is 41, or *rat*
The ace of clubs is 11, or *tot*
The 10 of clubs is 10, or *toes*
The 10 of hearts is 30, or *mass*

Only the face cards remain. How shall we bring them into our system? So far we have used only the words from 10 to 49 of our Basic List. All the words between 50 and 100 are still unused and at our disposal. Let us try this plan: for face cards we add 5 to the suit numbers. Thus we get the following suit values for the face cards:

clubs $(1+5)=6$, or in the sixties
diamonds $(2+5)=7$, or in the seventies
hearts $(3+5)=8$, or in the eighties
spades $(4+5)=9$, or in the nineties

If we value:

the jack　　2
the queen　3
the king　　4

and we follow the same system that we used for the number cards:

club-queen (or the queen of clubs)	becomes 6 and 3, or 63, or *chime*
diamond-jack (or the jack of diamonds)	becomes 7 and 2, or 72, or *can*
spade-king (or the king of spades)	becomes 9 and 4, or 94, or *bar*

In this way all the cards are replaced by words of the Basic List. This also means that we can perform numerous exercises once we master the translation of playing cards into Basic List words or, better, Basic List pictures.

Some of these experiments or exercises are good entertainment, and at the same time they are an excellent means of memory training. Therefore, in your spare time, get into the habit of translating cards into Basic List words. Shuffle a deck and take them in random order, one by one translating them into numbers, then translating the numbers into the Basic List words, until you become so adept at it that you can almost skip the numbers and directly translate the cards into the Basic List words. As a first exercise you might try the following:

Suppose you are at a party where there are ten persons besides yourself. They have already been introduced to you so that you know their names. Take a deck of cards, shuffle them or have them shuffled by someone else. Then, holding the deck face down, turn the top card face up so that you can see it and give that card to one of the guests, while at the same time making your association between the card—i.e., the Basic List word—and the person you give it to. Then you repeat the same thing with another person and continue until each of the ten persons has a card which you ask them to hide from your view. Let us suppose the names of the guests and the playing cards are as follows:

Mr. Barkowitz	5 of clubs
Miss Foley	10 of hearts
Mrs. Rich	7 of spades
Mr. Benchley	5 of diamonds
Mr. Gaetano	10 of spades
Mrs. Waters	ace of diamonds
Miss Levy	2 of clubs
Mr. Bellino	2 of diamonds
Mrs. Cordier	8 of hearts
Mr. Korsiak	4 of diamonds

Try to form your own associations before you read the following:

A dog *barks* (Barkowitz) while twisting his *tail* (5 of clubs).
Plenty of *folks* (Foley) represent a *mass* of people (10 of hearts).
Someone who is *rich* (Rich) *rakes* in the money (7 of spades).
To fix a *bench* (Benchley) you need *nails* (5 of diamonds).
Horses are brought to the *gate* (Gaetano) for the *race* (10 of spades).
You fish in *water* (Waters) using a *net* (ace of diamonds).
Many *leaves* (Levy) are *tan* (2 of clubs) in the fall.
See a little *bell* (Bellino) being rung by a *nun* (2 of diamonds).
Use a *cord* (Cordier) to hold a *muff* (8 of hearts).
Take a *course* (Korsiak) with professor *Nero* (4 of diamonds).

Your associations enable you to call out afterward the names of the persons and the cards they are holding. It is not possible to confuse the basic word with the name of a person because you know that the basic word can only represent a card. If you try this exercise at a party you will find that it is easier than the test given above because you will be dealing with living persons and, as you know, they offer more possibilities for associations than do printed names of fictitious persons. After some experience in small parties you can do this exercise with twenty, thirty, or even fifty-two persons; and, again, it is both fun and good memory training. It is, of course, necessary to master the translation of cards into basic words to such a degree that card and word are virtually identical in your mind.

THE MISSING CARDS

A very interesting card exercise, which seems more difficult than it actually is, is called "The Missing Cards."

You shuffle a deck and remove a small number of cards without looking at them. Then you look over the remaining cards just once. Take about six minutes for this scanning. Having finished this, you must be able to name the missing cards —that is, the cards which you had removed earlier. It is obvious that this exercise can be performed only by substituting words of the Basic List for playing cards. But to do "The Missing Cards" effectively, we also have to hook the Basic List words or, better, the word pictures to one and the same object or person. A person is preferred over an object. It is especially easy to make the associations with yourself.

When trying this exercise for the first time, you can make it a bit easier for yourself by excluding the twelve face cards. From the forty remaining cards you take out, say, ten cards and put them aside; these are then the so-called "missing" cards.

Next you look at the thirty cards which are left in the deck one by one and associate them with yourself. If the first card is the 7 of hearts (37—or *mike*), you see yourself talking into a microphone. If the next card is the 9 of diamonds (29 or *nap*), you picture yourself taking a nap, and so on. When you are through with all thirty cards, you then recall to yourself the words of the Basic List, starting of course with number 10, since the numbers from 1 to 9 do not represent playing cards. As you recall the words of the Basic List you ask yourself whether or not you made an association with that word. If so, you go on to the next and so on till you come to a word for which you have no association. This means that you have now located one of the "missing" cards. You might write down this card and continue this process until you have reached No. 49 of the Basic List. You should now have identified all the (ten) "missing" cards. You can find out whether you were correct by checking off the "missing" cards against your list.

After some more practice and becoming more confident, you

no longer have to exclude the face cards. The only difference it makes is that, after going through the Basic List words from 10 to 49, you also go through the words for the face cards, which are 62–64, 72–74, 82–84, and 92–94.

Especially in the beginning, do this exercise only once a day. Later on, you can do it as often as you want as long as you keep changing the person with whom you make your associations every time you start a new exercise.

No doubt, performing this exercise gives you a feeling of accomplishment, and it should. So why not take the next step and perform this feat before your relatives or friends? To give your performance more authenticity, let one of them shuffle the cards and let another one take out the ten or twelve "missing" cards.

This exercise can be done in various ways that can lend an extra attraction to your performance. For instance, the cards can be dealt to four persons as in a bridge game. Three of the four then call out their cards, slowly enough for you to form your associations. You then call out the hand of the fourth person.

A variation on this bridge-fashion exercise can be added by associating the cards not with one person but by associating the cards each person is holding with that particular person, so that you can afterward let anyone mention a card and you in turn can identify which of the four persons is holding that card, including those in the hand of the "dummy," or "missing" cards.

CHAPTER 29

"Mind Reading"

"MIND READING" WITH PLAYING CARDS

a) *By the Hook Method*

If you could hand someone a deck of playing cards and be able to tell him exactly which was the seventeenth, twenty-sixth, or forty-third card or, for that matter, any card in the deck, it would certainly be an impressive feat.

This can be accomplished by memorizing the deck with the help of the Hook Method. It becomes even more spectacular if a third person, who has not even seen the cards, can identify them. This looks and sounds like "mind reading."

Since you are familiar with remembering items in numerical order—think of the errand list and the magazine exercise—you probably realize immediately that the answer lies in associating the cards with the number they have in the (shuffled) deck. This is indeed correct. However, by using the Basic List for both the sequence of the cards from 1 to 52 and for the cards themselves, you would necessarily have to make two different associations with the same Basic List words, and that would be confusing.

Let us clarify this with an example. Assume that the twelfth card in the deck is the 2 of hearts. That gives you the association:

t<u>a</u>n (twelfth card) and m<u>a</u>n (for the 2 of hearts)

No problem so far. But as you go on and come to the thirty-second card, which happens to be, say, the 7 of spades, you associate:

m<u>a</u>n (thirty-second card) and r<u>a</u>ke (for the 7 of spades)

Thus we get two different associations with the word *man*. And because every number from 10 to 49 represents a playing card and at the same time a number in the deck sequence, such double associations happen forty times if you work with a full deck.

To eliminate this confusion we avail ourselves of the Secondary List for the cards and keep the Basic List for the sequence.

It takes a little practice but it is not as difficult as it looks at first sight. If a full deck is too much of a task in the beginning, you can try it first with ten or twenty cards and gradually increase the number as you become more experienced, until you master an entire deck.

To show you how it works we shall use the Secondary List words as given in Chapter 19. If you have a different Secondary List, you should, of course, use your own.

Suppose you shuffle a deck and the first twenty cards appear in the following order:

1. the 9 of diamonds	11. the 9 of hearts
2. the 8 of spades	12. the 8 of clubs
3. the 4 of diamonds	13. the 5 of diamonds
4. the 10 of hearts	14. the 8 of diamonds
5. the 6 of diamonds	15. the queen of clubs
6. the ace of spades	16. the 3 of hearts
7. the queen of diamonds	17. the 5 of spades
8. the 6 of clubs	18. the 2 of diamonds
9. the 2 of spades	19. the 2 of hearts
10. the ace of hearts	20. the 6 of spades

1. The first card is the 9 of diamonds.
   You associate *tea* (1) with *pillow*, which is the secondary word for the Basic List word *nap*—29.
2. The second card is the 8 of spades.
   Associate *Noah* (2) with *stone* (secondary word for *reef*—48).
3. The third card is the 4 of diamonds.
   Association: *May* (3) with *fiddle* (secondary word for *Nero*—24).
4. The 10 of hearts: *ray* and *candle* (secondary word for *mass*—30).
5. The 6 of diamonds: *law* and *statue* (secondary word for *niche*—26).
6. The ace of spades: *jaw* and *bread* (secondary word for *rat*—41).
7. The queen of diamonds: *key* and *brush* (secondary word for *comb*—73).

8. The 6 of clubs: *fee* and *box* (secondary word for *tissue*—16).
9. The 2 of spades: *pea* and *umbrella* (secondary word for *rain*—42).
10. The ace of hearts: *toes* and *rug* (secondary word for *mat*—31).
11. The 9 of hearts: *tot* and *flag* (secondary word for *map*—39).
12. The 8 of clubs: *tan* and *candy* (secondary word for *taffy*—18).
13. The 5 of diamonds: *tam* and *hammer* (secondary word for *nail*—25).
14. The 8 of diamonds: *tar* and *ship* (secondary word for *navy*—28).
15. The queen of clubs: *tail* and *bell* (secondary word for *chime*—63).
16. The 3 of hearts: *tissue* and *jewelry* (secondary word for *mama*—33).
17. The 5 of spades: *tack* and *train* (secondary word for *rail*—45).
18. The 2 of diamonds: *taffy* and *church* (secondary word for *nun*—22).
19. The 2 of hearts: *tap* and *cigar* (secondary word for *man*—32).
20. The 6 of spades: *nose* and *medicine* (secondary word for *rash*—46).

You noticed that we gave you only the words which are to be associated—the Basic List words for the sequence of the cards and the Secondary List words for the cards themselves—without offering any suggestions as to how to form your associations. Having gone this far in this book, you will have no difficulty at all in making these associations.

The purpose of the above listing was to show you that the use of the Secondary List avoids any confusion you might otherwise encounter by double associations for the numbers between 10 and 49.

To do this exercise effectively, you must be able to identify playing cards with their Secondary List words. The next thing that is required is quick association by visualization of the Basic List word *picture* for the number of the card in the deck, with the Secondary List word *picture* for the card itself. It has to be done quickly because there is only limited time to scan the deck. Bear in mind, however, that these visualizations do not have to become too deeply ingrained in your memory anyway since the association is to last only for a short time.

When you are asked to identify, say, the eleventh card, you recall your association of *tot* and *flag* and know instantly that flag is the secondary word for *map,* 39, which stands for the 9 of hearts. To prove that you were correct, you or somebody else can count the cards from the top of the deck and turn up the eleventh card in order to show everybody around that it is indeed the 9 of hearts. Thereupon you put the card back in the same place where it was before and continue with your performance.

Once you are capable of handling an entire deck, you can also tell your audience where the four aces are, or the four kings, or for that matter any four of a kind in the deck.

For the sake of illustration, assume that you are asked where the aces are in the twenty cards we used before. You would check mentally the associations you made with the Secondary List words for *tot, net, mat,* and *rat,* which are *toy, veil, rug,* and *bread.* You would establish that you made no association with *toy,* which means that the ace of clubs was in the unused part of the deck. The same is the case with the ace of diamonds, since you do not recall any association with *veil.* Then you proceed to *rug* and recall your association with *toes,* which means that the ace of hearts is the tenth card. You also find that you associated *bread* with *jaw,* and thus that the ace of spades is the sixth card in the deck.

The "mind reading" element can now be added. For this you need a partner. Your partner does not have to know the sequence of the cards or the Basic List. All that is required of the partner is that he or she knows the Number Code and knows how to translate playing cards into numbers.

Instead of calling out the card yourself, you say a few words which make an innocent-sounding sentence. The first two words of the sentence must be selected in such a way that the first consonant of the first word indicates the number of the suit, and the first consonant of the second word indicates the number of the card. It works like this:

Let us assume that you have memorized in sequence the twenty cards listed above. Now you are asked, "Which is the twelfth card?" Mentally, you check your association: 12=*tan,* associated with *candy,* which is the Secondary List word for *taffy,* whereupon you say, for instance: "<u>T</u>ry, <u>f</u>ind this card." Your partner instantly calls out: "It is the 8 of clubs," because the first consonant of the first word <u>T</u>ry stands for 1, or the first suit, which is clubs, and the first consonant of the second word find stands for 8, which combined indicates: clubs 8, or the 8 of clubs. The more subtle these little sentences sound, the more effective the performance becomes.

Suppose you are asked, "Which is the fifteenth card?" Promptly the following sequence comes to your mind: 15=*tail, tail—bell, bell—chime.* You need not translate the word *chime* into numbers and the numbers into the card, you merely use one word starting with a *sh* sound and another word starting with an *m.* You could say, for instance, "Show me what you know about this card," addressing your partner. But you could also address the person who asked you the question, or anyone else for that matter, and say something like: "You sure make it difficult for me." Either way your partner will come up with the correct answer, translating 63 into the queen of clubs. Notice that we threw in the word *you.* Of course, it does not make any difference because it contains no consonant. You must have an understanding with your partner that any such word—like *you, I, how, a,* etc.—has no number value and should therefore be ignored.

It is not difficult to teach someone the Number Code, the sequence of the suits (clubs=1, diamonds=2, hearts=3, spades=4), and to explain the procedure in this exercise so that he or she can act as your partner.

As a start you could memorize the twenty cards listed above in the sequence given. If you take these twenty cards out of a deck and put them in the same sequence, you are ready for your first exercise. With some more experience you will gradually be able to take on more cards and eventually handle an entire deck. You will be the life of the party wherever you perform this feat.

Some of our students have found it easier to use the Basic List for the cards and the Secondary List for the sequence of the cards. There is no objection at all to this reversed procedure.

At this point turn to Chapter 1, pages 10–11, and take Test No. 6 again. Compare your present score with your previous one. The improvement must be remarkable.

b) *By the Chain Method*

Another card exercise, which may seem somewhat similar to

the one just described but is actually quite different, is done by using the Chain Method.

It does not require any knowledge of the Secondary List; we use only the Basic List.

For the purpose of explanation, let us assume that we have taken from a deck twenty cards which happen to be the same cards we used in the previous exercise and also that they are in the same sequence. This time we memorize the sequence of the cards by chaining each card with the following one, ignoring which card is the first, second, etc. For that reason we translate the cards into the Basic List words, not the Secondary List words as we had to do in the previous exercise.

The top card is the 9 of diamonds. You put this card—face up—on the table. The next card is the 8 of spades which you put—always face up—on top of the previous card. The basic words for these cards are respectively *nap* and *reef.* Thus you put yourself in the picture and *see* yourself taking a *nap* on a *reef.*

The next card is the 4 of diamonds, basic word *Nero.* Association: you see *Nero* landing on the *reef.*

Next is the 10 of hearts—*mass. Nero* brings along a *mass* of people. And so the chain continues:

6 of diamonds—*niche:* The mass of people gather in front of a niche.
ace of spades—*rat:* In the niche they discover a rat.
queen of diamonds—*comb:* The rat is playing with a comb.
6 of clubs—*tissue:* You put the comb in tissue paper,
2 of spades—*rain:* which gets wet in the rain.
ace of hearts—*mat:* The rain falls on your mat.
9 of hearts—*map:* When you take up the mat, you find a map.
8 of clubs—*taffy:* The map is glued together by taffy
5 of diamonds—*nail:* which you pry open with a nail.
8 of diamonds—*navy:* You give the nail then to a navy man
queen of clubs—*chime:* who is ringing some chimes,
3 of hearts—*mama:* which he got from your mama.
5 of spades—*rail:* She will be arriving by rail;
2 of diamonds—*nun:* near the rail stands a nun
2 of hearts—*man:* who is comforting a man,
6 of spades—*rash:* suffering from a rash.

Scan these twenty cards a few times, recalling your associations. Then see if you can reconstruct your chain without looking at the cards. It is surprising how quickly you will master this little chain.

Now you are ready for the exercise. Spread the cards in your hands like a fan with the backsides of the cards toward you, and ask somebody to take out one card. Make sure that you separate the cards exactly at the point where the card was taken out, so that you have the top part of the chain in one hand and the bottom part in the other. Bring the cards together again by placing the top part of the deck beneath the bottom part and glance as surreptitiously as possible at the bottom card. The card that is now at the bottom is the one that in your chain precedes the card that was taken out. Since you know by your chain which card follows any other card, you can tell immediately which card has been taken out. In order to restore the correct sequence of the cards, according to your chain, you must put the card that was taken out back in its proper place before repeating the same procedure with someone else. The proper place for the card that was taken out is at the bottom of the deck as you are holding it.

Let us see how it works with the twenty cards we have chained as above. Assume that somebody takes out a card. You split the deck at the point where the card was taken out; you bring the top part of the deck under the bottom part and notice that the bottom card is the 9 of hearts, the basic word for which is *map*. You remember that in your chain *map* was followed by *taffy* (the map was glued together by taffy). *Taffy* represents the 8 of clubs. So you tell your friend: "You took out the 8 of clubs," and enjoy the surprised look at his face.

To give your performance an additional touch of mystery, you can cut the cards (after you have returned the card that was taken out to the bottom of the deck) as many times as you want. If it makes the impression on others that you are shuffling the cards, so much the better. Of course, you actually do not shuffle the cards, because that would completely disturb the sequence and your chain would no longer be of any help to you. Cutting, however, does not change the sequence. Every card will still follow the same one as you had chained them.

The only thing you have to keep in mind is that the last card in your chain will be followed by the first card. In other words, you need to make one additional link, as in our example between *rash* (last card—6 of spades) and *nap* (first card—9 of diamonds). You could think of getting tired from scratching the rash and taking a nap to recover.

The "mind reading" element enters into the performance in a way similar to the previous exercise. Once you establish which card has been taken out, you can signal to a partner exactly which card it is. Taking the same example as before, upon seeing that the bottom card is the 9 of hearts (*map*), which in our chain is followed by *taffy*, or the 8 of clubs, you can say in an offhand way, for instance: "**D**o you **f**ind it hard to believe that I can tell you which card you took?" Thereupon your partner calls out, "You took the 8 of clubs."

Only if the same card or cards of the same suit should be drawn out of the deck twice in a row might your audience get a clue as to how you are divulging the cards to your partner and then only if you keep using the same words to start your sentence. To avoid this repetition you can change your choice of the first two words. Below you find a selection of words for each suit and each card:

1	2	3	4	5
Try	Know	Am	Really	All
Tell	New	May	Ready	Like
Think	Now	Must	Are	Love
Do	Name	Make	Hear	Let
Take	Nothing	Mind	Read	Leave
It	Naturally	More	Urge	Allow

6	7	8	9	10
Shall	Can	Have	Pay	See
Should	Could	Feel	Put	Say
Sure	Give	Find	Please	Ask
Just	Get	If	Bet	Sense
Show	Guess	Fine	Believe	Select
Generally	Concentrate	Full	Promise	Seem

The above words are only examples; you can add many of your own choice. It is clear, however, that there is quite a variety of possible combinations which make it easy to form sentences.

Judging by the reports from former students who have performed these card exercises for family and friends, and even for large audiences, they have been amply rewarded by the warm reception and admiration they have received on these occasions. And then, to realize that most of these students took our memory course because they thought they had such a "bad" memory!

"MIND READING" WITH OBJECTS

If you and your partner master both the Basic List and the Secondary List, "mind reading" games can be extended far beyond playing cards. You can, for instance, identify articles or objects that people wear or carry on their persons.

This is another form of entertaining your friends by the use of your knowledge of the Secondary List.

Suppose you ask your guests for any kind of object they may have in their pockets or pocketbooks. Your partner turns around or is blindfolded, to assure the audience that he or she cannot possibly see what the objects are. Let us assume that the first article you are handed by one of the guests is a ribbon. You and your partner know that *ribbon* is the Secondary List word for *tam* or 13. So you ask: **T**ell **m**e, what am I holding in my hand?" Your partner then, knowing that *t* (tell) *m* (me) translates into 13 or *tam,* for which the Secondary List word is *ribbon,* calls out: "You are holding a ribbon."

In this case as in the "mind reading" with playing cards, discussed earlier, your partner has only to watch for the first consonants of the first two words of your sentence and translate them into the Basic List word, which leads him to the Secondary List word as the answer.

When you say, "**N**ow **c**oncentrate on this object," your partner will know that it is a tie, because *n* (now) and hard *c* (concentrate) is 27, and the Secondary List word for neck is *tie.*

If you really want to go all out for this application, you should adapt your Secondary List for that purpose and bring in as many words as possible that represent objects which people may give you during such a performance. As long as you and your partner agree on which words are to be used to identify certain objects, you can select any word whatsoever that is easy to associate with the Basic List word. Invariably it will happen that among the objects which people are holding out there is one that is not on your Secondary List. However, since there are usually so many to choose from, you can always disregard it and select those you can handle.

With a little training you can even signal to your partner objects which are not contained in the Secondary List. You may need two questions in such cases. You can make it clear to your partner that you are going to ask him two questions on the same object by saying something like: "Be doubly careful now." In addition your partner may have to use some ingenuity and imagination to come up with the right answer. An example: You give the signal: "Be doubly careful now," followed by: "<u>P</u>lease, <u>r</u>eveal what I am pointing at?" <u>P</u>lease <u>r</u>eveal gives him 94 or *glass* (Secondary List word for *bar*). Your partner answers, "It is a glass." You then say, "I<u>f</u> you <u>c</u>an, tell me what the gentleman is drinking," which indicates to him *olive* (Secondary List word for *fig*). Should not your partner then have enough information to arrive at "martini"?

In order to be able to use two words for the numbers 1–9, you treat them as 01, 02, 03, etc. If someone hands you a ring, which is the Secondary List word for *key* (7), you can say: "A<u>s</u> <u>c</u>lever as you are, I doubt . . ." which gives him the clue to *ring* (Secondary List word for *key*—07).

"MIND READING" WITH MUSICAL SELECTIONS

Some of our former students have applied the Hook Method to musical selections. They made up a list of popular music pieces and identified each one with the Basic List. Mrs. Joan Goldberg gave her permission to cite a few of her selections as examples. Here are the pieces listed under the numbers 21 to 30 with her suggested associations:

Number	Title	Association
21	Wedding March	The *net* reminds us of the bride's veil
22	Oh, How I Hate to Get Up in the Morning	Mrs. Goldberg's Basic List word for 22 is *noon;* contrast: morning—noon
23	Margie	association obvious
24	Roamin' in the Gloamin'	Similarity of sound: Rome (associated with *Nero*)—roaming
25	If I Had a Talking Picture of You	Picture hanging on a *nail*
26	When the Lights Go On Again	A light in a *niche*
27	Don't Sit under the Apple Tree	See an apple falling on your *neck*
28	Blue Skies	See a *navy* ship under the blue sky
29	Sleepy Time Gal	*nap*—sleep
30	Hail, Hail, the Gang's All Here	a gang seen as a *mass* of people

In this manner 100 pieces can be connected with the Basic List. The procedure for the game is about the same as with the playing cards and the objects. One of the partners, who has a sheet on which all the titles are listed in numerical order, asks somebody in the audience to point to any one of them without mentioning either the number or the title. Now, let us assume that the title selected is "Sleepy Time Gal" (No. 29). The partner then says to his musician-partner, "Now play something for this lady (or this gentleman)," which makes clear that it is No. 29, Basic Word *nap,* which is associated with "Sleepy Time Gal."

If you want to extend the list to 200 pieces, you simply use the Secondary List. When a number between 101 to 200 is requested, the sentence to be used should be prefaced by a word like "Attention!"

Listed below you'll find selections that would fit the numbers 150 to 159, using the Secondary List words from 50 to 59:

Number	Title	Association
150	Do, Re, Mi . . .	Secondary word for 50 (*lace*) is *needle*. Association "Sol, a *needle* pulling thread"
151	Green, Green Grass of Home	Secondary word for 51 (*lot*) is *grass*. Association obvious
152	Autumn Leaves	Secondary word for 52 (*lane*) is *trees*. Association obvious
153	Cocktails after Dark	Secondary word for 53 (*lime*) is *soda*
154	Born Free	Secondary word for 54 (*lair*) is *lion*
155	Days of Wine and Roses	Secondary word for 55 (*lily*) is *vase*
156	Back in the Saddle Again	Secondary word for 56 (*lash*) is *horse*
157	Up a Lazy River	Secondary word for 57 (*lake*) is *sailboat*
158	Edelweiss	Secondary word for 58 (*leaf*) is *flower*
159	Little Green Apples	Secondary word for 59 (*lap*) is *basket*

Again, whatever titles you might prefer over the ones given above is immaterial. As long as both partners agree on the association, the performance will be effective and entertaining for all concerned.

Meetings

CHAPTER 30

How to Carry One's Viewpoint Effectively in Meetings and Conferences

Whether in a business conference, a P.T.A. meeting, or a social gathering, if we want to take part in the discussion, it is of the utmost importance that we carry our viewpoint effectively. You will recall from previous chapters how the Chain Method can be utilized as an invaluable aid in this respect.

However, in order to address yourself to the questions which other persons have raised, or the points they have made, it is imperative that you remember those points and questions.

We also know for a fact that if we can refer to the previous speakers by name it lends great impact to the presentation of our own views.

One more thing to bear in mind is that, rather than reviewing opinions put forward earlier by others in their chronological order or in a helter-skelter fashion, it is advisable to group or classify such opinions. This makes them much easier to deal with and usually adds considerably to the clarification of the issues involved.

In order to show you how you can handle such a situation, there is no better way than to relate the proceedings in one of our classes at which the subject, chosen for the purpose of this exercise, was "Memory Training."

Since this exercise requires the application of nearly all of the techniques we teach in our course, it is usually in one of the last sessions that we undertake this kind of "meeting" exercise.

As is obvious to the reader at this point, the following techniques are involved:

1. Association of persons and questions
2. Classification of questions
3. Formulating the answers to the questions
4. Linking the answers to form an effective speech

Whenever numerical data are part of the discussion, the Number Code comes into play also.

Usually someone gives a speech on a certain topic. However, since the subject of "Memory Training" was so familiar to all the class members, we made only some introductory remarks about the procedures and what was expected of all students, emphasizing that they were to ask a variety of questions about the subject, regardless of whether they did or did not know the answers to the questions already.

The names of the participants and their questions follow here in the order in which the questions were asked:

1. Mr. Fischetti: What is the distinction in the practical application of Hook and Chain Methods?
2. Mr. Walker: I am a businessman. How can I apply this system to remembering the prices of merchandise?
3. Mrs. Spiegel: How can a speaker remember which person asked a certain question, if he does not know the name of the person?
4. Miss Fraenkel: Is it good memory training to memorize prose or poetry verbatim?
5. Mr. Kolinsky: I am a policeman. How can I remember several car license numbers if the cars follow each other in quick order?
6. Miss Baird: What are the age limits in learning this system?
7. Mr. Pagano: Who invented the first system of memory training?
8. Miss Halpern: Can I apply the Chain Method to memorizing poetry?
9. Mr. Dykes: Does this system help to fight self-consciousness?
10. Mrs. Taylor: How can I remember the names of people to whom I am introduced at a party if there are many foreign names, such as Slavic or Hungarian?
11. Miss O'Neill: Can I apply this system to memorizing music?

12. Mr. Minamoto:	Have people ever tried to ascertain by scientifically conducted tests by what per cent our system improves memory capacities?
13. Mrs. Impersine:	Does this system help against stage fright?
14. Mr. Bernstein:	What is the quickest way to remember telephone numbers?
15. Mr. Stafford:	What is the distinction between an outline as I learned it in school and our chain?
16. Mr. Pontecorvo:	Will this system help me to forget things which I want to forget?
17. Miss Sullivan:	How can I remember the best-selling books every week?

We must point out that nobody was permitted to take notes and that we called on the students at random—not in the order in which they were seated—to ask their questions. (The questions listed above have been numbered only to be able to refer to them later.)

Subsequently all students were asked to write down the questions, in brief form, with the names of those who had asked those questions, without regard to the sequence in which they were asked.

After that, every student had the opportunity to check whether he or she had made any mistakes and to correct them, since it was necessary for the continuation of the exercise. Usually very few mistakes are detected at this stage. Forming effective associations between persons and facts—in this instance between students and questions—has by this time become second nature to the students, near the end of the course. For the same reason the reader of this book, having had ample practice by doing the exercises in previous chapters, will have no difficulty in this respect either.

The next step, classification of the questions, was a little more difficult, especially since the time allotted quite naturally was limited; in this case to approximately ten minutes.

As the reader is apt to expect, the classifications at which the students arrived varied considerably. As we have pointed out before, there is no such thing as "the only perfect classification." There are always various viewpoints on how to group things together and one may be just as good as the other, as long as we bring things together which belong to the same topic. Generally speaking, any classification is acceptable as long as it permits the construction of a chain whose links enable us to speak with confidence, touching upon each and every issue involved.

When looking over the various questions asked, it is important to see which one lends itself to a good beginning, but still more important, which question will be best to leave for a forceful ending.

One of the best examples of classification in this class session was submitted by Mr. Hugh Bigelow, who afterward also summarized the questions and, in answering them, shaped his talk into an exemplary speech. Here then is first his classification:

Introduction
Who invented memory training?   (Question 7)

I. *Questions relating to the general topic of memory training*
Is memorizing prose or poetry verbatim a good means for
memory training?   (Question 4)
Have tests been conducted about memory improvement
through our system?   (Question 12)
Does this system help against self-consciousness?
                                                 (Question 9)
Does this system help against stage fright?   (Question 13)
What are the age limits for learning this system? (Question 6)
Can this system be applied to music?   (Question 11)

II. *Questions pertaining to Hook and Chain Methods*
What is the distinction in the application of Hook and
Chain Methods?   (Question 1)
How can I remember the best-selling books every week?
                                                 (Question 17)
What is the distinction between outline and chain?
                                                 (Question 15)
Can the Chain Method be applied to poetry?   (Question 8)

III. *Questions pertaining to the Number Code*
How to remember prices of merchandise?   (Question 2)
How to remember telephone numbers?   (Question 14)
How to remember the license numbers of cars?   (Question 5)

IV. *Questions pertaining to names and faces*
How to remember many foreign names at a party?   (Question 10)
Without knowing the names of the people in his audience,
how can a speaker remember a person who asked a question?

(Question 3)

Conclusion
How to forget   (Question 16)

Following this outline, Mr. Bigelow then gave the following speech:

The story goes that a building in ancient Rome collapsed during a festival, killing all the guests except Simonides, who was outside at the moment of the catastrophe. The bodies of the guests were crushed beyond recognition, and the task of identification proved impossible. Simonides, however, was able to recall the names of all the guests by picturing the dinner table and reconstructing the seating in his mind. Thus he associated each chair with its occupant and used for the first time what we now call the Hook Method. Simonides, a Greek poet, introduced his so-called topical system in the 5th century B.C.

(Question 7)

Whenever we conduct such an exercise, we think about connections, and we know that each part of an association will help us to find the missing part. Memorizing in this way means constructive thinking. We must concentrate in order to form the association, and we must concentrate again in order to recall it. If our mind wanders, such an exercise is doomed to failure. Just the opposite holds true if we try to remember a poem or a piece of prose by mere repetition. After having repeated it a few times, parts of it must necessarily stick in our mind. This mind of ours, however, is always seeking something new. Therefore, if we repeat things which we already know, such repetition will become automatic and our mind will start wandering. For this reason, memorizing poetry or prose verbatim by mere repetition and without thinking is more conducive to mind-wandering and absentmindedness than to concentration and memory training.

(Question 4)

The value of memory training has been proved by many tests in different classes as well as at leading colleges and universities. The results of these tests have shown an improvement of from 200 to 400 per cent, depending upon the time and effort spent by the individual student as well as upon the given topic, such as words or numbers or names.   (Question 12)

Whatever the exact percentage, an improvement like this is bound to affect the entire personality. Many students in our class as well as in previous classes started this work as timid and self-conscious persons, doubting whether they could ever accomplish anything beyond the narrow limitations of their jobs. The memory feats which they learned to accomplish proved to them as well as to their families and friends that they could achieve much more than they ever expected. And since nothing succeeds like success, their self-consciousness was gone before this course came to an end. (Question 9)

Self-consciousness and stage fright are closely related. A person who feels self-conscious is always afraid to face a gathering and to make a speech. But once he is convinced that he can trust his memory, that there is not the slightest possibility of forgetting or getting stuck in the middle of a sentence, and that he can master his topic completely, he gains new confidence. He will realize that stage fright in itself is no handicap if it is counterbalanced by enough self-assurance. (Question 13)

The earlier he starts, the better for him. Time and again I have heard remarks from classmates like "I wish I had known this in high school" or "If I'd only known this when I was in college." And often enough I have thought so myself. Of course, not every feature of this system can be understood by children, but I know of various cases of parents who took the course and conveyed as much of it as they could to their children. I have heard of several ten-year-olds* who could memorize a hundred pages of a magazine; and, on the other hand, I heard of a gentleman in Philadelphia† who was seventy-eight years old when he took this course. (Question 6)

For a long time it seemed as if music could not be remembered by the Hook, Chain, or any similar method. But not long ago a prominent musician took this course and was able to apply its principles to music. (Question 11)

---

* Mr. Bigelow referred to Mary Lou Aistrup, who was ten years old, and Helen Needleman, who was eleven, when they proved to an audience of about three hundred persons that they had memorized a hundred pages of a recent magazine. Both were too young to join any of our classes, but Mary Lou was instructed by her parents, Mr. and Mrs. L. T. Aistrup, of Teaneck, New Jersey, and Helen got her knowledge from her aunt, Mrs. Sally Borosen, of Brooklyn, New York. In both cases (and many others) the adults had taken this course and had taught it to the children.

† Mr. Heinrich Rosenbaum took this course in Philadelphia at the age of seventy-eight. Brigadier General Russell C. Langdon took it in New York at the age of seventy-six. Both were outstanding members of their classes.

The fundamentals of Dr. Furst's system are the Hook and the Chain Methods. In principle we use the Chain Method for remembering connected items for a long time, the Hook Method for items which are disconnected and have to be remembered for only a short time.

(Question 1)

The Hook Method, for instance, would be used for recalling the best-selling books of any given week because there is not much sense in remembering them for longer than the current week.

(Question 17)

The distinction between the Chain Method and an outline is easy to see. In both cases we select cue words or sentences which are suitable for recalling the original ideas. In contrast to an outline, or, better, beyond the function of an outline, the Chain Method connects these cue words or sentences in such a way that each one must recall the following one.

(Question 15)

The closer we wish to remember the original text, the more cue words we have to use. The limit of cue words will be reached when we have to learn something verbatim, be it prose or poetry.

(Question 8)

In direct contrast to poetry are figures, which are completely abstract and most elusive for the average person's memory. However, in many instances of everyday life they are important, and it helps or at least saves time to know them by heart. The Number Code makes it easy to do so. If there is time enough to look for a code word which fits its purpose, we use the *Number Dictionary,* which is very helpful for finding good words as substitutes for numbers and which comes in very handy for remembering prices of merchandise or telephone numbers.

(Questions 2 and 14)

If there is not time enough to use the *Dictionary*—for instance, if a policeman wants to remember the license numbers of one or several cars in a hurry—we must use the Basic and Secondary Lists, which we always have on tap in our mind.

(Question 5)

Even more important than numbers are the names of people. We know how to associate name and person, and if the name is especially difficult, as are many foreign names, be they Slavic or Hungarian or of any other foreign origin, we must try to find a substitute which comes close in sound to the foreign name and which has a meaning in our mother tongue.

(Question 10)

As you all know, it was not difficult to remember all the questions and the class members who asked them because we learned how to associate persons and facts. However, if I were to lecture at a gathering of strangers, whose names I did not know, I am confident that I could do the same thing. Whoever would ask a question would have to be visible to me on the platform, so that I could see him as he rose. Instead of forming my association with his name, I would connect his question with his face, his appearance, or his place in the lecture hall. I could even use his wearing apparel since I have to remember his question for only a short time—only until my final remarks in the question-and-answer period. During that time he certainly would have no chance to change his clothes! (Question 3)

This entire system, in all its various phases, proves definitely that it is not so difficult to remember as many people think it is. The question remains whether it is just as easy to forget. But again the answer is in the affirmative. The things we cannot forget are usually those about which we made mistakes. They bother us because we left some business unfinished. The best cure, of course, is to finish it, to bring it over the threshhold from the subconscious to the conscious mind, and that again means: to remember! (Question 16)

The applause which followed this speech proved that the class fully appreciated Mr. Bigelow's ability to classify as well as construct good cue words and to use them, especially since he made it a point to direct each answer to the student who had asked the particular question.

It is needless to state that the ability to summarize questions and statements put forth in a business meeting will definitely improve a man's presentation of his own viewpoint, especially if he can address other speakers by their correct names.

It is a matter of applying the techniques taught in this book. With practice comes mastery.

Applications of Memory Techniques in Various Professions and Occupations

CHAPTER 31

The Importance of Memory to the Scientist

by Dr. John P. Nielsen, New York University

This chapter deals with the important role which a good memory plays in the work of the scientist. The major portion of this book is directed to the everyday needs of the average man or the practical professional man: the businessman, the lawyer, the doctor—in fact, to almost anyone who is seeking a firmer grip on those items that would help him in his work, were he to keep them better in mind. But here I wish to concentrate on the scientist.

Outside his professional activities the scientist is no different from anybody else. He has his difficulties remembering to take care of his car, answer correspondence, and balance his checkbook. In his work, however, he uses natural or developed abilities of a special kind, such as mathematics and logic, manual dexterity for certain experimental work and report writing, and he synthesizes information from various sources. The faculty of a good memory is not usually thought of as a specific requirement for the scientist, as it is for the actor or the lecturer. But bear with me and I think I can show that good memory is, in fact, one of the important qualifications for success in science.

When I was still in high school I attended a lecture on fluorescence given by a member of the staff of one of the General Electric laboratories. The lecture was accompanied by a number of colorful and dazzling demonstrations, such as the subject called for. But in spite of these vivid demonstrations I left the lecture hall more impressed by the mental performance of the speaker than by his graphic display. It seemed to me that he hopped, skipped, jumped, and somersaulted with the greatest of ease in a sort of mental gymnastics. As I remember it, he began with a historical introduction, reaching far back into the centuries, and mentioned item after item depicting the development of the science of fluorescence. When it appeared necessary he digressed into details of mythology and ancient history. When he had finished with history he plunged into the fundamentals of light, never hesitating to give the wave length of a particular line in the light spectrum, some basic formula, or a generous list of substances that exhibit certain fluorescent properties. To prove, it seemed to me, that he was indeed a versatile fellow, he launched upon a dissertation on the structure of the human eye and described its operations in response to color and light. This, it turned out, was merely a preliminary step to a survey of the use of illumination in our everyday life, on which note the lecture closed.

The entire talk of perhaps an hour and a half was made without the use of any notes. This was indeed a handsome display of mental power to me, who failed regularly on such questions in school as: What was the Boxer Rebellion and when did it occur?

Gradually my own interests gravitated toward scientific fields, and several years later I was graduated from college with a Bachelor of Science degree. So, of course, the lecture on fluorescence was not the last scientific lecture I attended; in fact, I attended scores of such lectures. I soon learned the disquieting fact that performing feats of memory is the stock in trade of scientists. These scientists were all as adept in memory as the first lecturer I had heard. It was a pleasure to listen to them but a distinct displeasure to reflect that I also was a scientist—or at least was intending to be one. Today I, just as do most of my associates at the university, find myself lecturing through an entire class period, and occasionally a double class period, without the use of notes; and I, too, make the necessary digressions into historical, biological, and practical aspects of my subject when necessary. It is not a question of brilliance at all; it was simply a case of necessity for me to develop my memory if I wished to keep up with my colleagues.

Are most scientists gifted with the natural ability to remember? In many cases, perhaps, there is a natural ability to remember things related to their field; but from my own observation I know that, like Roscoe Pound, many of them were forced to develop this faculty, whether they themselves were aware of it or not.

The scientist's day-to-day work is not lecturing but investigating—or sleuthing—for some elusive information that will add to the pattern of organized knowledge in his field. He is constantly on the lookout for clues; and the greater the array of information he has stored in his mind ready for recall, the more clues he recognizes along the path he is following. It is in his investigations that memory plays one of its most important roles.

The scientist's bread and butter is the collection of features that characterize his particular branch of science. They are called the principles, laws, and theorems of that science. Anyone who has so much as looked into the subject of chemistry and physics knows that in them one finds formal-looking, sometimes heavily typed or italicized passages labeled Newton's laws, Boyle's law, kinetic theory, the principle of relativity, and the like. The Pythagorean theorem is just one out of many hundreds that must be constantly on tap in the mind of any competent mathematician. Such basic principles, laws, and theorems are not too abundant, but they branch out into lesser ones which, like the particular cases to which they apply, are so numerous that one does not stop to count them. The scientist who remembers the right ones at the right time moves along in his work at a brisk pace.

Some time ago I heard an associate of mine claim that were he to forget everything he had ever learned except the scientific method, his loss would be unimportant. This would be all right as long as he wants nothing else but to exercise his mind. The smallest operations, however, such as multiplying or adding, without the aid of memory would be lavish time-consumers, leaving precious little time to apply the scientific method to the particular problem under consideration.

Remembering numerous little items, such as numerical constants, formulas, definitions, compounds, alloys, or whatever the particular field may call for, makes up the handy kit of tools for the scientist.

The principles, laws, and theorems, and all their subdivisions are the big things the scientist must keep in mind, while the pertinent and incidental details are the little things. But he has little to offer if he busies himself with these and comes up with discoveries that have been made before. He can justify his position in a research organization only if he gives promise of producing *new* and worthwhile information. Hence, before he outlines his program of work, he must make a "literature search."

He starts out, usually a little too ambitiously, by reading abstracts of papers written twenty or more years ago, making notes of the papers he should read in some detail. To complicate matters, some of the important papers are in German, French, or Russian, with no translations available. The number of papers to be read begins to mount, at which point he probably reflects with envy on the research worker of not too many years back whose literature research consisted of wading through only two or three shelves of books and a dozen or so scientific journals. Eventually he reads as many of the important papers as he dares spend time on and then assembles his findings into a survey in his notebook.

When this phase of his work is completed, he is in a position to draw up a program of investigation that will fill up some gap in his field. But everything that he has read has some bearing on his problem and he must remember as much of it as he can, or at least have it in his notebook. The sort of thing he has been exposed to during his reading, such as experimental techniques, analytical devices, names of other investigators working on somewhat similar problems, all have a potential use; any one of the little items he has read might be just the open sesame at a critical point in his work. *The more he remembers, the more likely he will be to catch that one little clue which will be a turning point in the solution of his problem.* It is too much to expect to remember everything, so he hopes that the right things will fortuitously stick in mind. Some workers patiently and with commendable thoroughness enter and organize countless items of information picked up in the library, but that does not necessarily make them available at the fleeting moment when they are most needed. No, the workers who are making significant achievements are those who avoid being bogged down by note-taking chores and who keep a handy stock of useful information in their heads.

And now, if the scientist whose trail we are following remembers, in addition, various items he hears at technical meetings, the sources of any number of pieces of equipment, instruments, and materials he needs in his experimental work; if he keeps mental tab on the appearance of his specimens before he destroys them in a test, some incidental observation he made a month ago and, without continually looking them up, some notes he made in his notebook, he has the substance that goes into a first-rate investigator.

Lest the reader think I may have laid too much stress on the memory faculty of the scientist, I hasten to add that the scientist must first be a logician at heart and have the instincts of pursuit. Memory is his labor-saving device. It leaves him free of chores which would otherwise make of him nothing more than a drudge.

Psychologists have claimed that the basic retentive powers of the mind are somewhat fixed in the individual. There is no doubt that a destructive process is constantly going on in the cellular structure of the body. Our body temperatures are rather strictly maintained at 98.6° F.; and, according to thermodynamic principles, matter above absolute zero—459.6° F., is constantly tending toward complete destruction. Hence, rocks crumble, smoke dissolves into the atmosphere, muscles become atrophied from disuse, and vegetation decays. On the other hand, living matter works against this tendency; it is constantly building and constructing, and during lifetime outsteps the thermodynamic destructive rate. This outstepping of the destructive rate is no doubt going on in our brain structure; and keeping ahead by just so much is controlled by the set of habits we have acquired. Probably what the psychologists mean by *fixed memory powers* is this keeping ahead by so much, which tends to be constant in any one individual but differs from individual to individual. Our hope to improve our memory is then dependent on how well we can discourage certain bad habits and encourage certain good habits. Our habits of observation, concentration, and association—as described earlier in this book—are the important ones.

We might ask at this point whether or not such habits are really under our control. Habits in general can be acquired or gotten rid of, but it requires effort on our part. People have acquired good manners, learned to drive carefully, developed punctuality for appointments, stopped smoking, and learned to control their tempers. As to memory, some of my acquaintances through training have shown marked improvement over a period of time. I know of some who have developed good memory through necessity, although they gave little thought to the basic principles of memory training. My acquaintance with Dr. Furst introduced me to such principles, and, whereas previously I was slowly becoming more efficient in studying, I find that I now move along at a considerably faster pace.

Before describing any particular techniques, I might mention briefly a general policy I follow. I frequently find it necessary to study a subject in which I have no great natural interest. Such subjects I always find rather difficult and hard to retain in mind. Previously I merely bent my will to studying a subject of this kind and accepted the very likely possibility of forgetting it shortly after the immediate need was satisfied. This was, for one thing, quite an inefficient procedure, for I found that in a number of cases I had to restudy the same subject several times. I now take the time out to develop what I call "interest" in the subject. In the class which I attended, Dr. Furst told the story of three travelers who, although they were together throughout their trip, gave quite different descriptions of the journey on their return. They brought back reminiscences of only those things that interested them individually. Since interest plays such an important role in memory, it behooves us to develop at the start a high interest in the subject we wish to study.

I increase my interest in a subject by examining it for every possible benefit it may have for me. I consider both the immediate and the possible long-range benefits. I ask myself how it will improve my work and enhance my income. I become active in the general field of the subject by attending a lecture or two on it and by speaking and perhaps even corresponding with people connected with it. I ask as many questions as I dare. I bring up the subject at the lunch table if I have the opportunity. As a consequence, I invariably find that the subject is really more interesting than I had realized, that it is connected with many subjects I am already interested in, and that there are in fact many ways it can benefit me. Having thus created a genuine interest, I proceed by selecting a textbook or some comprehensive technical paper covering the subject.

Over the years I've learned, at least for myself, that I can master almost any textbook by what I call the inductive method. Having selected the book (or paper) I wish to master, I arrange for chunks of time, say, three hours, for each study session. Then I select the first portion of the book that I know from previous experience I can master in one session. Let's say that it is the first chapter. The inductive method requires that I start with the smallest intelligence detail comprising the material to be studied: the new words, concepts, or terms that I encounter in reading the chapter. I look up these new words and terms in the dictionary, encyclopedia, or any other source at my disposal. Once knowing the "language" of the chapter, I reread the chapter, each sentence in isolation, making sure that I can construct in my mind the message of each statement. This puts me in the position to understand the author and his style of exposition. On the third reading I concentrate on the paragraphs (or sections) and capture the "point" developed for each. A good author groups his sentences into coherent units of paragraphs and sections, the coherency being necessary to establish some major point in each unit. The final reading is to connect these points into a story. There is always some kind of story being told in a chapter. Not quite the "boy-meets-girl, boy-loses-girl, boy-wins-girl" type, but surprisingly a story of some novel interest. At this point I sense that as far as that chapter goes I can take a "doctoral exam" in the subject.

Throughout all this I use countless mnemonic devices—as all scholars do. I myself pattern my mnemonics on the ideas described by Dr. Furst earlier in this book, using hooks and chains of all varieties. For example, if I had to take a doctoral examination (and I consider all presentations made by me at a conference as a kind of doctoral exam) on some material I have just studied in the manner just described, I would classify the material and commit it to memory.

The following example is taken from a book on advanced physics and represents a rather difficult section:

Einstein's theory of relativity states that the laws of physics are the same when determined relative to one inertial system as when determined relative to any other. Insofar as the laws of dynamics are concerned, Einstein's pronouncement contained nothing new, for the equations of accelerated motion have the same form when referred to a secondary inertial system as when referred to the primary inertial system. Insofar as electromagnetic and optical phenomena are concerned, however, it had been supposed that the primary inertial system occupied a unique position, in the case of the first on account of the appearance of velocities in the electromagnetic equations and in the case of the second on account of the fundamental significance of the velocity of light. If, now, we accept Einstein's principle, the speed of light is the same constant, independent of position, direction, or time, whether measured in one inertial system or another. Obviously, if this is the case, the so-called Galilean transformations or relations between measurements of distances and intervals of time in different inertial systems, which had been tacitly assumed, require radical modification.

For these rather complicated thoughts I have found the following classification:

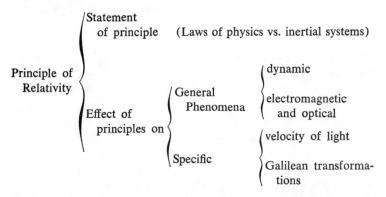

This paragraph can easily be remembered with the help of the Chain Method (Chapters 9 and 10). The cue words are as follows:

>relativity
>principle
>consequences
>general effects
>specific effects
>dynamics
>radiation
>velocity of light
>Galilean transformations

We can chain these cue words into a few lines as follows:

Relativity in *principle* has *consequences* which are *general* as well as *specific* in their *effects*. A *diamond radiates* at the *velocity of light,* getting *gals* into a *trance.*

For the purpose of passing the exam I would have no difficulty putting on the blackboard the complete outline of the paragraph. Once the outline is on the board, and having previously studied the material inductively, I would have no difficulty in answering any questions the examiners might possibly wish to ask me. Would the examiners be impressed? I assure you they would be. I once coached a doctoral candidate before his exam and we worked up three or four elaborate mnemonics in any area we were sure he would be asked about in the exam. He passed the exam handily. Also, I was told by one of the examiners that the candidate made a fabulous impression by listing eighteen ways a certain effect could be measured experimentally. I smiled inwardly as I recalled how easily we had chained together the eighteen methods just two days before.

To give this chapter a practical note for the scientist, I should like to show how the periodic table of the elements can be memorized. Every scientist worth his salt, particularly the chemist, physicist, geologist, ceramist, biologist, and metallurgist, should know this table, or at least large portions of it. There are two stages in learning the table. One is the deliberate and conscious learning with mnemonic aids. The second stage is the learning by usage, whereby parts (the useful ones) become reinforced by additional and less deliberate associations. This extends the short-term mastery to one of long term. I will present here a sample technique for learning the periodic table of the elements. I have chosen the Thomson or long form arrangement, which is somewhat more popular and useful than the historically significant Mendeleev table.

We begin with the frame, an 18-column, 8-row lattice, for entries into the table, shown in Figure 1. The columns and rows are numbered on the outside as shown. The numbers 8 and 18 are numbers easily associated with the elements. Eight, as every high school boy soon learns in his chemistry course, is the number of electrons that complete the majority of outer electron shells. (Chlorine has seven outer electrons and needs one to complete the shell, making it a valence one type of element). Eighteen is next to eight in the series 2, 8, 18, 32, 50, etc., or the series obtained by doubling the squares of the integers ($2 \times n^2$). This series is important in the periodic table. It represents the increases

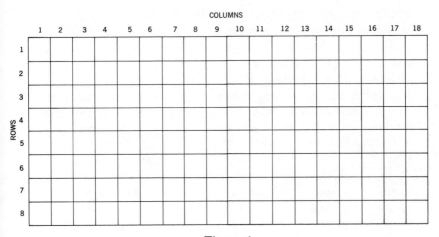

Figure 1

in atomic number for the last-column elements, that is, the inert gases. These increases, in repeated pairs, are indicated on the outside to the right of the table in Figure 2.

We will now proceed to enter numbers in the cells in the table, each number representing one specific element, and in fact each number representing the atomic number of an element. No. 1 is placed in the first cell, column 1, row 1. No. 2 is placed in the opposite corner at the top. The gap between 1 and 2 will be

COLUMNS

ROWS	1	2	3	4	5	6	7	8	9	10	11	12	13	14	15	16	17	18	$2 \times n^2$
1	1																	2	
2	3	4	5											6	7	8	9	10	>8
3	11	12	13											14	15	16	17	18	>8
4	19	20	21	22	23	24	25	26	27	28	29	30	31	32	33	34	35	36	>18
5	37	38	39	40	41	42	43	44	45	46	47	48	49	50	51	52	53	54	>18
6	55	56	57-71	72	73	74	75	76	77	78	79	80	81	82	83	84	85	86	>32
7	87	88	89-103	104	105	106	107	108	109	110	111	112	113	114	115	116	117	118	>32
8	119	120	?	?	?	?	?	?	?	?	?	?	?	?	?	?	167	168	>50

Figure 2

considered void, and therefore a line is drawn through these cells to x them out. We use the outside numbers at the right to build up column 18 down to atomic number 168. Next we go to row 2 and start to count off 3, 4, 5, and stop. We stop because obviously, if we continue the count-off, we will go way over No. 10 in the last column in the row. We therefore start with 10 and count off backward to No. 6. This completes this row, and we draw a line through the gap, from columns 4 through 13. We apply the same procedure for row 3 and obtain the same type of gap to be x'd out. Rows 4 and 5, however, have exactly 18 cells each, and the full count-off from left to right gives the numbers 36 and 54 for the last column. We attempt to count off for row 6, and by the third column, No. 57, we recognize that we have more numbers than cells in order to come up with 86 for column 18 of this row. As before, we count off backward and find that we meet No. 57 with No. 72 in column 4. This means that we must compress 14 numbers into column 3, from 57 through 71. Number 57 suggests the word l̲i̲k̲e, from the Number Code, and this in turn suggests that the 14 elements have l̲i̲k̲e chemical properties, and so it is fitting that they all are put into one cell. Row 7 is a repeat of this same procedure because the 32-number jump for column 18 is the same as for row 6. What about row 8? In some way 50 atomic numbers will have to be squeezed into 18 existing cells to end at No. 168 at the lower right corner. This we leave for the future, since, to date, we have discovered only the first 104 elements.

Having completed the numbering of the cells, we have in a real sense completed the periodic table of the elements. The elements are designated by their atomic numbers, or number of protons in the nucleus. This same number is the electron count in the orbits around the nucleus for the stable atom. A physicist or chemist who knows atomic structure in depth can give the electron distribution for each atom type, such as $1s^2$, $2s^2$, $2p^6$, $3s^1$ for element No. 11. The superscripts add up to this number 11. These symbols may seem complicated but really are not. However there is not sufficient space in this chapter to explain the code.

The inert gases are represented by column 18 and the numbers in this column indicate the completion of electron orbits for the various rows. To the discerning scientist many interesting relationships exist in columns, rows, and clusters of numbers. For example, odd-numbered metallic atoms are better conductors than even-numbered ones. (There is a complex theory behind this fact.) In committing these data to memory it is of great help to draw upon these underlying relationships.

Also, science is not all logic and numbers. History and the recognition of scientists making great discoveries play a role, and so we tend to use names rather than numbers for element designation. Hydrogen (H), atom No. 1, the lightest of all elements, is so called because water (hydrogene) is produced when burning it. (See Figure 3, page 296, for table of elements using symbols for names.) Helium (He), No. 2, is so named because it was discovered as being present in the sun or helios. Lithium (Li), No. 3, was discovered in stone (think of mono*lith*). Einsteinium (Es), Fermium (Fm), and Mendelevium (Md) for Nos. 99, 100, and 101 are named after great scientists. The Number Code can help us here by translating the numbers of the elements into meaningful words. For example, for No. 80 we can use <u>fu</u>sible, since Mercury (Hg) is the most fusible metal. <u>K</u>eep<u>s</u>ake, for No. 79 suggesting a Gold (Au) heirloom. <u>M</u>e<u>ss</u>ing, the German word for brass, an alloy of Zinc (Zn) with Copper (Cu), for No. 30. Naturally, the neighbor to the left of Zinc is found to be Copper. Copper and Nickel (Ni) are common coin metals, and so Nickel is found to be Copper's neighbor. Nickel suggests a magnetic metal, and there are two other magnetic elements, Cobalt (Co) and Iron (Fe), all found together. No. 8 is for <u>f</u>lame (or <u>f</u>ire), which always requires Oxygen (O) to support it. Speaking of fire, we are reminded of brimstone, or Sulfur (S), the neighbor just below Oxygen. Sulfur reeks sharply when burned, and two other elements have the same property, Selenium (Se) and Tellurium (Te), found in the same column, Nos. 34 and 52. By the way, there is another reason why Oxygen and Sulfur are associated as neighbors. There are two basic types of minerals used for ores: oxides and sulfides. Oxygen is an ingredient of air, as is also Nitrogen (N), and so we find them as neighbors. Nitrogen is a fertilizer element, as is Phosphorus (P), in the same column. This column has importance in agriculture, for we find Arsenic (As) right below Phosphorus.

COLUMNS

ROWS	1	2	3	4	5	6	7	8	9	10	11	12	13	14	15	16	17	18
1	1 H																	2 He
2	3 Li	4 Be	5 B											6 C	7 N	8 O	9 F	10 Ne
3	11 Na	12 Mg	13 Al											14 Si	15 P	16 S	17 Cl	18 Ar
4	19 K	20 Ca	21 Sc	22 Ti	23 V	24 Cr	25 Mn	26 Fe	27 Co	28 Ni	29 Cu	30 Zn	31 Ga	32 Ge	33 As	34 Se	35 Br	36 Kr
5	37 Rb	38 Sr	39 Y	40 Zr	41 Nb	42 Mo	43 Tc	44 Ru	45 Rh	46 Pd	47 Ag	48 Cd	49 In	50 Sn	51 Sb	52 Te	53 I	54 Xe
6	55 Cs	56 Ba	57-71 R.E.	72 Hf	73 Ta	74 W	75 Re	76 Os	77 Ir	78 Pt	79 Au	80 Hg	81 Tl	82 Pb	83 Bi	84 Po	85 At	86 Rn
7	87 Fr	88 Ra	89-103 A.S.	104	105	106	107	108	109	110	111	112	113	114	115	116	117	118
8	119	120	?	?	?	?	?	?	?	?	?	?	?	?	?	?	167	168

R.E.:

57 La	58 Ce	59 Pr	60 Nd	61 Pm	62 Sm	63 Eu	64 Gd	65 Tb	66 Dy	67 Ho	68 Er	69 Tm	70 Yb	71 Lu

A.S.:

89 Ac	90 Th	91 Pa	92 U	93 Np	94 Pu	95 Am	96 Cm	97 Bk	98 Cf	99 Es	100 Fm	101 Md	102 No	103 Lw

Figure 3

Going back to Zinc, No. 30, we know it is a low-melting-point metal. A truly remarkable low-melting metal is Gallium (Ga), No. 31—as it melts in the palm of your hand—right next door to Zinc. The neighbors of Gallium are all low-melting metals, e.g., Indium (In), No. 49, and Tin (Sn), No. 50. Tin suggests solder and its alloy partner is Lead (Pb). Tin has two crystalline forms, one of which is diamond, and so we look for Carbon (C) at the head of its column. Carbon is both an insulator (diamond form) and a conductor (graphite form). This dichotomy suggests semi-conductivity. The two leading semi-conductors in the table are Germanium (Ge) and Silicon (Si), both members in the same ·column. The compressed group, 57–71, comprises 14 elements, sometimes called the Rare Earths (R.E.), or the Lanthanide series. Their symbols are found just below the table. The Actinide series (A.S.) compressing elements 89 through 103 in one cell are also listed below the table. Here are included the radioactive elements, Thorium (Th), Uranium (U), Plutonium (Pu), etc. There is one radioactive gas, Radon (Rn), No. 86, and it would naturally be found at the bottom of a column, as are all radioactive (or unstable) elements.

By now we have given names to a couple of dozen elements and we need go no further. The reader, if interested, can develop his own associations. *Association,* please note, is the key.

With the aid of mnemonics—built up by referring to chemistry texts, dictionary, and encyclopedia sources—we can commit the entire table to memory. It is not so difficult as it seems; it frequently makes learning a pleasure, and it is certainly an indispensable tool of every scientist who knows his field well.

Another way to memorize the entire periodic table is by applying phonics, which means substituting words that sound alike for the names of the elements. We can form a little sentence or chain for each period and identify the periods by using the words of the Basic List.

Every student should make up his own chains because we remember our own creations much better than those suggested by someone else. A few examples follow to illustrate how it can be done:

Period I Hydrogen Helium
For *tea* (I) *high* *heels* are proper.

Period II Lithium Beryllium Boron
Noah (II) asked *little* *Beryl* if he could *borrow*
  Carbon Nitrogen Oxygen
her *car* for the *night*. He bumped into an *ox*
  Fluorine Neon
and *floored* a *neon* light.

Period III Sodium Magnesium
Around the *May* (pole) in *Sodom* the *magnates*
  Aluminum Silicon Phosphorus
used to pay *alimony* handing out *silky* *fox furs*
  Sulphur Chlorine Argon
while *suffering* in *choleric agony*.

By making the sentences rhyme they tend to become more effective as memory aids.

The Number Code can be very helpful in the scientist's work. For instance, when I begin a new series of experiments in the laboratory, I often find it useful to memorize the physical constants which I will be using frequently. The following metals were melted in one experimental program and I memorized their melting points by translating the numbers into words:

iron	1530	**tall mast** (Eiffel Tower—iron)
copper	1081	**soft** (this actually translates into 081, but that is enough since I know that copper melts above 1000 degrees)
lead	326	**ammunition**
tin	235	**enamel** (tin oxide is used in enamel)
aluminum	658	**jellify** (hydroxide jellifies)

All these are only incidental examples, but I am convinced they sufficiently illustrate the advantages of this system in studying as well as in teaching.

Having learned some important material in this way, do not worry that parts of it become vague and are forgotten. Down among the neuron paths of your brain cells the associations are lying dormant. As you grow in your science profession, little bits of new associations will naturally develop, reawaken, and reinforce the old ones. A time will come when you will be as familiar with comprehensive material such as the periodic table as you are with the furnishings of your home or the streets in your neighborhood. Your command of certain aspects of your field will at times astound your associates. But that is not your purpose. Memory is a tool and if you will be a scientist this tool must always be kept sharp and in good working order.

CHAPTER 32

Memory and Anatomy—
the Human Skeleton

*by Dr. Julius Dintenfass**

The prayer of many a student is: "Oh, that the brain were composed of stuff as soft as putty to receive impressions and that it could be transformed into marble in order to retain them!"

Study requires the student to collect facts and retain them. The student who tries to cram all the facts into his head shortly before an examination finds that the facts fly away soon afterward. Resorting to rote memory is a much less satisfactory means of retaining facts than using the principles of mnemonics elaborated by Dr. Furst.

The intricacies of human anatomy have always been a stumbling block to students. The body contains hundreds of important details which must be thoroughly known by the physician, dentist, chiropractor, or other professional man dealing with it. Too often the doctor, just a few years out of school, declares he has forgotten most of anatomy, and finds it necessary to resort to textbooks again. Here is a way to retain this information so it can be useful for long periods of time.

THE CRANIAL NERVES

The average student usually depends on memory by rote. In desperation he invents certain impromptu mnemonic devices which, although helpful, are difficult to retain for any period of

---

* Member, New York State Board of Chiropractic Examiners; Director of Chiropractic, Medical Assistance Program, Department of Health, New York City; author, *Chiropractic—A Modern Way to Health*, Pyramid Books.

time. For example, the following jingle is often used to memorize the twelve cranial nerves:

> On Old Olympic Towering Top
> A Finn And German Viewed A Hop.

The first letter of each word is the same as the first letter of each of the cranial nerves. This has the disadvantage of giving only *one* letter which coincides with the first letter of each nerve—hardly enough to recall the difficult names of the nerves. Besides, there are three nerves which start with the letter *o* and two which start with the letter *t*.

I have found that both the Hook and Chain Methods can be applied to remember the cranial nerves. In both cases I use a substitute word which comes close enough in sound or sense to the name of the nerve to bring it to mind. As substitutes I have found:

I.	Olfactory	sounds like	Oil factory
II.	Optic	" "	Optician
III.	Oculomotor	" "	Occupant
IV.	Trochlear	" "	Truck
V.	Trigeminal	" "	Three gems
VI.	Abducens	" "	Abduction
VII.	Facial	" "	Face
VIII.	Acoustic	" "	Ear (There is no similarity in sound, but *ear* and *acoustic* belong together.)
IX.	Glossopharyngeal	" "	Glossy photograph
X.	Vagus	" "	Vague
XI.	Spinal Accessory	" "	Spinal
XII.	Hypoglossal	" "	Hypocritical

If I use the Hook Method, I form associations like:

1. *Tea*	Oil Factory	(Association: the similarity of tea and oil)
2. *Noah*	Optician	(Association: Noah looking through his eyeglasses)
3. *May*	Occupant	(Association: We occupy a new house in May)

and so on.

The *advantage* of the Hook Method is that I immediately know the number for each nerve. The *disadvantage* is that these associations may weaken if I use the Basic List for other purposes. Since I wish to remember these cranial nerves permanently, I prefer the Chain Method and I form the following sentences:

> At the *oil factory* the *optician* looked
> for the *occupant* of the *truck*.
>   Connecting link: Why does he look?
> *Three gems* were *abducted* by a man
> who was hiding his *face* and *ears*.
>   Connecting link: When his picture was taken.
> A *glossy photograph* was taken,
> which was rather *vague*; even the
> *spine* was not clear to a *hypocritical*
> eye.

These three sentences have the advantage that each one contains four nerves: the first sentence, nerves 1-2-3-4; the second sentence, nerves 5-6-7-8; and the third sentence, nerves 9-10-11-12. Therefore it is easy to know the number for each nerve without much counting.

THE SKELETAL SYSTEM

Dr. Furst's method can be applied equally well to the skeletal system. Here we can take advantage of classification and the Number Code. The human skeleton can be classified into two general divisions as follows:

1. Axial Skeleton	Skull	29	bones
	Vertebral Column	26	"
	Ribs and Sternum	25	"
2. Appendicular	Upper Limbs	64	"
	Lower Limbs	62	"
	Total	206	bones

These numbers* can be remembered by the following sentences:

The k<u>n</u>o<u>b</u> (29) of the body is the skull.
A <u>n</u>u<u>dg</u>e (26) in the back (vertebral column) can be painful.
We <u>i</u>n<u>hale</u> (25) with the ribs and sternum.
A <u>ch</u>ai<u>r</u> (64) is a restful seat; especially an armchair.
<u>Ch</u>ai<u>n</u>s (62) are uncomfortable about one's legs.

For the total number I can substitute:

The student who remembers all the bones in the body makes quite a se<u>n</u>sa<u>t</u>ion (206).

However, knowing the numbers of bones is not enough. We must also know the names of the bones and where they belong. Here is the entire list:

Bones of the Head or Skull

A. The Bones of the Cranium

1 Occipital	2 Temporals
2 Parietals	1 Ethmoid
1 Frontal	1 Sphenoid

B. The Bones of the Face

2 Nasals	2 Palates
1 Vomer	2 Maxillas
2 Inf. Turbinates	1 Mandible
2 Lachrymals	1 Hyoid
2 Malars	

C. The Bones of the Ear

2 Malleus
2 Incus
2 Stapes

Bones of the Trunk

7 Cervical Vertebrae	1 Sternum
12 Thoracic Vertebrae	24 Ribs
5 Lumbar Vertebrae	
1 Sacrum	
1 Coccyx	

* See Chapters 13 and 20.

Bones of the Upper Extremity

1 Clavicle }
1 Scapula   } Shoulder girdle
1 Humerus (Arm)
1 Radius }
1 Ulna   } Forearm

8 Carpus (Wrist)
5 Metacarpus }
14 Phalanges } Hand

Bones of the Lower Extremity

1 Hip Bone (Ilium)
1 Femur (Thigh)
1 Patella
1 Fibula }
1 Tibia   } Leg

7 Tarsals (Ankle)
5 Metatarsals }
14 Phalanges   } Foot

The standard textbooks present the skull from various positions, as: the top, front, back, lateral, and lower surfaces of the skull. If, however, we study the bones of the skull in logical sequence, we see that it makes the study of this structure relatively simple.

Let us start with the cranial bones and the facial bones. Following the cranial bones in logical sequence from front to back, we find one large bone in front in contact with four smaller bones which, in turn, are in contact with one large bone in the back of the head. The large bone in front is the *frontal* bone, which is in contact with two pairs of bones. At the sides, in the region of the temple and the ear, are the two *temporal* bones; on the top of the head, the two *parietal* bones. These four are in contact with the last bone of the skull, the *occipital* bone. There are two hidden bones located inside the cranium. One is a large bat-shaped bone situated at the bottom of the skull which holds all the main skull bones together on the inside—the *sphenoid* bone. The second is the *ethmoid* bone, a small bone also located in the base of the skull, in the region of the nose. In addition, there are three bones located inside the ear. These are the malleus (hammer), *incus* (anvil), and *stapes* (stirrup). It is easy to learn all these bones by remembering the following sentences, which contain substitute words for the anatomical names.

The cranial bones:

> *Frontal*   *Temporal*   *Parietal* *Occipital*
> In the front of the temples the parrots osculated.

> *Sphenoid Ethmoid Malleus*   *Stapes*   *Incus*
> Inside the Sphinx   Ethel   hammered the stirrups on the anvil.

The facial bones (check the list given above):

> *Hyoid*   *Mandible Maxillas Malars*   *Lachrymals*
> Hy and that man   Max   maltreated the lackey at the

> *Palates*   *Nasals*   *Vomer*   *Inf.*
> palace. It was so nasty one could vomit from the infernal

> *Turbinates*
> turbid odor.

The vertebral column (the bones of the spine) is the central axis or backbone of the skeleton. On top of it sits the skull. It gives attachment to the rib cage and the pelvis and the upper and lower limbs. It is divided into four regions:

1. Cervical (neck)
2. Dorsal or Thoracic (thorax)
3. Lumbar (hollow area of the lower back)
4. Sacral and coccygeal (area where the lower back protrudes and the tail bone).

The first region contains 7 bones; the second, 12; the third, 5 (remember $7+5=12$); the fourth, the sacrum, is 1 large bone; and the coccyx is the tail bone at the tip of the spine. This equals 26.

The ribs are attached to the thoracic region of the spine, which contains 12 bones; therefore it is easy to remember that there are 12 pairs of ribs. In the front of the rib cage, 7 pairs of ribs are attached to the sternum or breast bone. An association with the number of bones in the cervical region (also 7) is easy.

To remember the bones of the extremities, we should note the important anatomical fact that the lower limbs are homologous with the upper limbs. Such similarity of structure can be used to good advantage as a memory aid. Since *shoulder—arm—forearm—wrist—hand* form a logical chain, there is no need to construct another one. Let us try the following comparisons:

Upper Limbs	*Lower Limbs*
1. Shoulder Girdle (Clavicle and Scapula) The shoulder shows a *scar* caused by the *claw* of a cat.	1. Hip Girdle (Pelvis)
2. Arm (Humerus) A *human* arm.	2. Thigh (Femur) Strong thighs make fighters *famous.*
3. Forearm (Radius and Ulna) The forearm is a straight line like the *radius* in an *ultra*-large circle.	3. Leg (Patella-Tibia and Fibula) *Pat* tells legends and *fibs* about *Tibet.*
4. Wrist (Carpus or carpal bones) We need a flexible wrist to catch *carp.*	4. Ankle (Tarsals or tarsal bones) Ankle-deep in *tar.*
5. Hand (Metacarpus and Phalanges) All hands are holding *metallic* shields in a *phalanx.*	5. Foot (Metatarsals and Phalanges) Notice that we have to add *meta* to *tarsal* in the same way as we added *meta* to *carpal* for the upper limbs; then we repeat *phalanges.* If you still prefer a sentence, remember: Bulgarian soldiers on foot *met Tartars* in a *phalanx.*

This procedure makes it easy to tie up the structures of both extremities.

The principles of Dr. Furst for memorizing have proved to be very successful not only for me but for others. In experimenting with a group of students, I found that 90 per cent of the group succeeded in memorizing the names of all the bones of the skeletal structure in thirty minutes.

CHAPTER 33

Sermons and Memory

by Rev. Edward Hofmann,*
Leonia, N.J.

I was formerly forced to read my sermons from manuscript because I was unable to keep them in mind. A sermon differs from a lecture on secular topics in that it must follow the prepared script more closely. While it is not necessary to know the sermon verbatim, the minister should stay as close as he can to its original wording. Consequently I have found Furst's Chain Method very helpful in my work. For the reason mentioned above, I find it necessary to use more cue words than for a secular lecture or talk, but, by linking the cue words together, it is very easy to keep the chain in mind.

Knowing the chain means knowing the entire sermon, and I no longer find it difficult to speak without manuscript. The immense benefit resulting from this fact is, of course, that I can keep my eyes on my parishioners instead of on voluminous notes. As an example, let me cite the way in which I constructed and learned the chain for the sermon "A Christian's Joy," which I recently delivered. Here is the sermon:

A CHRISTIAN'S JOY
(Philippians IV:4–6)

The last words of famous personages, attributed to them shortly before death, are always of interest, particularly when the person in question was very dear to us.

We have often meditated on the seven last words spoken on the cross or those great words of comfort given during the forty-day period preceding our Lord's final departure on Ascension Day.

Today let us turn to what may easily have been the last words of

* Former Pastor of Emmanuel Episcopal Church, Weston, Conn.

St. Paul—his letter to the Philippians. Written in prison during, or just before, a trial that seemed pretty hopeless, Paul in his letter turns (and what could be more natural?) to the parish dearest to his heart. Here, in the face of death and departure, the Apostle speaks out—no, he sings his message in what may have been his swan song. The keynote he strikes again and again is one of pure joy. This note of joy rings out most convincingly in the famous passage which we have chosen for our text:

"Rejoice in the Lord always, and again I say, Rejoice."

What is the secret of this joy? Is it different from any other joy? Can it actually be obtained? And how can it be kept always? These are questions that arise in our minds as they might have arisen in the hearts of the Christians of those early days.

First of all, it is no secret in the strict sense of the word. No one is excluded from this joy unless he excludes himself. The call for constant rejoicing goes to everyone, everywhere, not only to the readers in Philippi in the days of St. Paul. They must have understood the Apostle of All Nations when he continued: "Let your moderation be known unto all men. The Lord is at hand." He meant that all men may begin to wonder why you are so happy and to ponder whether they, too, might not share this happiness with you. Happy people are really "gracious" towards one another. They are not selfish. They cannot help inducing others to take part in their happiness. They want to share their overflowing joy. For them rejoicing means spreading joy as well as being joyful.

Naturally, we are not speaking of the joys that are of this world. They come and go just as do the feelings, likings, and moods that create them—just as the manifold accomplishments of man's own devising pass and do not last forever. Only in the Lord can one rejoice always.

And why is it that so few of us live up to this ideal? Well, this spiritual rejoicing to which Paul attributes such importance throughout his letter is not so easy to obtain. Therefore his repeated admonition. One must not only hear the good news but accept it wholeheartedly and with humble faith. This calls for a complete change in our way of life. The message is as simple as it ever was, but it is still a stumbling block to some and meaningless to others. After all, it requires sacrifice and self-denial and a kind of suffering entirely alien to most of this world's "wise and understanding" people.

Small wonder, then, that Christ thanked His Father for having "hidden these things from them" and having revealed them to babes. Were not these the very ones who welcomed our Lord at His entry into the holy city and into the temple? No one could stop their joyful singing and exalted hosannas. It is the children and the simple folk who are always first when "the Lord is at hand." They are not sad or sorry, too busy or asleep when the call comes. They were the first to welcome Him after His coming into this world. They are the ones whose "faith had made them whole," whenever the Lord passed by. They are the members of the little flock which Christ urged to rejoice because their "names were written in heaven." Yes, our commonwealth is truly in heaven and from there we await a Saviour.

"The Lord is at hand." Here we find the key to this great rejoicing. We are reminded of the *maranatha,* the password of the early Christians and their constant prayer of hopeful longing: "Come, Lord Jesus, come!" And why such joyful expectation? Out of the deep love for and knowledge of Him who first loved us.

They really knew what Paul was talking about when he told them: "Rejoice in the Lord always. . . . Be careful for nothing . . . in everything pray with thanksgiving." There was for them, as there is for us, much to be thankful for. If we spent more time in prayer and meditation on thanksgiving, all our requests would melt away and nothing but rejoicing could prevail.

We must keep this spirit of joy and gratitude toward our Lord alive in our hearts. Sooner or later we will surely face the test: Is our joy really based on a strong belief in the reality of the nearness of our Lord?

Now, if we let our light so shine in the world, we will find that people take sides. We will not only win but also lose friends. We may even have to be ready, at least potentially, to be called to martyrdom. All this should not come as a shock to a Christian. The road to resurrection leads through suffering and tribulation. And that is true for the disciple as well as for the Master. We have before us not only the example of this writer to the Philippians—Paul—who certainly endured to the bitter end, but also that ever-joyous and thankful soul, St. Francis. In our day, what better example can we have than the Serbian Bishop Nicolai, whose joyful spirit was not broken but strengthened during the four years he spent in concentration camps? These men, and many more brave men and women, tell us "it can be done."

It can be done and it is certainly worth doing. Rejoice and be glad, for your reward will be great in heaven. Never be discouraged. A little while—and the Lord will come again. And right now, with His helping hand, He is always as near to us as we desire Him to be.

Forget what lies behind. Strive forward to what lies ahead! Amen.

For this sermon I constructed the following chain, in which the cue words are always linked together by questions:

Cue Words	Linking Thoughts
The last words	
	By whom?
St. Paul	
	To whom?
Philippians	
	Where?
In prison	
	About what?
"Rejoice in the Lord"	
What is the secret of this joy?	
Is it different from any other joy?	
Can it be obtained?	
How can it be kept always?	
	Who knows the answers?
No secret	
Nobody excluded	
"Let all men know"	
	What is the effect of knowing?
Happy people let others take part	
Rejoicing means spreading joy	
	What kind of joy?
Not the joys of this world	
	What else?
Spiritual joy	
Not easy to obtain	
	How to obtain it?
Sacrifices	
	Who is willing to make them?
Simple folk	
	What did they do?
They welcomed Him into the world	
	Contrast to world?
Names written in heaven	
	How to approach heaven?
Through prayer of thanksgiving	
	Is it dangerous?

Cue Words	*Linking Thoughts*
Our faith will be tested	
We will lose friends	
Ready for martyrdom	
	Who has to be ready?
Disciple as well as Master	
	Examples?
St. Francis	
Nicolai	
	Final goal for all this?
Reward will be great	

After I selected these cue words and constructed my chain, I was able to remember the sermon without difficulty. By using the Chain Method I can speak for hours without a manuscript or notes.

CHAPTER 34

Law and Memory

by William Barlow, LL.B.
Member, New York Bar

A lawyer must either have an excellent memory or rely on voluminous notes. In his office, surrounded by reference books, digest
systems, and case histories, he can (even though the process be
time-consuming) trace citations and secure the law and facts as
to a case; but many an occasion arises, most frequently in court,
in which a new point of view is raised, when it is of considerable
advantage to be able to quote previous decisions from memory.

Furthermore, if one is required to take voluminous notes while
his adversary is making his plea or argument, it becomes exceed-
ingly difficult to concentrate on the more important task of preparing a counterargument. It need hardly be added that constant
reference to notes during the presentation of an argument does
not make for smooth or effective delivery.

My work with Dr. Furst in memory and concentration has
sharpened my memory and provided me with a key to greater
development in my field. I now find that I can remember citations of cases with less effort than heretofore. To be more specific,
let me cite some cases, giving the book and page number and how
I remember the citations.

In Haupt *v.* the United States, 67 S.C. 874, the court affirmed
a father's conviction for treason in sheltering his son, a German
spy. Instead of remembering the numbers, I remember the phrase,

<u>Sh</u>eltered <u>c</u>ulprit, <u>f</u>ather's <u>c</u>onviction <u>r</u>ightful.
 6   7   8 7   4

United States *v.* John L. Lewis and the United Mine Workers,
67 S.C. 677, was a case involving a contempt action against
John L. Lewis and the United Mine Workers for calling a strike

and the shutdown of coal mines in violation of a court injunction during a period in which the mines were under the control of the United States Government. I use the following phrase to remember the citation of the case:

<u>Sh</u>utoff <u>c</u>oal <u>sh</u>owed <u>c</u>ourt <u>c</u>ontempt.
  6   7   6   7   7

In Patton *v.* Mississippi, 68 S.C. 184, the court held that systematic exclusion of Negroes from jury venire because of race denies equal protection of laws to Negroes. Instead of trying to remember the numbers 68 S.C. 184, a task which is as difficult for me as it is for most people, I remember the simple phrase,

<u>J</u>ury <u>f</u>avoritism <u>d</u>evised <u>f</u>or <u>r</u>ace.
 6   8   1   8   4

Perhaps of even more importance than remembering the citation of a case is remembering the law and facts of important decisions. Since thousands of decisions are handed down by the federal and state courts each year, it is a considerable task to remember even a small portion of the decisions. Here the Chain Method advocated by Dr. Furst opens up a new avenue of remembering a great many decisions. By way of example, let us take the aforementioned case of Patton *v.* Mississippi, in 68 S.C. 184. I am quoting first the entire case which I selected to form a chain.

PATTON v. STATE OF MISSISSIPPI
68 S.Ct. 184
Mr. Justice BLACK delivered the opinion of the Court.

The petitioner, a Negro, was indicted in the Circuit Court of Lauderdale County, Mississippi, by an all-white grand jury, charged with the murder of a white man. He was convicted by an all-white petit jury and sentenced to death by electrocution. He had filed a timely motion to quash the indictment alleging that, although there were Negroes in the county qualified for jury service, the venires for the term from which the grand and petit juries were selected did not contain the name of a single Negro. Failure to have any Negroes on the venires, he alleged, was due to the fact that for a great number of years previously and during the then term of court there had been in the county a "systematic, intentional, deliberate and invariable practice on the part of administrative officers to exclude Negroes from the jury lists, jury boxes and jury service, and that such practice has resulted and does now result in the denial of the equal protection of the laws of this defendant as guaranteed by the 14th amendment to the U. S. Constitution." In support of his motion petitioner introduced evidence which showed without contradiction that no Negro had served on the grand or petit criminal court juries for thirty years or more. There was evidence that a single Negro had once been summoned during that period but for some undisclosed reason he had not served, nor had he even appeared. And there was also evidence from one jury supervisor that he had, at some indefinite time, placed on the jury lists the names of "two or three" unidentified Negroes. In 1940 the adult colored population of Lauderdale County, according to the United States Census, was 12,511 out of a total adult population of 34,821.

In the face of the foregoing the trial court overruled the motion to quash. The Supreme Court of Mississippi affirmed over petitioner's renewed insistence that he had been denied the equal protection of the laws by the deliberate exclusion of Negroes from the grand jury that convicted him. 29 So.2d 96. We granted certiorari to review this serious contention.

[1] Sixty-seven years ago this Court held that state exclusion of Negroes from grand and petit juries solely because of their race denied Negro defendants in criminal cases the equal protection of the laws required by the Fourteenth Amendment. A long and unbroken line of our decisions since then has reiterated this principle, regardless of whether the discrimination was embodied in statute or was apparent from the administrative practices of state jury selection officials, and regardless of whether the system for depriving defendants of their rights was "ingenious or ingenuous."

[2] Whether there has been systematic racial discrimination by administrative officials in the selection of jurors is a question to be determined from the facts in each particular case. In this case the Mississippi Supreme Court concluded that petitioner had failed to prove systematic racial discrimination in the selection of jurors but in so concluding it erroneously considered only the fact that no Negroes were on the particular venire lists from which the juries were drawn that indicted and convicted petitioner. It regarded as irrelevant the key fact that for thirty years or more no Negro had served on the grand and petit juries. This omission seriously detracts from the weight and respect that we would otherwise give to its conclusion in reviewing the facts, as we must in a constitutional question like this.

[3] It is to be noted at once that the indisputable fact that no Negro had served on a criminal court grand or petit jury for a period of thirty

years created a very strong showing that during that period Negroes were systematically excluded from jury service because of race. When such a showing was made, it became a duty of the State to try to justify such an exclusion as having been brought about for some reason other than racial discrimination. The Mississippi Supreme Court did not conclude, the State did not offer any evidence, and in fact did not make any claim, that its officials had abandoned their old jury selection practices. The State Supreme Court's conclusion of justification rested upon the following reasoning. Section 1762 of the Mississippi Code enumerates the qualifications for jury service, the most important of which apparently are that one must be a male citizen and "a qualified elector." Sections 241, 242, 243 and 244 of the state constitution set forth the prerequisites for qualified electors. Among other things these provisions require that each elector shall pay an annual poll tax, produce satisfactory proof of such payment, and be able to read any section of the state constitution, or to understand the same when read to him, or to give a reasonable interpretation thereof. The evidence showed that a very small number of Negro male citizens (the court estimated about 25) as compared with white male citizens, had met the requirements for qualified electors, and thereby become eligible to be considered under additional tests for jury service. On this subject the State Supreme Court said:

"Of the 25 qualified negro male electors there would be left, therefore, as those not exempt, 12 or 13 available male negro electors as compared with 5,500 to 6,000 male white electors as to whom, after deducting 500 to 1,000 exempt, would leave a proportion of 5,000 nonexempt white jurors to 12 or 13 nonexempt negro jurors, or about one-fourth of one per cent negro jurors,–400 to 1. . . . For the reasons already heretofore stated there was only a chance of 1 in 400 that a negro would appear on such a venire and as this venire was of 100 jurors, the sheriff, had he brought in a negro, would have had to discriminate against white jurors, not against negroes,—he could not be expected to bring in one-fourth of one negro."

[4] The above statement of the Mississippi Supreme Court illustrates the unwisdom of attempting to disprove systematic racial discrimination in the selection of jurors by percentage calculations applied to the composition of a single venire.

The petitioner here points out certain legislative record evidence of which it is claimed we can take judicial notice, and which it is asserted establishes that the reason why there are so few qualified Negro electors in Mississippi is because of discrimination against them in making up the registration lists. But we need not consider that question in this case. For it is clear from the evidence in the record that there were some Negroes in Lauderdale County on the registration list. In fact, in 1945, the circuit clerk of the county, who is himself charged with duties in administering the jury system, sent the names of eight Negroes to the jury commissioner of the Federal District Court as citizens of Lauderdale County qualified for federal jury service. Moreover, there was evidence that the names of from thirty to several hundred qualified Negro electors were on the registration lists. But whatever the precise number of qualified colored electors in the county, there were some; and if it can possibly be conceived that all of them were disqualified for jury service by reason of the commission of crime, habitual drunkenness, gambling, inability to read and write or to meet any other or all of the statutory tests we do not doubt that the State could have proved it.

[5, 6] We hold that the State wholly failed to meet the very strong evidence of purposeful racial discrimination made out by the petitioner upon the uncontradicted showing that for thirty years or more no Negro had served as a juror in the criminal courts of Lauderdale County. When a jury selection plan, whatever it is, operates in such way as always to result in the complete and long-continued exclusion of any representative at all from a large group of Negroes, or any other racial group, indictments and verdicts returned against them by juries thus selected cannot stand. As we pointed out in Hill v. State of Texas, our holding does not mean that a guilty defendant must go free. For indictments can be returned and convictions can be obtained by juries selected as the Constitution commands.

The judgment of the Mississippi Supreme Court is reversed and the case is remanded for proceedings not inconsistent with this opinion.

These are the cue words which I selected and which enable me to keep the entire case in mind and ready for use whenever I need it:

Cue Words	Linking Thoughts
Indicted—White jury	
	Indicted—convicted
Convicted—White jury	
	White—Negro
No Negroes on venire for thirty years	
	Thirty years—sixty-seven years
Sixty-seven years ago Negro exclusion held denial of protection of law	

Cue Words	*Linking Thoughts*
	Law—statute
Statute or practice	
	Qualifications
Mississippi court considered one venire	
	One venire—all venires
Supreme Court considered all venires	
	Result?
Long-continued exclusion from venire	
	Proves
Racial discrimination and denial of equal protection of law	

The cue words which I selected form a chain of connecting links. By the use of each, I am able to quote the entire case in its important details. Just remembering the few connecting words enables me to reconstruct the entire case. The process can perhaps be likened to erecting an edifice around a scaffold.

As I became more adept in the use of the Chain Method, I found I could apply it to remembering the points advanced by my adversary. I used to take notes so that I would not miss a single point in my reply, but writing takes time and while writing it is difficult to listen. And very often I lost some of the remarks made. Furthermore, there was no time left to organize my own thoughts. Using the Chain Method obviates taking voluminous notes, thereby saving valuable time and enabling one to listen closely to the argument advanced and to prepare one's own argument and deliver it without being distracted by constant reference to lengthy notes.

Once mastered, the Chain Method not only is helpful in remembering what you expect to say but also forces you to think logically and precisely. The Chain Method makes for a smoother and more effective delivery. It makes it much easier to follow the learned counsel of Roscoe Pound, the eminent Dean of Harvard Law School, who said:

"It is the lawyer's duty to help the court by presenting his client's case in a logical, orderly, systematized fashion, seeing that nothing is omitted that appears on the case, that what bears on the case is put in its proper setting and that what does not bear on the case is not brought in to waste time and distract the attention of the tribunal."

CHAPTER 35

Engineering and Memory

by J. George Adashko
Electrical Engineer

An engineer is no better than his memory and, next to his education, his most valuable asset is the ability to recall quickly facts and figures that he has encountered before. It can even be said that anything normally meant by "engineering experience," "engineering judgment," "sound practice," and all the other timeworn expressions used to describe successful engineers can be traced to one common factor—a well-ordered memory.

When we talk of an engineer who is a "good theoretician, well versed in fundamentals," we mean, of course, a man who remembers readily most of the formulas and derivations that apply to the particular problem, and who can therefore arrive quickly and readily at a solution by analytical means. On the other hand, the "sound, practical engineer" usually described as possessing "plenty of good common sense" is the man who answers questions promptly because he remembers, without having to refer to his books or slide rule, that in the past he or somebody else has already solved a similar problem.

Both the good theoretician and the good practical engineer (as well as the many good ones who combine in varying proportions the qualities of the two extreme types) are adept in employing their particular skill, which again is nothing but a variant of good memory, to solve engineering problems quickly and accurately. In research, production, administration, estimating, design, or whatever engineering function he performs, the "experienced" engineer relies most frequently on his memory to guide him. He remembers which materials are costly and which are not; he recalls which procedures are wasteful and which are not; he knows what size and type of apparatus are best for a particular job; and so on indefinitely.

Theoretically, an engineer should be able to design, say, the Brooklyn Bridge merely by starting with Newton's laws of mechanics and deriving step by step all the necessary equations describing the stresses in the cables and beams, etc. Such an engineer, who must of necessity be gifted with a logical mind bordering on the supernatural, would need to remember very little, but he would also certainly accomplish very little in his lifetime. All others must cut their work short by remembering what has been done before. Every engineering equation, every table, every chart, and every curve are nothing but the engineer's mnemonic aids, designed to put at his fingertips what has been learned, discovered, or derived before.

It is quite clear, therefore, that what is commonly known in engineering as "acquiring experience" is really nothing but memorizing a great number of facts, and that is, of course, what all engineers do throughout their professional lives. Unfortunately, too many go about it in a haphazard manner without realizing the enormous benefits that can be derived from a systematizing of the memorizing process, such as is outlined in this book.

As he tackles the problem of memorizing, an engineer is on the one hand under many disadvantages as compared with, say, a salesman, but on the other hand he also has many advantages. The disadvantage is that he must memorize "for keeps." The salesman remembers his price list only until the prices are changed or the line discontinued. The engineer draws on his "experience"—which is his memory—constantly, and the older he gets and the more responsible position he holds, the more is demanded of his memory. On the other hand, the salesman's price list may contain items and numbers that are utterly unrelated, while there are very few engineering tables that do not follow some predetermined order, as set by a formula or a physical law, and therefore contain in themselves valuable memory-aids that can be used to advantage.

This leads us to two basic and important observations: first, the engineer, because he has to memorize things practically all his life, must learn to consider his memory system as a machine that has to turn out many products constantly; he cannot afford to tie it up with only one or two things. To be more specific, if he uses the Basic List to memorize a series of figures, he must arrange to learn these figures in a very short time and release the Basic List quickly so that he can apply it promptly to the next problem. In other words, the Basic List must be used only during the process of memorizing; but, as soon as something is learned, the memory process must become so automatic that the Basic List is no longer required and can be released for the next problem.

The second important observation is: because engineering data are not haphazard but usually follow some definite order, it is necessary to take advantage of this order in memorizing. We must not follow the Basic List blindly but learn to modify it to suit conditions. It is important to study each memorizing problem individually and devise the most suitable means of memorizing for the particular job confronting us. The Basic List is most useful but must not be taken too literally, because it is often possible to devise short cuts that are even more useful than the Basic List.

As an example of how to memorize a table of engineering data, I choose the Annealed Copper Wire Table, showing gauge numbers and areas in circular mils. The table is as follows:

Gauge No.	Area (mils)	Gauge No.	Area (mils)	Gauge No.	Area (mils)
0000 ..	211,600	12 ..	6,530	27 ..	201.5
000 ..	167,800	13 ..	5,178	28 ..	159.8
00 ..	133,000	14 ..	4,107	29 ..	126.7
0 ..	105,500	15 ..	3,257	30 ..	100.5
1 ..	83,690	16 ..	2,583	31 ..	79.70
2 ..	66,370	17 ..	2,048	32 ..	63.21
3 ..	52,640	18 ..	1,624	33 ..	50.13
4 ..	41,740	19 ..	1,288	34 ..	39.75
5 ..	33,100	20 ..	1,022	35 ..	31.52
6 ..	26,250	21 ..	810.1	36 ..	25.00
7 ..	20,820	22 ..	642.4	37 ..	19.83
8 ..	16,510	23 ..	509.5	38 ..	15.72
9 ..	13,090	24 ..	404.0	39 ..	12.47
10 ..	10,380	25 ..	320.4	40 ..	9.888
11 ..	8,234	26 ..	254.1		

To those familiar with the Furst method of memorizing, this table holds no terror whatsoever. None of the numbers contains more than four significant figures (that is, disregarding the zeros at the end). Using the Basic and Secondary Lists,* we can easily form the necessary associations. For example, Gauge No. 1 can be remembered by associating *tea* (1), *fame* (83), and *game* (69). "A *famous* man playing a *game* after *tea*" is a ready way of correlating No. 1 with 8369. All that is necessary is to add a mental note that no zeros are added to the areas of gauges from No. 11 up, one zero is added for Gauges 1 to 10, and two zeros are added to the end of the areas of Gauges 0, 00, 000, and 0000. It is also very easy to devise a simple list for these latter four gauges. For example, we can use words beginning with s, such as seat for No. 0, sun for No. 00, sum for No. 000, and sore for No. 0000.

The Furst method is simple and foolproof, and in many cases it is really the only one by which such a list of numbers can be memorized quickly and permanently. But the engineer must take advantage of the nature of the table and try to make his task even simpler if possible. He is called upon to remember so much that he must not ignore any possible labor-saving device.

Looking at our table, we observe several things that make it more than just two unrelated lists of numbers. The gauge numbers keep on increasing, while the areas in circular mils decrease. This in itself is of some help, since it is always easier to remember numbers that are arranged in an ascending or descending sequence. Closer examination of the table discloses the following:

The area of No. 0 wire is 105,500 circular mils, or approximately 100,000.
The area of No. 10 wire is 10,380 circular mils, or approximately 10,000.
The area of No. 20 wire is 1,022 circular mils, or approximately 1,000.
The area of No. 30 wire is 100.5 circular mils, or approximately 100.
The area of No. 40 wire is 9.888 circular mils, or approximately 10.

Thus we see that, for every increase of ten in the gauge number, the area in circular mils is divided by ten. If we remember the area of any one number, the area of the wire with a number

* See Chapters 14 and 19.

greater by ten is approximately one tenth of that area. Thus, the area of Gauge No. 12 is approximately one tenth the area of Gauge No. 2; the area of Gauge No. 27 is approximately ten times the area of No. 37, etc. This enables us to divide the list into several sections, a classification which is very useful in the final act of committing the table to memory.

The complete procedure would therefore be approximately thus:

A. Divide the table into five parts—0000 to 0, 1 to 10, 11 to 20, 21 to 30, 31 to 40.
B. Memorize thoroughly the portion of the table from 31 to 40, using the Furst method with the Basic and Secondary Lists.
C. Proceed with the second portion of the table, from 21 to 30. Bear in mind that the areas will be very much alike, except for being ten times larger. This will be both useful association and a quick check on memorizing, to prevent errors.
D. Memorize the remaining portions, as in C.

I have gone through this table at some length merely to show that while the basic process is no different for the engineer than for any other person, engineering data usually follow a very well-ordered pattern, and a little expenditure of time and study before beginning to memorize will be of considerable help and will materially reduce the time needed to complete the work.

To sum up briefly, the following are the salient points to be kept in mind about the engineer's memory problems:

A. The things the engineer has to remember usually have to be learned permanently. Therefore memorizing has to be done very thoroughly, so that it becomes automatic. The basic number list or whatever hook is used must be discarded as quickly as possible.

B. The engineer has to memorize things practically all his life. He cannot afford to waste too much time on trivia. There is no point in systematizing every little problem. Apply the system only to the difficult problems.

C. Engineering data usually contain valuable hints in themselves that can facilitate memorizing. Take a little time to find out what you are trying to remember, and half the problem of *how* to remember is solved.

CHAPTER 36

Salesmanship and Memory

by Robert Nestler

I am a salesman. The firm I represent in a selling capacity manufactures an original line of bedspreads.

I can say without exaggeration that I have used every feature of this memory system, and to my advantage. In traveling I have found Classification and the Chain Method a tremendously time-saving device. I have found that the things which I have to remember before approaching a new customer can be organized in the following way:

1. *The City*
   A. The population of the city
   B. How many stores use my merchandise?
   C. Hotels, restaurants, entertainment spots to which I can take my buyer

2. *The Buyer*
   A. His name, interests, and hobbies
   B. The assistant buyer's name, interests, and hobbies
   C. The type of buyer and assistant buyer
      (1) Does he follow the taste of other people, or is his taste independent?
      (2) Does he want something new, or does he prefer things which are already established?
      (3) Is he quick-minded (annoyed by repetition), or is he slow-grasping (frequent repetition necessary)?

3. *My Own Firm*
   A. When, where, and by whom established?
   B. The history of the firm
   C. The owner's name
   D. The names of the department heads

4. *Competitive Firms*
   A. When, where, and by whom established?
   B. Names of owners
   C. Why should the buyer prefer my merchandise?
      (1) Lower price?
      (2) Better quality?
      (3) Better known to the public?

5. *The Merchandise*
   A. Price
   B. Styles and colors
   C. Construction and factory
   D. Who uses it?
   E. How is it selling?
   F. Remarkable points about this merchandise
   G. Delivery date

Of course, each of these items has to be supplemented by accurate figures and facts, but I have found that these are easily remembered as soon as I have the cue word.

The Hook Method and Number Code proved just as valuable to me as Classification and the Chain Method. I quote an incident that happened at the time when I had just finished Dr. Furst's memory course and that proved to be a turning point in my career:

As I stated before, I represent a manufacturer of bedspreads. Each new season a complete line of new models is presented to us. At the time I'm talking about, a catalogue with rough sketches was sent to our New York office. This catalogue contained seventy-three new designs, each with style number and price. I memorized them page by page in the way I had learned to memorize a magazine.* A few days later the actual bedspread samples arrived. The boss and all the salesmen, including myself, assembled to look at the new line. As each bedspread was revealed, I was able to quote its style number and price without consulting any written matter.

Afterward, the boss called me into his office and asked me how I had managed to know all this by heart, since I had never seen the spreads before. I told him how I had studied the sketches and

* See Chapter 17.

gave him an idea about our Number Code. As an example I quoted the following items:

"No. 1028 is a design that shows wavy lines and costs $9.50. Since all the numbers start with 10, it is enough to remember the last two digits. The wavy lines remind me of the ocean, which is easy to associate with *navy*. For $9.50 I find a<u>ppl</u>au<u>s</u>e. Therefore the sentence

'The navy gets applause'

takes care of style-number, design, and price.

"No. 1093 shows a design of a house and costs $6.50. I associate the house with *lighthouse* and *beam,* and I substitute <u>j</u>ewe<u>ls</u> for $6.50. *Beam* and *jewels* are easily associated since both are sparkling. Therefore

'Beam—jewels'

takes care of design, number, and price.

"No. 1034 shows an animal and costs $3.75. I associate this animal with the horse, or *mare.* I substitute <u>me</u>e<u>kl</u>y for $3.75 and I have

'The mare follows meekly.'

"No. 1050 has a lattice design and costs $5.75. I associate the lattice with *lace,* substitute <u>lo</u>c<u>al</u> for $5.75 and arrive easily at the sentence

'Making lace is a local art.'"

My boss was fully convinced, and this conversation led to a series of talks at the end of which he told me that I was to take care of all our sales problems in the future. That means that I was promoted to sales manager with a corresponding raise in salary. Therefore I can truthfully state that this memory system finally gave me the opportunity I had been looking for ever since I started work.

CHAPTER 37

The Stage and Memory

*by Tonio Selwart**

An actor depends entirely upon his memory. If it fails him, there is nothing he can do but give up his career. I took this memory course not so much because I was dissatisfied with my memory, but because I was constantly looking for short cuts which would make it easier for me to memorize my lines and save valuable time that I could put to better use.

The Chain Method met and even surpassed my expectations. I now realize that it was a time-wasting procedure to learn my lines merely by endless repetition. Today I read the entire play through three or four times and get acquainted with all its characters, especially with the one I am to portray. After having formed a good over-all picture, I again read my own lines several times—often enough to know the gist of my part while I'm on stage. Knowing the gist of my lines makes it easy for me to express the thoughts, first in my own words, and then to adjust these words verbatim to the text of the play.

I follow the same procedure when I encounter long sentences. That is, I impress the main idea of the sentence on my mind and afterward fill in the details. For instance, when my lines read: "The other day, I think it was Wednesday, I met your Aunt Betsy, and though I was very pleasant to her, she was as usual very disagreeable," I remembered first: "The other day I met your Aunt Betsy and she was very disagreeable." Later on I filled in the words which are missing in this basic sentence.

Compared with memorizing by rote, this type of learning not only is more efficient but really calls for thinking in the same

---

* Well-known stage and screen actor who originated the role of the "bundling hero" in *Pursuit of Happiness*.

way as does the character I'm playing, and so it makes me feel almost identical with him.

All this is especially important when the time between accepting a new role and the first performance is very short, as happens frequently at summer theaters. A few years ago during the Drama Festival in Ithaca, New York, I had exactly three days to memorize my part in *Topaze*. My lines filled 110 pages, and I don't think I could have learned them without using this system.

Here's another instance: I played the part of the Nazi Haas in the moving picture *Hangmen Also Die*. Haas is the man who succeeded Heydrich as "Protector" of Czechoslovakia. During the forenoon of the last day of shooting, Director Fritz Lang suggested that I speak a very lengthy bit directly into the camera. This meant that I could not read it as I had theretofore. Following the rules which I have just described, I was ready for camera and sound that same afternoon.

On the stage as well as in television it is not enough for an actor to know his lines; he must know his cues, too. A cue in the theater is the last word spoken by one of the characters before an actor speaks his own lines. Usually there is a natural association between this last word and the actor's first sentence, but sometimes it is lacking and the actor's lines could start a few minutes earlier or later. In cases like this, I form an artificial association, which may rest on meaning or sound or whatever presents itself.

In *Candlelight,* for instance, there is no natural connection between my cue word "He is away" and my line "I want to say something." Here I use the rhyme "away" and "say" to form an artificial association.

I have found it helpful, too, to connect my words with movements or actions which I have to make at the same time. If there is no natural association between words and action, I form an artificial one. I recall a dinner scene. In it I am called on to pass various dishes in a certain order. While I pass the salad I have to say: "Your father seems to have grown very stout lately." Knowing that salad is frequently recommended for reducing, I use the contrast to connect my line and action.

All these various memory-aids grow in importance when I play in a foreign language, as happened recently in French Canada. I recall a sentence spoken by another character which ended with *l'autre jour j'ai vu un bateau* ("the other day I saw a liner"). I interrupt the story he is about to tell by speaking of a weekend excursion. There is no logical connection between his words and my remark. I formed an artificial connection by seeing myself aboard a steamer for a weekend excursion, and this association never failed me.

Finally, there's the matter of names and faces. I know that remembering them is important for everyone, but it is absolutely vital in my profession. Take the fan who comes to see me backstage in Ottawa and will see me again two or three years later when I happen to be in the neighborhood again. To remember or not to remember him (or her) almost equals, from an actor's point of view, Hamlet's "To be or not to be . . . !"

CHAPTER 38

Miscellaneous Applications
Musical Dates and Memory

*by Mitchell Sadewitz**

I have found the Number Code extremely helpful in remembering not only the birth and death dates of all the noteworthy composers, but also the most significant dates in their lives as well as the dates of important musical events in general. This has enabled me to answer many questions put to me by students without taking time out to consult reference books.

Knowing exact dates is important because, in the interpretation of a musical composition, it is often necessary to know the time and the circumstances under which it was written. Beethoven's Third Symphony, for instance, is more highly appreciated if we know that it was completed in 1804 and originally dedicated to Napoleon Bonaparte, whom Beethoven had regarded as a savior of mankind. He was shocked and disillusioned when Napoleon declared himself Emperor and in a rage tore off the dedicatory inscription from the manuscript. It is now known as the "Eroica" Symphony.

Here is the way I use the Number Code: in selecting the substitute words I sometimes use one word and sometimes the initial consonants of several words, depending on which association seems easier. With the exception of birth dates, I leave out the centuries because they are understood.

The Life of Ludwig van Beethoven

1770	Born	**G**reatest **c**omposer's **s**tart in life
1775	Began music study	**C**a**ll** (heard the divine call)

---

* Well-known pianist and teacher who has traveled extensively through the United States on his "one-man campaign" tours for the benefit of the American Cancer Society and the American Heart Association.

1783	Appointed to play in court orchestra—without salary	**Fa**me
1784	Appointed as second organist—with a salary	**F**ee **r**eceived
1785	Studied violin with F. A. Ries	**Vio**lin
1788	Start of lifelong friendship with Count Waldstein and Stefan Breuning	**F**inds **f**riends
1792	Beethoven's father dies	**B**ad **n**ews
1798	Discovered his incipient deafness	**B**itter **F**ate
1800	First Symphony performed in concert. Defeated Steibelt in an improvisation contest	**S**tarts **s**ymphonies or **S**ymphony—**S**teibelt
1801	Fell in love with Giulietta Guicciardi, to whom he dedicated "Moonlight" Sonata	**S**wee**t**
1804	In a rage he tore off the title page of Third Symphony. The title "Eroica" Symphony is substituted	**S**o**r**e or **S**ymphony "E**r**oica"
1805	Composed the soul-stirring "Appassionata" Sonata	**S**ou**l**
1808	Finished Fifth Symphony	**S**ymphony **F**ive
1811	Met Maelzel, inventor of the metronome	**T**ick **t**ock
1815	His brother Karl died and he assumed guardianship of his troublesome and wayward nephew	**T**roublesome **l**oafer
1823	Completed Ninth Symphony	**N**o **m**ore or **N**inth **m**asterwork
1827	Died	**N**o**c**turne

I am also interested in remembering the dates of world premieres of operas and their composers. I found it easy to learn them by using meaningful substitutes for names which have no meaning and by applying the Number Code to the year. I omitted the centuries because they are rather obvious to a musician. Here are a few examples:

Tales of Hoffman is **often** (Offenbach) v̲iewed̲ (1881)
Carmen is **busy** (Bizet) k̲il̲ling (1875)
The Mastersingers **wagon̲** (Wagner) with the c̲hief̲ singer (1868)
The Girl of the Golden West **puts** (Puccini) the d̲ice on the bar (1910)
The Barber of Seville places **roses** (Rossini) in̲ a d̲is̲h̲ (1816)

Denominations of
United States Currency

by Ruth Howe

I had just completed Dr. Furst's memory course when I listened one night to a quiz program over the radio. I heard the question, "Whose picture is on our American five-dollar bill?" And I felt very much ashamed when I didn't know the answer. Neither did the contestant.

Isn't it terrible? I thought to myself; here we handle these bills every day and we don't pay any attention to the men whose pictures are shown on them! Since I had just learned how to handle such a task, I set to work and found the following associations. I am sure I shall remember them for years to come, and I'm quite sure that readers of this book will too.

$1	George Washington First President of the United States. Took first presidential oath	Oath
$2	Thomas Jefferson Drew up the Declaration of Independence	Independence
$5	Abraham Lincoln	Lincoln
$10	Alexander Hamilton His ideas to establish the public credit on a firm basis have endured to this day	Ideas
$20	Andrew Jackson Well known for his honesty	Honesty
$50	Ulysses S. Grant	Ulysses

$100	Benjamin Franklin He proved the thesis of the identity of lightning and electricity in his famous kite experiment	<u>Thesis</u>
$500	William McKinley McKinley was assassinated by a man named Czolgoz (Cz=s)	Czo<u>l</u>goz a<u>ss</u>a<u>ss</u>in
$1000	Grover Cleveland Cleveland was twice sustained in presidential elections (1884 and 1892)	<u>T</u>wi<u>c</u>e <u>s</u>ustained

I have heard that five- and ten-thousand-dollar bills are also in circulation, but I decided to wait with these until my husband brings a few home in his pay envelope.

Appendix

DECLARATION OF INDEPENDENCE

When, in the Course of human events, it becomes necessary for one people to dissolve the political bands which have connected them with another, and to assume among the powers of the earth, the separate and equal station to which the Laws of Nature and of Nature's God entitle them, a decent respect to the opinions of mankind requires that they should declare the causes which impel them to the separation.

We hold these truths to be self-evident, that all men are created equal, that they are endowed by their Creator with certain unalienable Rights, that among these are Life, Liberty and the pursuit of Happiness. That to secure these rights, Governments are instituted among Men, deriving their just powers from the consent of the governed. That whenever any Form of Government becomes destructive of these ends, it is the Right of the People to alter or to abolish it, and to institute new Government, laying its foundation on such principles and organizing its powers in such form, as to them shall seem most likely to effect their Safety and Happiness. Prudence, indeed, will dictate that Governments long established should not be changed for light and transient causes; and accordingly all experience hath shewn, that mankind are more disposed to suffer, while evils are sufferable, than to right themselves by abolishing the forms to which they are accustomed. But when a long train of abuses and usurpations, pursuing invariably the same object, evidence a design to reduce them under absolute Despotism, it is their right, it is their duty, to throw off such Government, and to provide new Guards for their future security. Such has been the patient sufferance of these Colonies; and such is now the necessity which constrains them to alter their former Systems of Government. The history of the present King of Great Britain is a history of repeated injuries and usurpation, all having in direct object the establishment of an absolute Tyranny over these States. To prove this, let Facts be submitted to a candid world.

He has refused his Assent to Laws, the most wholesome and necessary for the public good.

He has forbidden his Governors to pass Laws of immediate and pressing importance, unless suspended in their operation till his Assent should be obtained, and when so suspended, he has utterly neglected to attend to them.

He has refused to pass other Laws for the accommodation of large districts of people, unless those people would relinquish the right of

Representation in the Legislature, a right inestimable to them and formidable to tyrants only.

He has called together legislative bodies at places, unusual, uncomfortable, and distant from the depository of their public Records, for the sole purpose of fatiguing them into compliance with his measures.

He has dissolved Representative Houses repeatedly, for opposing with manly firmness his invasions on the rights of the people.

He has refused for a long time, after such dissolutions, to cause others to be elected: whereby the Legislative powers, incapable of Annihilation, have returned to the People at large for their exercise; the State remaining in the meantime exposed to all the dangers of invasion from without, and convulsions within.

He has endeavored to prevent the population of these States; for that purpose obstructing the Laws of Naturalization of Foreigners; refusing to pass others to encourage their migrations hither, and raising the conditions of new Appropriations of Lands.

He has obstructed the Administration of Justice, by refusing his Assent to Laws for establishing Judiciary powers.

He has made Judges dependent on his Will alone, for the tenure of their offices, and the amount and payment of their salaries.

He has erected a multitude of New Offices, and sent hither swarms of Officers to harass our people, and eat out their substance.

He has kept among us, in times of peace, Standing Armies, without the Consent of our legislatures.

He has affected to render the Military independent of and superior to the Civil power.

He has combined with others to subject us to a jurisdiction foreign to our constitution and unacknowledged by our laws; giving his Assent to their Acts of pretended Legislation: For quartering large bodies of armed troops among us: For protecting them by a mock Trial from punishment for any Murders which they should commit on the Inhabitants of these States: For cutting off our Trade with all parts of the world: For imposing Taxes on us without our Consent: For depriving us in many cases of the benefits of Trial by Jury: For transporting us beyond Seas to be tried for pretended offenses: For abolishing the free System of English Laws in a neighbouring Province, establishing therein an Arbitrary government, and enlarging its Boundaries so as to render it at once an example and fit instrument for introducing the same absolute rule into these Colonies: For taking away our Charters, abolishing our most valuable Laws and altering fundamentally the Forms of our Governments: For suspending our own Legislatures and declaring themselves invested with power to legislate for us in all cases whatsoever.

He has abdicated Government here by declaring us out of his Protection and waging War against us.

He has plundered our seas, ravished our Coasts, burnt our towns, and destroyed the lives of our people.

He is at this time transporting large Armies of foreign Mercenaries, to complete the works of death, desolation and tyranny, already begun with circumstances of cruelty and perfidy scarcely paralleled in the most barbarous ages, and totally unworthy of the Head of a civilized nation.

He has constrained our fellow Citizens taken Captive on the high Seas to bear Arms against their Country, to become the executioners of their friends and Brethren, or to fall themselves by their Hands.

He has excited domestic insurrections amongst us, and has endeavored to bring on the inhabitants of our frontiers, the merciless Indian Savages, whose known rule of warfare is an undistinguished destruction of all ages, sexes and conditions. In every stage of these Oppressions We have Petitioned for Redress in the most humble terms. Our repeated Petitions have been answered only by repeated injury. A Prince, whose character is thus marked by every act which may define a Tyrant, is unfit to be the ruler of a free people. Nor have We been wanting in attention to our British brethren. We have warned them from time to time of attempts by their legislature to extend an unwarrantable jurisdiction over us. We have reminded them of the circumstances of our emigration and settlement here. We have appealed to their native justice and magnanimity, and we have conjured them by the ties of our common kindred to disavow these usurpations, which would inevitably interrupt our connections and correspondence. They too have been deaf to the voice of justice and of consanguinity. We must, therefore, acquiesce in the necessity, which denounces our Separation, and hold them, as we hold the rest of mankind, Enemies in War, in Peace Friends.

WE, THEREFORE, the Representatives of the United States of America, in General Congress, Assembled, appealing to the Supreme Judge of the world for the rectitude of our intentions do, in the Name, and by authority of the good People of these Colonies, solemnly publish and declare. That these United Colonies are, and of Right ought to be, Free and Independent States: that they are Absolved from all Allegiance to the British Crown, and that all political connection between them and the State of Great Britain is and ought to be totally dissolved: and that as Free and Independent States, they have full Power to levy War, conclude Peace, contract Alliances, establish Commerce, and to do all other Acts and Things which independent States may of right do. And for the support of this Declaration, with a firm reliance on the protection of Divine Providence, we mutually pledge to each other our Lives, our Fortunes, and our sacred Honor.

INDEX OF NAMES

INDEX OF SUBJECTS